A
Marquetry
Odyssey

A Marquetry Odyssey

Historical Objects and Personal Work

Silas Kopf

HUDSON HILLS PRESS

MANCHESTER AND NEW YORK

This book is dedicated to the memory of my mother, Jane Walker Kopf, who had an eye for beautiful objects and first introduced me to design. It was she who encouraged me to pursue a career in furniture, and she always showed enthusiasm about whatever project I was working on.

First Edition

Copyright Page © 2008

All rights reserved under International and Pan-American Copyright Convention.

Except for legitimate excerpts customary in review or scholarly publications, no part of this publication may be reproduced or transmitted in any form or by any means, electronic or mechanical, including photocopying, recording, or information storage or retrieval systems, without written permission from the publisher.

Published in the United States by Hudson Hills Press LLC, 3556 Main Street, Manchester, Vermont 05254.

Distributed in the United States, its territories and possessions, and Canada by National Book Network, Inc. Distributed outside of North America by Antique Collectors' Club, Ltd.

Executive Director and Publisher: Leslie Pell van Breen
Designer: Deborah Fillion
Editor: Rick Mastelli
Proofreader: Linda Bratton
Production Manager: David Skolkin
Indexer: Rick Mastelli
Color separations by Pre Tech Color, Hartford, Vermont
Printed and bound by TWP, Singapore
Founding Publisher: Paul Anbinder

Library of Congress Cataloging-in-Publication Data

Kopf, Silas.
    A marquetry odyssey : historical objects and personal work / Silas Kopf ; foreword by Glenn Adamson.
      p. cm.
    ISBN 978-1-55595-287-7
    1. Marquetry. I. Title.
    NK9920.K67 2008
    745.51'2 dc22
                              2008003172

Half-Title Page:
Detail of Figure 72: Garden Cabinet (1998) Silas Kopf

Frontispiece:
1. Music Cabinet (1990) Silas Kopf
English brown oak and marquetry; 71 × 46 × 23½ in.
Photo: Dean Powell

Contents

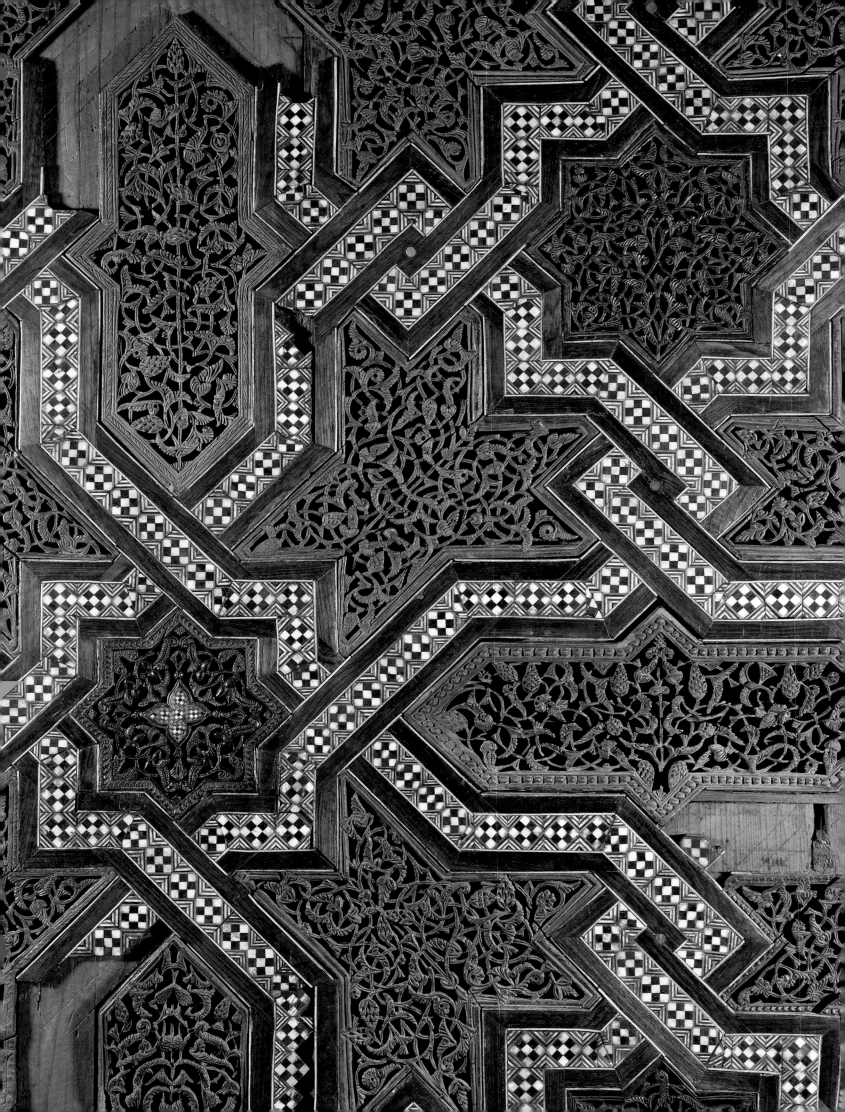

Acknowledgments

A book like this is the product of many individuals. I first had the idea for a book on marquetry more than ten years ago, but many pieces were not in place, and this effort is stronger for having waited.

I owe a huge debt of gratitude to William A. Lincoln. His book, *The Art and Practice of Marquetry,* introduced me to the craft and was so well written that it gave me the confidence that I could actually learn marquetry.

Pierre Ramond has been generous with his vast knowledge of marquetry technique and history. I am proud that we have a friendship going back twenty years now. His books opened the door to several areas that had been unknown to me.

Wendell Castle gave me a job when I had few skills to offer. I learned craftsmanship in his shop and have tried ever since to live up to his standards.

My furniture has been the product of many helpers. Tim Faner and Tom Coughlin raised the level of cabinetmaking in my shop to an extraordinary level. Over the years I had additional help from Henry Edquist, Jay Stanger, Rex Brodie, Bill Hill, Julie Godfrey, Mike Chermisino, Bill Hewitt, Spider Johnson, and Tony Sadlowski. From time to time I have relied on Tom Raredon for metalworking expertise and Tom Johnson for excellent finishing.

Many people contributed to the research of this book. Collecting the photographs was at times a daunting task and people sprang up to help at important times. Brian Considine and others on the staff of the J. Paul Getty Museum were very helpful and generous in allowing the use of images from the museum's collection.

When I first entered the craft world, a woodworker with much more experience said, "Get good photography. More people will see your work on a printed page than will ever see the actual piece." I have been fortunate to work with a number of excellent photographers, most importantly David Ryan, Dean Powell, and Kevin Downey. Dave Dumas of Pivot Media helped to make the images ready for print.

Yannick Chastang, Patrick Edwards, Jon Harr, Geoffrey Killen, and Arnold Skolnick all offered timely advice.

I owe a considerable debt to my editor, Rick Mastelli, and designer, Deborah Fillion. Rick also took all the illuminating photographs in the technical appendices, and the clarity of those essays owes as much to his skill behind a camera as with a sharp pencil. At times when I was willing to say, "Oh, it's good enough," both Rick and Deborah pushed to refine and go one step further. This book is surely a result of their caring about making it the best it could be.

Finally, I would like to thank my wife, Linda, for being a sounding board about this book from its conception. She has always been enthusiastically positive about the project, and it bears her behind-the-scenes imprint.

DETAIL OF FIGURE 216:
THREE MILE ISLAND DESK (2004) SILAS KOPF

☙

Foreword

A BIG, BEAUTIFUL demilune table in the Metropolitan Museum of Art has a veneered top in which alternating flitches of flame mahogany and figured maple are arranged in a fan shape. Like most old furniture—it was made around the beginning of the nineteenth century in Salem, Massachusetts—the object's appearance is vastly different today from what its maker intended, or what its original owners saw when they looked across their parlor. In this case, however, time has brought considerable improvement. What was once a dramatic color contrast of dark and light woods has mellowed over the course of two centuries, as what are probably many layers of oil finish have darkened and cracked with age. More strikingly, the top has buckled and heaved as a result of

wood movement. A surface that would once have been dead flat, like an architect's drawing, now has the gentle swell and ripples of a becalmed sea. It is as if a kind of organic melody has emerged from the table, playing against the underlying rhythm of the cabinetmaker's original geometric composition.

While this table does not have the pictorial characteristics that one associates with marquetry, it is nonetheless an example of the art, and in its current state it captures something of the intrinsic interest of such furniture: a give-and-take of image and material, in which neither can quite gain the upper hand. Every work of marquetry, from the relatively simple fan on the Metropolitan table to the most complex pictorial, ornamental, or geometric designs, has at its heart the

attempt to pull recalcitrant matter together into a unified pattern. Few things in the world of furniture making are harder to do. Elsewhere in this volume Silas Kopf writes, "one of the things that interests me about marquetry is the artistic limitations." And indeed, when compared with its closest artistic cousins—drawing and painting—these "pictures in wood" do seem to be absurdly troublesome. The palette of colors available to the marquetry artist is restricted. The process of material preparation and assembly is laborious. Achieving fluidity and verve in line, which come so easily with a pen or brush, are in marquetry a nearly impossible task that only the most accomplished of artisans can realize. And then, as the Metropolitan's demilune vividly attests, there is the wood itself. The

2. PIER TABLE (1800–1810)
MAKER UNKNOWN, SALEM, MASS.
Mahogany, maple, casuarina, holly, and ebony; 29¼ × 59½ × 26½ in.
Metropolitan Museum of Art, New York;
Purchase, Anthony W. and Lulu C. Wang,
Louis and Virginia Clemente Foundation, Inc.,
and Computer Associates Gifts; and
Friends of the American Wing Fund (1996.245);
Photo: Metropolitan Museum of Art

DETAIL OF FIGURE 50:
STUDIOLO FROM THE DUCAL PALACE OF
FEDERIGO DA MONTEFELTRO AT GUBBIO

DETAIL OF FIGURE 27:
CABINET (1900) LOUIS MAJORELLE

material reasserts its status as once-living tissue, still subject to the vicissitudes of its environment, even after it has been laboriously assembled into a smooth and tidy panel.

And yet, as Kopf intimates, it is precisely the limitations of marquetry, its inefficiencies, that make it so fascinating. In the greatest achievements of the craft—the Italian Renaissance masterwork the Gubbio studiolo, also in the Metropolitan (figure 50); the mighty cabinets and elegant tables of André-Charles Boulle (figure 3); or the delicate creations of the Art Nouveau furnituremaker Louis Majorelle (figure 27)—something always transcends mere technical achievement. Such works operate not only on the level of perfect technique, but also in a more suggestive, culturally resonant

register. Somewhere between the trees from which veneers must be cut and the picture held in the maker's mind, marquetry must strike a balance. And in this effort, self-awareness and subtlety are often the result. This is most apparent in the case of trompe l'oeil marquetry, of which the Gubbio studiolo is perhaps the most significant historical monument. In this fabulous hybrid between a library and a walk-in still-life painting, what appears visually to recede is in fact quite flat (in a kind of reversal of the demilune's undulating top). The color, grain, and figure of every bit of wood in the studiolo's interior is exploited for its ability to imitate some other material—a systematic denial of reality that is, at the same time, a glorification of the actual qualities of timber.

A similar degree of compositional control was achieved by baroque cabinetmakers in France, but with a less playful and more authoritative effect. A cupboard now in the collection of the Victoria and Albert Museum is of uncertain authorship, but it typifies the upper echelon of the genre that Boulle invented (figure 3). It typifies the way that the absolutist court of Louis XIV exerted its control over everything in its orbit, including nature itself. Thus the interior of the doors on this monumental piece, composed of engraved pewter against a mahogany ground, are like a rendering in marquetry of the layout of one of the gardens at Versailles.

At the other end of the spectrum, the naturalism of Art Nouveau work presents the full cycle of the art in a beautifully resolved metaphorical style. For Majorelle's atelier to produce a cabinet, trees had to be sliced into thin sheets which were in turn cut into tiny bits and then reassembled—all to create an object with the variety and delicacy of the trees from which it was fashioned.

Silas Kopf is a lifelong observer of objects such as these. He is easily America's most adept practitioner of marquetry, and a keen student of the craft's history as well. In this respect he is unusual among contemporary studio furniture makers, who tend to pick and mix their allusions to historical precedent rather freely. Kopf, by contrast, has a profound respect for precedent. He came by this attitude honestly. The first two artists in the field that Kopf encountered (not counting the famous maker/designer/entrepreneur George Nakashima, who sent him packing summarily) were Richard Scott Newman and Wendell Castle. Newman is not a marquetry specialist, but in many respects he looks back to the same works that Kopf reveres: the courtly furnishings of

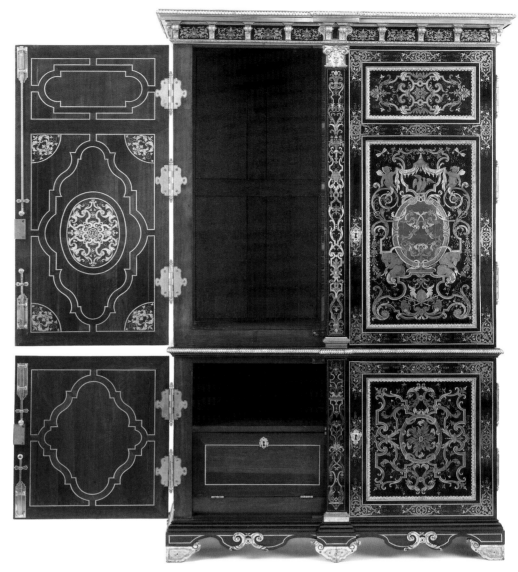

3. ARMOIRE OR CUPBOARD (C. 1685–95) MAKER UNKNOWN, FRENCH (PARIS)
Oak veneered with ebony, tortoiseshell, brass, pewter and clear horn with turquoise blue pigment behind, gilt bronze mounts with crossed L's and cipher of Louis XIV; 100¾ × 63½ × 24¼ in.
Victoria and Albert Museum, London; Photo: V&A Images/Victoria and Albert Museum

the ancien régime, rather than the rough-and-ready country chairs, earnest Arts and Crafts oak sideboards, or Danish Modern designs of the 1950s that many other contemporary makers tend to favor. Castle, meanwhile, is a historical encyclopedia unto himself; his points of reference have ranged from, again, the masterworks of the European *ébénistes* to German Expressionist films to the sculptures of Constantin Brancusi.

Yet it is difficult to imagine either Newman or Castle sitting down to

write an actual history of their discipline. This is a sign, I think, of the fundamentally self-reflective nature of Kopf's practice. It is an attitude that is consistent with his pieces of furniture, which are meditations on the relation between maker, object, and image. Sometimes his creations are simply witty, in a Postmodern, reflexive way—a favorite example of mine is the *Aloha Cabinet,* which depicts seahorses floating in a wash of bubbly bird's-eye maple, and features naturalistic seaweed (an insider's pun on "seaweed" marquetry, a dense vegetal

DETAIL OF FIGURE 214:
ALOHA SHIRT CABINET (2003) SILAS KOPF

style popular in England and the Netherlands during the late seventeenth century). Others, particularly his self-portrait pieces, lean towards a more frank depiction of the struggles and pleasures of his craft—he has shown himself pressed against the picture plane of the top of a chest, in the guise of a bricklayer building a cabinet slowly but surely from the inside, and (in a piece that aptly conveys what a hard day in the studio must feel like) chewing sideways on the end of a stick (figure 4).

In other pieces, Kopf betrays his inner historian more obviously. He has made several works in direct homage to the Gubbio studiolo, lifting from its seemingly inexhaustible supply of motifs. Classical French marquetry has had special importance for him, because of his stint as a student of the École Boulle in Paris, which still teaches the art of marquetry in

4. PRIMAL WOODWORKING (1985) SILAS KOPF
Oak, oak burl, and marquetry; 17 × 52 × 19 in.
Photo: David Ryan

the traditional way. Afforded the opportunity to master the specialized tools of the French *marqueteur* (such as the *chevalet*, which allows the sawing of a stack of veneers simultaneously) and to study objects in museum collections, Kopf drank this tradition in whole. It could be said to form the basis of his technique and visual vocabulary since. As for Art Nouveau, one need only cast a cursory glance at the spectacular decorations for a Steinway piano that Kopf executed to see the influence that Majorelle, Émile Gallé, and their contemporaries have had on his work (figure 195).

As the book you hold in your hands demonstrates, these points of reference are only the tip of the iceberg in terms of Kopf's lexicon of marquetry. Like his furniture, this volume offers an approachable introduction to a craft that may seem recondite—technically baffling at first, and perhaps a marginal subject within the broader current of art history. In Kopf's hands the subject comes almost literally alive. What's more, this book offers a rare chance to get inside a furniture maker's head, because of its piece-by-piece narration of Kopf's own development as an artisan, designer, and artist. Furniture historians of the future will be delighted with this unusually detailed overview (if only Boulle or Majorelle had thought to write a similar account!). Meanwhile, students of furniture today, whether they approach the subject as makers, collectors, or scholars, will doubtless feel the same way. It is a book of many pieces: history, technique, autobiography, and travelogue. But, like any great piece of marquetry, the whole is more than the sum of its parts.

— *Glenn Adamson,*
Head of Graduate Studies
and Deputy Head of Research,
Victoria and Albert Museum,
London

DETAIL OF FIGURE 199:
MORNING GLORIES (1989) SILAS KOPF; MODEL L, STEINWAY AND SONS PIANO

5. Hadley Chest with Tulips (1988) Silas Kopf
Mahogany and marquetry; 33 × 44 × 22 in.
Photo: David Ryan

Introduction

A CAREER IN THE ARTS can be thought of as a journey of growth, refinement, and increasing self-confidence—with a series of stops along the way to explore creative side roads. No one who attempts to make beautiful or at least interesting objects starts off producing a masterpiece. An artist is being too cautious if diversionary searches don't at least occasionally lead to dead ends. Perhaps more than the successful work, these "mistakes" can serve as opportunities for development.

Artists who focus on craftsmanship have the added challenge to become better technicians within their chosen medium. Craft involves a long-term relationship with materials and tools, discovering what can and can't be done with them. Like musicians practicing scales, craftspeople need to gain command of their techniques through repetition, as hands and fingers develop a memory that allows for ease of production. Once you are comfortable with the tasks, you can begin pushing boundaries, and that's how you grow.

The philosopher George Santayana famously wrote, "Those who cannot remember the past are condemned to repeat it." It could equally be said, "Those who do not know the past *cannot* repeat it." Much can be gained from becoming familiar with the great objects that have been made through history. I don't know if the anecdote is correct, but I was told that Sam Maloof, the great American furniture craftsman, once told a group of students that years ago he was proud of himself for having come up with a new form for a chair. Shortly thereafter, looking through a book, he saw a picture of an Egyptian throne and realized that the essence of his design was right there in that 4,000-year-old object. Little in design is really revolutionary. Most things we think of as new are but a small step away from established precedents. It can be intimidating to realize what great things have been produced throughout history, but it can also be wonderful to feel connected to a continuum of creativity, of people striving to make beautiful, interesting, and useful things.

We are fortunate to live at a time when so much material is becoming so easy to study. Beautiful books and magazines are printed every day illustrating masterpieces of furniture. Museums exhibit furniture as art. And now the

6. FALL FRONT DESK (1986) SILAS KOPF
Laurel, curly laurel, and marquetry; 58 × 40 × 18 in.
Photo: David Ryan

internet provides access to information from all corners of the globe. Cabinetmakers of the past had no such advantages. They might have been able to see a new piece at a neighboring workshop, or perhaps they had access to a book of styles. Growth as a designer-craftsman was usually a slow, restricted process.

Wood, originally a living material that is not structurally homogeneous, can be a challenge to work. Nevertheless, it has been invaluable for making things since before the dawn of history. It is plentiful in many parts of the world, and its uses have spanned the range from the merely utilitarian to the spectacular.

Woodworking offers many avenues of expression. Wood can be sculpted with chisels and gouges. It can be turned on a lathe, revealing the very essence of the tree. Whether with hand tools or machines, it can be sized, shaped, and joined to form objects big or small, from buildings and furniture to utensils, musical instruments, and sculptures. One small corner of the field of woodwork takes diverse species of wood and pieces them together to form patterns and images. This is the essence of marquetry and inlay. The desire to embellish wood with contrasting inlays has been a part of making things for thousands of years. Some of the same skills required to fabricate furniture are used as well to decorate that furniture. The ability to hone an edge on a cutting tool and then to shape a piece of wood precisely is as essential to cutting an accurate inlay as it is to making a well-fitted dovetail joint. Surely the first inlay decoration was added by the same person who made the piece of furniture. It was only much later that inlay became a skill in its own right, and the one who designed

7. Table (c. 1680) Attributed to André-Charles Boulle
Oak veneered with marquetry tortoiseshell, pewter, brass, ebony, horn, ivory, boxwood, cherry, sycamore, cedar, beech and amaranth; 28½ × 43½ × 29 in.
The J. Paul Getty Museum, Los Angeles (inv. 71.DA.100)

and made the furniture might seek out the specialist in decoration. By the fifteenth century, inlay, or intarsia as it was called in Italy, had become a trade distinguished from the rest of woodcraft. The skills at cutting intarsia spread throughout northern Italy. As the craft grew, new techniques were developed, and modern marquetry was born.

Marquetry and inlay are technically distinct. In a true inlay a recess is cut into a surface, the cavity is filled, and then the surface is made flush. Marquetry is created by piecing together contrasting materials of the same thickness (or thinness) and then overlaying the assembled sheet onto another surface. The process is akin to assembling a jigsaw puzzle. Historically, the key to making elaborate marquetry was the ability to use a fretsaw with enough accuracy to cut the shapes. The art and craft of marquetry reached its height in seventeenth- and eighteenth-century France. Some of the furniture produced for the French aristocracy is mind boggling in its complexity and technical finesse. Eventually marqueteurs added exotic materials to their designs: metal, tortoiseshell, horn. New materials presented new challenges, adding new opportunities as well. Surface decoration enhanced increasingly complicated furniture designs. The craftsman who could offer the most elaborate and innovative ideas had an advantage, and he would be sought after to create work for the most prestigious clients, in whose possession it would have the most influential exposure. Most craftsmen were no doubt motivated by economics to learn a new stylistic or technical distinction rather than personal expression. Money was to be made at the top of this fashionable world. Nevertheless, craft has always been a difficult way of making a living.

I have long been curious about the economics of craftwork. Chronicles of great artisans reaching the end of their careers in destitution trace a recurring theme. It is understandably galling to make luxurious objects for an elite class and be only modestly compensated. How much greater must have been that feeling, making something for royalty, and then going home to a hardscrabble existence in the working class neighborhoods of Paris.

❧

Creating a piece of marquetry entails a number of challenges. There is the technical challenge of accurately cutting the pieces of wood, which requires learning how to use the tools. If the marqueteur is the designer, he is also tested in creating the drawing that guides the work. Once an object is finished, the questions should be, "How can I make it better?" and "How can I make it more interesting?" Craftsmen have always been motivated by these two concerns. As designers push themselves, styles evolve.

Designing and making objects are separate concerns. A great craftsman isn't necessarily a great designer. But a great designer will understand the materials for which he is designing, and he will be aware of the limitations of the technician who realizes the plan. Often the designer and the craftsman are one and the same. Great things have been produced from the imagination of one individual who also has the skill to execute the design. Think of the great painters of the past who not only conceived the composition of their pictures, but also mixed the colors and manipulated the brush to get the desired result.

The making of a marquetry picture is much like painting. There needs to be a composition. Then the design is executed from a palette of colors and textures, not of paint but of available wood veneers.

One of the things that interests me about marquetry is the artistic limitations. The most obvious constraint is that wood has a very limited range of color. The tones are

8. Sloppy Paint Job (2003) Silas Kopf
Shedua, satinwood, and marquetry; 28 × 26½ × 20 in.
Photo: David Ryan

earthy; beige and brown predominate, with only an occasional bright hue thrown in. It is true that marquetry can employ dyed woods, but even so, the colors and tones are a restriction that most painters would shy away from. The marqueteur's task is in finding those harmonious relationships that can produce a pleasing picture in spite of the limitations. I imagine that photographers who work in black and white instead of color feel much the same way.

Wood does have a characteristic that paint doesn't have, and it makes marquetry unique. Wood has grain (a term used to describe various aspects of the structure and texture of wood) and figure (the shape of the grain patterns). No two pieces of wood will be exactly the same. Trees grow by continually adding wood fibers to their outer layer and extremities, the trunk and limbs getting wider and longer. The history of a tree can be discerned in its growth rings, and these rings show up in the cut boards. Different parts of the tree have different characteristics. A chunk of wood from a root spur or burl might not look anything like the straight-fibered board from the tree's trunk. Small limbs may have begun to grow and will show up as knots in a board. Color, texture, and figure vary for all kinds of reasons. Some trees have a layer of significantly lighter colored sapwood. Other trees' fibers will grow in a wavy manner and produce a figure we call curly. A board from yet another tree may exhibit a striped or ribbon figure because the grain of the annual growth rings naturally spiral in alternating directions. The variety in wood is endless and shows the organic nature of the material—both an asset and a liability to the maker.

Although the tree was dead when it was cut into lumber, it continues to react to its environment. The wood fibers absorb moisture, swelling in humid conditions, and shrinking when the air is dry. But the swelling and shrinking is not uniform dimensionally. While wood fibers, long and narrow like soda straws, expand and contract considerably in diameter, they change barely at all in length. So pieces of wood move, accordion-like, as the seasons change. Careful wood craftsmanship will take this fact into account. Contrary wood movement between components can cause a construction to self-destruct. Appropriate methods of joining wood have been developed over millennia, and the degree to which these constructions have stood the test of time is testament to their efficacy.

The raw material for marquetry is veneer. Veneers have been sawn from logs since ancient Egypt. Veneering is a way of making the most of rare and precious materials, and it is also a way of controlling wood movement. Thin wood can be glued in various grain configurations because thin wood exerts less force (as it moves in response to changes in humidity) against the glue bond. As sawing techniques advanced through the centuries, thinner, more consistent veneers could be produced with less waste. Early in the twentieth century, giant machines were built with knives that could actually slice sheets off a log with no waste at all. The machines further evolved to where they can turn a log on its axis and peel off the layers of veneer like paper toweling.

Most American craftsmen don't jump right into marquetry. They start as cabinetmakers, learning the basics of working with the tools and the traditional ways of building objects. This was the case with me. I wanted to learn how to craft a piece of furniture. To do so means putting yourself in a tradition that goes back to early civilizations. Many of the tools haven't changed over the centuries. Power tools can be more efficient, saving time and sweat, but the processes are the same. Often there is still no replacement for the chisels, saws, and planes that have been around through the ages. Learning to use the tools takes practice and patience. I imagine that most woodworkers have had the experience I had in building my first piece. I was thrilled that I was actually able to do it. At the same time I realized how flawed it was. Thus came the perennial questions, "How can I make it better?" and "How can I make it more interesting?" My second set of dovetail joints was an improvement. While learning the basics of the craft, I scrutinized furniture I could find in galleries and museums, as well as in the workshops of friends. I began paying attention to how craftsmen have used carving, inlay, and marquetry to embellish their work.

I found marquetry to be a great way to display the uniqueness of wood. The ideal in marquetry is to piece together a variety of woods to create a harmonious picture that takes advantage of the individual pieces of veneer. The challenge is in choosing the best piece of wood for the job. And then I had to learn to make the joints tight. Marquetry involves very different attention than does cabinetwork. Cabinetwork is three-dimensional construction; marquetry involves only two dimensions. I approach my marquetry designs as marqueteurs traditionally have: as a painter approaches a canvas. The furniture designer in me must think sculpturally. But both sensibilities come together to incorporate the marquetry in the furniture harmoniously. I have rarely made a panel that isn't integral with a piece of furniture. Marquetry's origin was in the context of furniture, and it is there that it feels most comfortable for me.

‹›

DETAIL OF FIGURE 89:
FOUR ARTS (2003) SILAS KOPF

My goal with this book is two-fold. I hope that craftsmen interested in marquetry will be inspired and enabled to design and produce their own work more confidently. I also trust there is an audience who will be interested in a provocative part of furniture history. I believe your experience with art will be enhanced if you understand how it was made, recognizing the rich context of its development through the ages. Fantastic objects in museums are passed by every day because people don't have an insider's perspective. I'm not a scholar; I don't have the temperament or the training to explore history the way an academic would. To write a scholarly text I would also need facility in a number of languages, not to mention being able to travel extensively. I have been fortunate to have spent some time in France (where I have a passing ability in the language), Italy, and England, and seen some of the great work first-hand.

But there are fantastic pieces in Germany, Holland, Spain, Russia, and elsewhere that I have seen only in books. Therefore my survey is not comprehensive, and it doesn't pretend to be. I hope this book may open the door for you to explore the history of the craft on your own. And I hope you return to your studio, or your living room, as inspired by your explorations as I have been by mine. Marquetry has a great past, and those who keep the tradition alive can create a great future as well.

— Silas Kopf
Northampton, Massachusetts
September 2007

9: **What a Knucklehead** (1999)
Silas Kopf
Wilsonart laminate and ebonized ash;
76 × 23 × 19 in.
Collection: Wilsonart International, Temple, Tex.;
Photo: Dean Powell

Some people find their life's work through being exposed to a field while growing up. Perhaps a parent passed along an enthusiasm for or commitment to their own vocation. This was traditionally how people were introduced to a career, particularly in the building trades. In earlier generations a young man would learn carpentry or cabinetmaking in his father's workshop. I had no such fortune. When I was growing up, there were probably a few screwdrivers and hammers around the house, but they would have been used only reluctantly for some basic home repair. The idea of actually making something lasting with your hands would have seemed impossible to my father, my brothers, or myself.

I was introduced to woodworking as a college student majoring in architecture at Princeton University. At the time Princeton offered little in the way of studio art. The act of painting or sculpting was considered un-academic. Studying art meant exploring the history of art. However, the university had a non-credit sculpture studio, where an economics professor provided some modest instruction in woodcarving. This teacher suggested I look at some of the work of Henry Moore (figure 10). I was only vaguely familiar with this giant of twentieth-century sculpture, even though there was a wonderful bronze sculpture of his on the campus. I got a book or two out of the library. Moore worked in many materials, including bronze and stone, but it was the wood pieces that really struck me. The grain and the knots seemed to give the work vitality and uniqueness. I became hooked on doing something with wood, and started by making some sculptures from small blocks. When it came time to decide whether to go to graduate school, I resolved that my future would not be designing buildings.

This interest in wood led me to investigate what others were doing in the medium. Living in New Jersey, I was not far from the Pennsylvania town of New Hope, where, someone told me, a man named George Nakashima made remarkable furniture. I visited his studio and was immediately struck by the beauty of his work, particularly the special quality of the timbers he used to make his distinctive tables and seating (figure 11).

10: INTERNAL AND EXTERNAL FORMS (1953–54)
HENRY MOORE
Elmwood;
103 × 34 × 36 in.
Albright-Knox Art Gallery Buffalo, N.Y.; Charles Clifton, James G. Forsyth, Charles W. Goodyear, Edmund Hayes, and Sherman S. Jewett Funds, 1955

That day Mr. Nakashima was at the showroom to meet with clients, and I spent about an hour awkwardly hanging around for a chance to speak to him. Finally, he was free and I mustered the courage to ask if there was a possibility of employment. I will never forget how he paused and looked me over as if I were the most impudent person he had ever encountered. He said something like, "I have you college people approach me all the time asking for work. You know nothing that could be of any help, yet you think you know everything. In the old days in Europe a boy was apprenticed to a master and was never even allowed to touch a tool. He slept under a bench and cleaned the workshop. Maybe after a few years he would be taught how to plane a board." He told me a story about how a musician would be taught in old Japan. He, too, might be apprenticed to a master, but instead of playing an instrument he would be given the job of gardening within earshot of the master while he was practicing his music. If the apprentice really cared, he would absorb the essence of the music by listening. The lesson was obvious. After these, perhaps apocryphal, stories Mr. Nakashima calmed down and lightened up. He told me that the European or Japanese apprentice system didn't exist here. His advice was to get some practical woodworking experience however I could. Ideally, I would apprentice to a cabinetmaker. He also referred to the college-level woodworking program at

11. CONOID BENCH WITH BACK (C. 1974) GEORGE NAKASHIMA
Walnut; 31 × 113 × 40 in.
Photo: George Erml

12. BLANKET CHEST (C. 1978) RICHARD NEWMAN
Mahogany; 20 × 44 × 20 in.
Photo: David Leveille

the Rochester Institute of Technology, with which he was vaguely familiar.

Shortly after my visit to Nakashima I was in my hometown in western Pennsylvania. I told my parents of my hope to go into woodworking. They were skeptical (to say the least) of this decision, concerned that I would be squandering an expensive education. But not long after, my mother told me she had seen an interesting piece of furniture in a gift shop in a nearby town. She suggested that if I were really interested in woodworking, I should go see it. I drove to the shop and was struck by the piece, a handmade wall-hung cabinet in a style that exhibited the organic curves and sensitivity to wood that attracted me to Henry Moore's work (compare figure 12). But here was a utilitarian object. I knew enough about the art world to realize how difficult it is to make a career in the fine arts. Perhaps if you could make the art functional, there might be more of a market. The proprietor told me that the maker of the piece was a friend of his named Richard Newman, from Rochester, New York. He gave me Richard's phone number and suggested I call.

It took me a while to muster the courage to telephone Richard. I was afraid I might get the same curt treatment I had initially received from Nakashima. I told Richard I was interested in learning woodworking and asked if I might visit his studio. The following week I made the three-hour drive to Rochester and found Richard to be very amiable and open about his work. To my untrained eye his furniture seemed constructed with great technical finesse. The wood was cut and joined with intricate dovetails and mortise-and-tenons, clearly requiring different skills than those I had been using to make wood sculpture. His tools were intriguing and intimidating to me: planes, saws, drills, and terribly scary power tools.

The trip confirmed Nakashima's recommendation; Richard was an RIT graduate who, before opening his own shop, had worked in the studio of one of the RIT professors—Wendell Castle. I was not at all familiar with Castle's work. Richard suggested that we take the short drive out to the suburbs to visit Wendell's studio. Wendell wasn't there that afternoon, but his assistant (another RIT graduate) showed us around. They were working on a spiral staircase carved in solid walnut, almost complete and ready for an oil finish (figure 13). I was stunned. It had all the elements I loved about woodcarving. A fifteen-foot-high sculptural object, with the organic shapes that I had found so appealing in Henry Moore's work, it was also a formidable technical and engineering challenge. Each tread was a little sculpture that had to be assembled in a craftsman-like manner into a staircase that would support people's weight.

Throughout the studio I was drawn to the organic quality of Wendell's work. Some of his forms looked literally like bones. In the studio I saw an unfinished floor lamp that looked like a femur from a dinosaur. I remembered that Moore had a collection of bones that he used as inspiration for his sculptures.

It wasn't until some time later that I became aware of just how prominent Wendell Castle was in the burgeoning field of studio furniture. His work had been exhibited all over the country, including an important show at the Renwick Gallery of the Smithsonian Institute. The exhibition *Woodenworks* in 1972 featured the furniture of Castle as well as Nakashima, and three other designer-craftsmen: Wharton Esherick, Sam Maloof, and Art Carpenter. I had a great deal to learn about the players in the field of woodworking, yet without really trying I had encountered two of them.

I wrote Wendell a letter and asked if he needed an employee. When we talked by phone, his only question was whether I had any woodworking experience. When I told him I had done only a little carving, he said I would be a much more valuable assistant if I had some shop experience and knew something about cabinetmaking. It was the classic Catch 22: No one would give me experience if I didn't have any experience. School seemed to be the only option.

I looked into the summer program at RIT, but it was full. However, there was an evening course that met twice a week, for two hours each night. The instructor was one of the students from the regular undergraduate program. I decided that it was at least a start, so I enrolled, found a small studio apartment, and moved to Rochester. The course was to run for ten weeks. I had no idea how little a novice could actually do in what amounted to forty hours of shop time.

My project was to make a dovetailed box with two little drawers. We were given basic instruction in the use of some of the power tools (jointer, planer, tablesaw), and I was shown how to lay out dovetails. It turned out to be impossible to complete the piece in the allotted time, but I got enough done that I was able to sand it up and put a finish on it in my apartment. There were serious problems with the craftsmanship, but it didn't really matter to me. I felt I had begun a journey.

The Rochester area had an active community of woodworkers, largely because of people having gone through the program at RIT. Before long I was able to get a job in the cabinet shop of an RIT graduate who specialized in architectural millwork and commercial installations. This wasn't the type of work I was ultimately looking for, but it was another step along the way. Slowly I gathered some modest skills and knowledge of tools and machinery. Every three or four months I'd call Wendell and again ask about work. Eventually my persistence paid off. After a year I got a call

13. SPIRAL STAIRCASE (1973) WENDELL CASTLE
Walnut
Photo: courtesy Wendell Castle

14. Dining Table (1973)
Wendell Castle
Walnut
Photo: courtesy
Wendell Castle

from him about an opening in his shop, and I jumped at the chance.

At that point in Wendell's career, his work was what I would call utilitarian sculpture, the same sort of thing that first appealed to me in Richard Newman's little cabinet. Art with a purpose. Wendell was making pieces of furniture out of stack-laminated blocks of wood that he then carved into organic forms (figure 14). The process involved bandsawing shapes and gluing them, layer upon layer, until the form was roughly complete but stepped rather than smoothly curved. Wendell would start carving the shape with an electric chainsaw and work through successively finer carving tools until the form was refined. Eventually, he'd turn it over to his assistants, who did the final sanding and oil finishing.

Wendell had a system of employing two workers, each of whom would commit to stay for two years. The starting time was staggered so that essentially a new person would come in every year. The more experienced of the two would help train the new person. This senior employee also got the more challenging jobs, sometimes even doing some of the shaping. The newer person would joint and plane the lumber, as well as oil the finished pieces.

I vividly remember one morning when Wendell came into the shop and spent several minutes studying the table that had just been turned over to me for sanding. He walked around it several times and finally picked up the chainsaw and cut off the bottom half of the piece! I was stunned. He said, "It isn't right. The base of the table needs to be rebuilt." The table already had about two weeks of his work into it. And it looked fine to me. But Wendell

had uncompromising standards. He would work to that goal, even if it meant a financial sacrifice. This is a lesson that I have recalled on many occasions when I wanted to stop short on a project, thinking that no one else would care. Ultimately the integrity of the piece is the maker's responsibility, and it should be built to a standard that satisfies the craftsman first. Presumably if he is content, then the client will be as well.

While I was working for Wendell, I maintained contact with Richard. Once, when I was visiting his shop, he commented that he thought he might have felt more at home in a shop in France at the turn of the twentieth century, "working for someone like Gallé or Majorelle." Not willing to acknowledge my ignorance of these two designers, I simply nodded thoughtfully and filed the names away. I had taken a class at Princeton with Robert Clark, a scholar of American decorative art, and I vaguely remember hearing reference to Gallé, but I thought of him as a glass artist, not a furniture designer. The discussion with Richard led me to the library to look up French Art Nouveau furniture. It came as a revelation. I learned that Gallé, best known for his glass, was also an outstanding furniture designer. Here was the beautiful organic carving integrated with functionality that I appreciated in Wendell's work, plus a new element: decoration done with inlaid pictures. Marquetry.

During the late 1960s and early 1970s Art Nouveau, particularly the French brand, was in vogue among studio furnituremakers. Many, including Wendell, imitated aspects of that compelling turn-of-the-twentieth-century movement. Carving and shaping were the most attractive techniques of Art Nouveau, inspired by designers like Guimard and Gallé. But no one seemed to be trying to decorate with marquetry or inlay. The finest of the French work often exhibited both carving and inlay. My first foray into the study of historic furniture was to learn a little something about Émile Gallé. As I found out, Gallé could be inspirational for more reasons than the beauty of his work. He was an exceptionally successful businessman, as well as an influential artist.

❧

Émile Gallé

Reading about Émile Gallé opened my eyes to one of the great artists of his era. Because his work is decorative, he is probably less well known than if he were a fine artist. His reputation is based on the diversity of his work in different media. Primarily a glass artist, he also designed ceramics and furniture.

Gallé was a proud citizen of the province of Lorraine in eastern France. France's window on Germany and the rest of eastern Europe, Lorraine is unique as a place where cultures meet. In the eighteenth century the capitol city of Nancy had developed as a center of the arts under the patronage of the Duke, Stanislas. Glassmaking and pottery attracted many talented designers. Gallé's father manufactured mirrors and glass tableware, with the business eventually expanding into faience pottery.

Born in 1846, Émile Gallé received a formal humanist education, studying classics, philosophy, poetry, art, and music. He had an obvious talent for art. Émile spent long hours drawing plants, which led to a life-long interest in botany. While still a teenager he produced decorative designs for the family business. His education took him to Germany for several years. At twenty-one he returned to Lorraine and began working full time at the faience factory.

After the Franco-Prussian War of 1870, Gallé began his own glassworks business. A few years later his father turned over the rest of the family business to him. Émile aggressively expanded the output of both glasswork and pottery, and in 1884 his work won a gold medal for design at a major exposition of decorative art in Paris. That notoriety led to the opening of a retail shop for the glass in Paris. This presence in the capital put Gallé in touch with the most influential figures in the French decorative arts.

In 1885 Gallé began designing furniture, having discovered wood quite by accident. Needing a special stand for one of his unique glass vases, he visited a dealer of fine and exotic woods and immediately fell in love with the material. He was attracted to the color of timbers, like amaranth and satinwood, and was captivated by the variety of grain and figure. He noticed the way light seemed to penetrate the surface and reflect back differently, depending on the angle of view. Gallé began designing for wood and found craftsmen to carve and inlay production furniture designs, as well as his one-of-a-kind pieces. The woodworking shop grew quickly. Soon it had a small sawmill for custom-cutting lumber, as well as storage sheds for timber and fine veneers.

Eventually the various Gallé factories in Nancy employed 300 workers with showrooms in Frankfurt, Germany, as well as Paris. This enterprise made Gallé a national hero. As wealthy clients clamored for unique, luxurious pieces of furniture and glass, the production lines ran at full capacity. Gallé was not wedded to a romantic notion of handcraft. He used the latest mechanized tools to save time and increase productivity. Machines were used to do the preliminary shaping on furniture parts, which would then be turned over to a master carver for only the final tooling by hand. The machines could be run by less skilled workers, saving the company significant money.

The marquetry designs that embellished the furniture were done in the traditional way, with line drawings. All the parts were keyed by numbers. This way the designs could be reproduced as long as the same woods were available. So, Gallé amassed a huge stock of veneers—at least 600 different varieties. It was one man's job to keep track of

15. Tuilpe de l'est (c. 1900) Émile Gallé
Pearwood, oak, and marquetry
Musée de l'École de Nancy, Nancy, France; Photo: O. Dancy

16. Aube et Crépuscule (1904) Émile Gallé
Rosewood and marquetry; 56 × 75 × 85 in.
Musée de l'École de Nancy, Nancy, France; Photo: C. Philippot

this inventory and to make sure that when the designer called for an oak burl with a particular density of pips, that veneer was available. This way the furniture ended up looking as the designer intended and wasn't left to the whim of the individual marqueteur to make the wood choice.

Nancy had become the focus of the decorative arts movement in France, and Gallé was its most prominent designer. Other notable artists included Auguste Daum, Eugene Vallin, Louis Majorelle, and Victor Prouvé. Prouvé's father had worked for Gallé's father, and Émile had known Victor since the two were boys. Prouvé later became a close collaborator with Louis Majorelle, the other giant of Nancy furniture design. Gallé was an inspiration to all the designers of Lorraine, who eventually exhibited together under the name *École de Nancy*.

The Paris International Exposition of 1900 was a watershed event for Gallé and the other designers of the École de Nancy. The curvilinear Art Nouveau style was seen by people from around the world. Some of Gallé's most important furniture pieces were exhibited at the Expo. Opportunities to open showrooms sprang up around Europe. Tragically, it was only a few years later, in 1904, that Gallé contracted leukemia and died. He had reached a pinnacle of success and one can only speculate about what a longer career might have produced.

Gallé's legacy as a furniture designer is enormous. His elegant designs were accessible to the middle-class market, while his one-of-a-kind pieces were treated as fine art. He mixed beautiful marquetry with beautiful carving. Behind the style was a great interest in the natural world and a desire to bring

17. Firescreen (c.1900) Émile Gallé
Ash with applied decoration in various woods
*Victoria and Albert Museum, London, CT9271;
Photo: V&A Images/Victoria and Albert Museum*

nature into the home through furniture design. For Gallé modern style involved making both fine and everyday objects inspired by nature, which he considered the wellspring of truth.

A small box, now in the Musée de l'École de Nancy, illustrates many of the finest qualities o f Gallé's sensibilities (figure 15). The box is designed around a theme of lilies, which is carried through in both the marquetry and the carving. The four trapezoidal shapes that form the sides of the box are joined by carved wooden lilies. The sculpting is realistic and very organic, the lines intertwining to form the structure. The background to the marquetry is quartersawn oak with a beautiful fleck pattern. Because the marquetry lilies are off-center and leaning over, the composition seems off balance. But the effect is purposeful, as nature is not always symmetrical. The interplay of the light, bright marquetry against the dark wood for the carving and background makes this a striking piece.

In 1900 Gallé designed a firescreen for the Paris Exposition, achieving a very unusual layered effect (figure 17). The screen is framed with a sinuous vine carved in pearwood and sprouting a few curvaceously carved leaves. At the top the vine sends down shoots across the face of the screen, a beautiful curly ash veneer. The vine traverses the background, at times protruding from the surface, at other times inlaid into the surface. The background includes the same kind of leaves and vines carved elsewhere in solid wood, only here cut in marquetry. Additionally, some leaves are inlaid into the surface and left proud, then carved to give them more three-dimensionality. The fully round carvings appear closest, then the inlaid and carved parts, and finally the marquetry in the plane of the background panel. It is a wonderful effect.

Shortly before his death, Gallé was commissioned to make a remarkable set of bedroom furniture. Gallé's frequent forays into nature and symbolism took full flight with this piece, entitled *Aube et Crépuscule* (Dawn and Dusk, figure 16). The headboard depicts a large insect spreading its wings over the landscape.

18. GALLÉ FACTORY (C. 1900) AUGUSTE HERBST
30 × 18½ in.
Musée de l'École de Nancy, Nancy, France; Photo: G. Mangin

The veneer chosen for the sky is darkest at the top and lighter toward the horizon, as if the setting sun is still illuminating that part of the picture. Small mother-of-pearl dots are inlaid into the veneer as stars. The footboard depicts another giant insect with elaborate wings. The body of the creature is a piece of glass that was created in the Gallé glassworks. The wings are carved in low relief, with veins running the length of the wing. Figured veneers are glued onto the sculpted panel, and then small pieces of pearl and abalone shell are inlaid in bands running perpendicular to the carving. The combination of carving and veneer work is an awesome technical accomplishment.

The work of Gallé inspired me greatly in my nascent career. He was an incredibly inventive and uncompromising designer, yet also a highly successful businessman, employing as many as 600 workers in his glassworks alone (figure 18). I assumed there were others in the history of the craft who had done fantastic things. I began my exploration of furniture history with a few books on Art Nouveau. Soon I would at least have something to talk about with Richard Newman.

☙

19. MARQUETRY JEWELRY BOXES (1980) SILAS KOPF
Photo: David Ryan

The use of marquetry in furniture design by Gallé piqued my interest in this decorative technique. Marquetry is not an important part of the American furniture tradition. If I were going to learn anything about the technique, the information would have to come from Europe.

I eventually found *The Art and Practice of Marquetry* by William A. Lincoln, an Englishman. I was lucky that the first book I located on the subject was so good. It gave a basic history of the craft and some excellent technical insight. The first thing I learned from Lincoln was that marquetry is not inlay. I had assumed that marquetry was produced by cutting a recess in a board and filling it with contrasting pieces of wood. But that technique Lincoln describes as inlay. In marquetry a veneered sheet is pieced together like a jigsaw puzzle, including the background of the picture or design. The whole is then overlaid onto a thicker backing. The resulting look can be the same in either inlay or marquetry, but the route to get there is different.

Lincoln's book informed me that the essential tool for cutting marquetry is a fretsaw with a very fine sawblade. The teeth on one of these blades can be so small, the blade appears to be nothing more than a wire. A fretsaw can be motorized and it is then called a scroll saw. Wendell Castle had an old scroll saw that he allowed me to use after hours and weekends. I started to make small pictures that could be used on little boxes.

Several things attracted me to marquetry. Émile Gallé's work had captured my imagination. The range of effects possible seemed limitless. I liked the obvious economy of working with veneers, in contrast to the expense and effort of working with large timbers such as those necessary to produce Wendell's carved objects. From a business standpoint, I didn't know of any American furniture makers who were focused on the technique. It appeared that those in the studio furniture movement who were successful had a signature look to their work that was readily recognizable. I thought of Wendell with his stack-laminated technique or George Nakashima with his live-edge slabs. Perhaps marquetry could be a similar signature that would constitute my niche in the field of studio furniture.

Lincoln's book is dedicated to a man named Ernest Oppenheim. He was identified as the past president of the Marquetry Society and the founder of the Marquetry School of Toronto. Toronto is not too far from Rochester. I was able to find Mr. Oppenheim in the phone book, and I arranged a visit. The school was a very modest affair, but Mr. Oppenheim was able to point me in the right direction. He sold sawblades and veneer tape which he said were hard-to-find specialty items. He also pointed me to an excellent source of veneer in Buffalo.

I collected an assortment of veneers from the company in Buffalo and then bought an old scroll saw. I began with small floral pictures in the style of Gallé. These small panels were excellent pieces to practice on. I was able to make finished objects without investing a lot of time or expense, while learning how to shape and join the parts with a bit of technical finesse (figure 19). I could also try different wood combinations and see how they looked together.

❧

Every piece I made used the marquetry method called bevel (or double-bevel) cutting. I had read about the technique in Lincoln's book. It was only a two-page entry, but bevel cutting looked like the easiest way to approach marquetry. In this method one piece of veneer is laid on top of the other. A fine sawblade cuts the line that will be the border between the two picture parts. The beauty of the technique is that the two parts are cut at the same time, along the same line. Even if the cutting deviates from the desired line, the pieces will still fit each other.

Marquetry pictures have been bevel-cut at least since the eighteenth century. The advantage of bevel cutting is that it can easily produce a picture without gaps. Bevel cutting developed out of Boulle work, where two contrasting parts are laid on top of one another and one cutting yields a pair of both figure and ground. Boulle panels have a gap around the picture parts the size of the saw kerf. Someone realized that if the saw cut is angled, the kerf can be eliminated. The compromise is that in bevel cutting, only one picture can be made at a time (see Appendix 4: Boule Work and Appendix 7: Bevel Cutting).

The equipment needed to get started doing marquetry is relatively simple: a saw, veneer tape to hold the pieces together, and a variety of veneers. My first designs were simple floral patterns—petals and stems and leaves. My intent was to use the color and grain of the wood to its best advantage. The floral designs called for a pleasing juxtaposition of wood tones. The same pattern could be used to make a dark flower on a light background or a light flower on a dark ground.

I started working on the floral patterns for two reasons. Most importantly they were the models that I had seen in the Art Nouveau examples of Gallé. Secondly, flowers are forgiving. If you miss the line, no one is going to know the newly created line wasn't intended; the petal will just be shaped a little differently. The ability to saw accurately is not paramount. For a novice bevel cutting is the perfect technique because the two parts can't help but fit together well. And flowers are the perfect subject to practice on.

After a few months I had run out of both the veneer tape and the sawblades. I called Mr. Oppenheim and was told that he had died and that with his passing the business had dissolved. All I was left with was the empty packet for the blades and the end of the little plastic reel for the tape. The sawblades were from a German company named Eberle, and the tape was from another German company called Ubro. A letter to the German Consulate in New York yielded an address for both companies. Ubro had a distributor in Memphis, Tennessee, so finding the tape was relatively easy. The sawblades were slightly more difficult. Eberle would sell me the blades, but there was a minimum order. The dollar amount was not too great, but the number of individual blades seemed enormous, something like twenty-five gross (with each pack having a dozen blades). Would I ever possibly use that many blades? I decided that if I wanted to learn the craft I had to take the plunge. (I've re-ordered two more times in the intervening thirty years!)

❧

Rochester was a great place for craftspeople. The School for American Craftsmen at the Rochester Institute of Technology had spawned a community of people doing handcraft. There was also an audience interested in the work. Rochester had one of the first art/craft galleries in the United States. The city had plenty of industrial space for rent. Colleagues were open about discussing their work. It was exciting to be part of the craft community.

There were two important influences on woodworking in the mid-1970s when I was becoming involved in the field. One was the publication of James Krenov's book *A Cabinetmaker's Notebook* in 1976. The other was *Fine Woodworking* magazine, which began in 1975. Each of these resources came on my radar screen and affected my direction.

James Krenov is a Russian immigrant to America who was trained as a cabinetmaker in Sweden. He returned to the States from Europe in the 1960s and taught at several schools (including RIT). The teaching experience probably led him to write the book and eventually two more. They had widespread influence on young woodworkers all over the country. I am sure there are copies in people's studios all around America to this day.

Krenov's work has the design sensibilities of Scandinavian furniture and Shaker furniture, with an emphasis on maximizing the unique potential of the wood out of which it's made (figure 20). Particular pieces of wood inspire Krenov's work, perhaps not as obviously as Nakashima's, but Krenov stresses the subtle care that should be taken in choosing and using wood as part of the design process. His doors, for instance, are often made with a re-sawn board in order to celebrate a revealed defect or special grain configuration. The construction is generally in solid wood. If it is veneered, the veneers are individually re-sawn, thick enough to have integrity. The furniture also displays great technical finesse, with joinery exposed and important to the design aesthetic. Numerous individual touches, such as carved pulls and handmade hardware, give the work a wonderful charm. It is simple, honest furniture—but intensely so. A reaction to mass-production and commercial values, these objects would never be mistaken for other than the late twentieth century works they are. For me, and many others, Krenov's work was exciting because it fit the image of the wholesome lifestyle we were pursuing. His approach to furniture making was a philosophical, political statement, an alternative to our throwaway society. This was a mission that I found particularly attractive. Thirty years later, Krenov's design influence can still be seen in the field of studio furniture.

I recently revisited *A Cabinetmaker's Notebook*. It was interesting to note that the book begins with a passage from the ancient Chinese mystic Chuang Tzu about a woodcarver. I was interested in Eastern religions when I first encountered the book, and Krenov tapped into those sensibilities. Good design was to flow from an understanding of how to build the object. It was necessary to become a master—of dovetails, mortise-and-tenon joints, and the tools and techniques involved in making them. The joints needed to be cut the way a musician learns scales, over and over until the finished work evidenced confidence. Some of this sounded like the talk Nakashima had given me. Krenov made his own planes. His finishes were handrubbed oil. It was clear from the photographs that Krenov would be an exacting task master and not settle for sloppy standards. If you were going to build something, it was worth doing it as well as you could. That meant learning about the properties of wood and the tools of the trade.

A Cabinetmaker's Notebook is not a how-to guide, unless you consider it how to live your life. There is very little telling you how to execute a particular joint. Krenov would explore the technical parts of cabinetmaking in future books. But for me his real influence was in convincing people to go about making things in such a way as to make them proud of what they've done. The book should be of interest to all craftspeople, regardless of their medium, because of Krenov's emphasis on process and excellence.

Another niche for aspiring woodworkers of the mid-1970s was filled by *Fine Woodworking* magazine. The publication went beyond the norm of most magazines catering to woodworkers. Other publications ran plans for building bookcases, and were dominated by routers and radial arm saws. *Fine Woodworking* had articles on hand tools and traditional joinery. The early issues offered an exciting mix of articles on techniques, history, wood technology, reviews of shows, as well as general information. There were articles on turning, antiques, and contemporary sculptural work. I looked forward to every issue. The magazine forged a community among far-flung woodworkers, who are by nature often isolated. Across America people had access to the same inspirational material.

It is interesting to go back and look at *Fine Woodworking* from the 1970s to see the type of work that was featured. Much of it looks remarkably naïve in terms of both design and craft. But the work seemed fresh and interesting. Many of the magazine's articles were written by readers. People were willing to share their developing talents and insights into the craft. This is very different from the traditional attitude of European craftsmen who, perhaps in the shadow of the guilds, would only reluctantly yield secrets of the trade. The editors went out and found the best people they could to provide authentic information. The names of contributors to those early issues read like a who's who of American woodcraft of the time: Krenov, Bob Stocksdale, Tage Frid, Jere Osgood, Mark Lindquist. Other articles were by people who would soon become well known: Alphonse Mattia, Roseanne Somerson, John Dunnigan, Timothy Philbrick, Stephen Hogbin, and Richard Newman. Leading figures such as George Nakashima, Wendell Castle, and Bill Keyser were profiled. The lone woodworker in his shop in Kansas was given access to the same material as someone in one of the big craft areas like Rochester or Oakland, California. The reader could use the magazine as a guide to new techniques that would otherwise remain remote. Additionally, picture galleries regularly featured what people were building throughout the United States and Canada. The skills of professionals and amateurs alike were ratcheted-up. We all grew to be better craftsmen by paying attention to the pages of *Fine Woodworking*.

20. Cabinet of English Brown Oak (1977) James Krenov
English brown oak, American spalted maple, Swedish ash; 54¾ × 28¼ × 8 in.
Photo: Bengt Carlén

21. GAME TABLE (1973)
WENDELL CASTLE
Walnut and maple;
30 × 40 × 40 in.
Photo: courtesy Wendell Castle

When I began working for Wendell Castle, most of his pieces were stack-laminated. While he had gained fame doing those pieces, he was experimenting with other techniques. He told me that he had received his own craft education while teaching at RIT and watching the other instructors explain some of the traditional aspects of woodworking. These things weren't part of his training as a sculptor. Wendell had been hired primarily for his skill as an innovative designer; when he arrived at school he wasn't a sophisticated technician.

In the early 1970s Wendell designed and built a game table and chairs that I found particularly attractive (figure 21). The top of the table was a highly figured veneer. The legs were dovetailed into the frame of the top in a pinwheel fashion. The chairs were made with bent-laminated hoops and finger joints. They were also sculpted in a very pleasing way. But it was the joinery that made the design very different from the stack-laminated pieces that were Wendell's mainstay. These were the pieces I was most interested in.

That first year working for Wendell gave me a chance to make a number of marquetry jewelry boxes. At the same time I was able to see how Wendell worked. I knew I needed to get much better at traditional woodcraft. My skills were quite limited. For a brief while I was the only apprentice in the shop. Another young man was hired, and my seniority gave me some new opportunities. Then Wendell expanded the workforce by hiring two more people, one of whom was a very talented Englishman. Steven Proctor had had excellent classical training in furniture design and woodworking at the Royal College of Art in London. He could build objects with remarkable finesse.

I understood the basics of joinery, but Steven was able to integrate interesting solutions in constructing Wendell's designs. My apprenticeship was turning into a terrific learning experience.

I knew I wanted to put marquetry and traditional woodworking joinery together in furniture. When I became comfortable with the style of floral marquetry, I attempted to make some furniture pieces to decorate with these simple designs. I made several coffee tables with simple marquetry tops and Nouveau-style carving (figure 22). I built blanket chests that were basically large jewelry boxes (figure 23). I attempted some cabinets that had shaped parts (figure 24) inspired by Art Nouveau designs (and perhaps a bit of Krenov).

None of the pieces I built at that stage was too challenging. I was developing a marquetry vocabulary, as well as practicing my furniture-making skills. The natural inclination is to imitate work we admire. I loved those French Art Nouveau pieces and their sinuous curves. I wanted to combine the carving and marquetry, as Gallé had done. Hopefully, I was not slavishly imitating but rather beginning to develop a look of my own.

In building these early pieces I was also trying to educate myself about aspects of the history of furniture, and more specifically about marquetry. I would look for used books on Art Nouveau that had good photos of furniture. Besides Gallé, the designer that most intrigued me was Louis Majorelle, also from Nancy. His work slowly grew on me, and I came to appreciate his designs even more than Gallé's.

❧

22. Dogwood Coffee Table (1979) Silas Kopf
Walnut and marquetry; 17 × 52 × 20 in.
Photo: David Ryan

23. Blanket Chest (1980) Silas Kopf
Cherry, satinwood, and marquetry; 18 × 36 × 20 in.
Photo: David Ryan

24. Bamboo Cabinet (1977) Silas Kopf
Cherry and marquetry; 52 × 19 × 13 in.
Photo: David Ryan

Louis Majorelle

25. MARQUETRY WORKSHOP AT MAJORELLE FACTORY IN NANCY, FRANCE (1906)
Photo: from the "Revue Industielle de l'Est," 1906

One of the preeminent furniture designers of the Art Nouveau period, Louis Majorelle came to woodwork naturally, as his father was also involved in furniture decoration. Auguste Majorelle was born in 1825 in the province of Lorraine, and trained in the decoration of faience pottery. When he was 33, he started his own faiencerie and became adept at lacquer work in the Asian style, popular in the mid-nineteenth century. Along with ceramic decoration Auguste began designing furniture.

In 1860 Auguste moved his growing family to Nancy, which prospered during the following decade. Local people were able to spend money on domestic consumption, such as furniture and other decorative objects. By 1870 the number of furniture merchants in Nancy had doubled.

Auguste Majorelle's son, Louis, was born in the small Lorraine town of Toul in 1859. As a teenager Louis was sent to art school in Nancy. The hope was that his training would enable him

to make a contribution in his father's business. So he attended to the decorative arts (including cabinetmaking) rather than fine art painting. When he was seventeen, he enrolled in the École des Beaux-Arts in Paris, where he met two people with whom he would form important bonds: Alexandre Charpentier, who would become one of the leaders of the Parisian Art Nouveau movement, and Victor Prouvé, a childhood friend of Gallé. Majorelle and Prouvé shared an interest in developing a decorative arts industry in Nancy. They hoped to return home and invigorate the province with the new ideas that were brewing in Paris.

In 1870 one of the many wars with Germany ended in a French defeat, and the far eastern province of Alsace was ceded to Germany. In a curious way this made Nancy even more important because now the city was the unmistaken leader of French culture in the east. At the same time many Alsatians, who didn't want to live under German rule, emigrated to

Nancy, bringing with them their money and their talents. By this time Louis had joined his father's prospering business. Although he was not the eldest son, he showed the most artistic talent and, when Auguste died in 1879, it was Louis who took over the firm.

Cabinetmaking skills in Nancy in the 1880s were considerable. The city was home to 200 or more well-trained woodworkers. Cabinetmaking masters, journeymen, and apprentices provided an invaluable pool of labor for producing Majorelle's designs. Nancy would become an international center for furniture making, and by 1906 the city included 800 to 900 woodworkers.

By 1899 Majorelle needed to update the family factory, and so he erected a modern building on the outskirts of the city—35,000 square feet, with high ceilings and windows that faced north to take advantage of the best light. Two large workshops were equipped with 40 benches each, and the marquetry atelier had twelve chevalets (figure 25). A sculpture shop accommodated 36 carvers. In all there were about 150 woodworkers and around 250 employees. Only four other firms in Lorraine employed more than 100 workers. One of them was the Gallé shop.

Gallé and Majorelle shared an interest in producing work that would be accessible to a wider audience than the luxurious furniture upon which their companies' reputations had been built. Maintaining the distinction of their pieces while lowering costs required creating a skilled workforce capable of using the most modern equipment. The Majorelle company produced many designs that were relatively easy to reproduce but still had the character that Louis cared about.

To the casual observer, the furniture of Gallé and Majorelle looks very similar. Both have the flowing, sinuous lines of the French Art Nouveau sculpted in the wood, often in an asymmetrical design. And marquetry panels decorate the planes of the piece. Characteristic of the Art

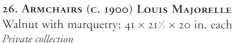

26. Armchairs (c. 1900) Louis Majorelle
Walnut with marquetry; 41 × 21½ × 20 in. each
Private collection

27. Cabinet (1900) Louis Majorelle
Wood stained purple, oak veneered with
kingwood and marquetry
*Victoria and Albert Museum, London; inv.:
1999–1990; Photo: Victoria and Albert
Museum/Art Resource, New York*

Nouveau style of Lorraine is the use of botanical motifs. Both men return again and again to plant forms for their marquetry designs.

Majorelle's work is rich and luxurious, yet based on a simplicity of line. He relied on the beauty of the materials, enhanced by engaging technique. Carving typically draws the eye around the work, but the focal point is often a marquetry panel. In a pair of beautiful armchairs with upholstered seats, the front rises and joins the arms to form the heads of geese (figure 26). This carving is placed so that sitting in the chair you are invited to run your fingers over the carved heads and beaks. The design is deliberately tactile. The curving lines flow into the back, which frames a marquetry panel of oversized flowers. One chair has irises and the other tulips. Both marquetry designs are somewhat off-center, giving them a more natural look. Other chairs in this series are identical, except for the marquetry. It would be interesting to know

if they were done as individual marquetry panels, or in small runs.

Majorelle designed a series of small cabinets around 1900 with challenging veneer and carved structural elements. One of them was made for the Exposition Universelle and is now displayed at the Victoria and Albert Museum in London (figure 27). It is one of my favorite Art Nouveau pieces, and an early inspiration. The cabinet has all the attributes of the period, with graceful carving that leads your eye over all the surfaces. Yet the focal point of the piece is a marquetry panel, placed at a height where you can easily see the detail of the picture and the beauty of the wood. It is a simple picture of a sailboat on a body of water.

Majorelle could also design pieces that were very elegant while making only limited use of marquetry. It is interesting to look at some furniture that he designed for himself, such as a bedroom set (figure 28) made with a highly figured Japanese ash (tamo). The

28. BEDROOM SUITE (1903–04) LOUIS MAJORELLE
Ash, Japanese tamo, copper, and mother-of-pearl
Musée de l'École de Nancy, Nancy, France; Photo: C. Philippot

shaping of the wood is not only visually engaging, it begs you to touch it. The only surface decoration is the copper and mother-of-pearl inlay in the corners of the head- and footboard. The decoration is even more subtle because the materials don't jump out the way they might on a less neutrally toned wood.

In 1903 Majorelle turned to Victor Prouvé, his old friend from his school days in Paris, to design the marquetry

for a piano (figure 29). Prouvé's solution was to make the marquetry look a bit like stained glass, with simple shapes and black outlines. Prouvé had designed a number of pieces for the glass workers of Lorraine. This design's translation into wood is somewhat muted compared to glass, because of the need to work with the palette of natural wood tones. Nevertheless, it is an effective solution. The scene is of

29. The Death of the Swan Piano (1903)
Louis Majorelle in collaboration
with Victor Prouvé
Mahogany and marquetry; 39 × 60 × 84½ in.
Musée de l'École de Nancy, Nancy, France;
Photo: C. Philippot

30. Buffet (1898) Louis Majorelle
Rosewood, chestnut, and marquetry;
94 × 62½ × 21½ in.
Badishes Landesmuseum, Karlsruhe, Germany

pond vegetation with water lilies and irises that run around the edge of the piano. The top also has marquetry with lily pads and vines. As is typical of Majorelle's work, the base is sculpted out of massive pieces of mahogany.

Majorelle did something with his marquetry decoration that none of the other French Art Nouveau designers did. He would cover surfaces with repeated patterns, composed sometimes of complex curved parts, sometimes of rectilinear parts, to make subtle backgrounds. Occasionally Majorelle would mix curved and rectilinear patterns on the same piece and even add in some pictographic marquetry, as with the buffet he designed in 1898 and now displayed at the Badishes Landesmuseum in Karlsruhe, Germany (figure 30).

Because Majorelle was trained as a cabinetmaker, he understood the advantages and limitations of wood—what you could do with it and what you couldn't. Many of the pieces are very complicated, with angles that would have challenged the cabinetmaker at the bench. The coordination between designer and craftsman, so important in creating a well-composed piece, was not a problem with Majorelle because he was a skilled cabinetmaker himself. His designs are always technically sensible. Yet he pushes the material to its limits.

☙

Northampton: In 1977 my wife and I were thinking of moving from Rochester. Her family is from Maine and mine is from northwest Pennsylvania, so we decided to look for something in between. At about this time *Fine Woodworking* published an article on a new woodworking school in western Massachusetts. They were looking for people to become resident craftsmen. It seemed like a great opportunity to move to a new location without having to set up a shop. We visited the school, called the Leeds Design Workshops, in Easthampton. We liked the area very much. From Easthampton we could explore the New England area and find the community where we would ultimately settle.

The Leeds Design Workshops was started by David Powell, an Englishman who had apprenticed in the Sydney and Edward Barnsley workshops in the Cotswolds. His intent was to give Americans a traditional English training experience. Side by side with the school, David wanted a community of furniture makers who would offer potential clients a variety of skills. The hope was that Easthampton could become a place where customers could commission high-quality custom pieces. Eventually there was to be a skilled turner, carver, perhaps an upholsterer. I was to fill the spot for marquetry in the community.

We ended up living in Northampton, a few miles from the school. Northampton offered many of the things we were looking for. With four colleges, plus the University of Massachusetts, within a ten-mile radius, cultural life is rich. Music, film, dance, and theater are all readily available. Visual artists and craftspeople make livings in the region. It has been such a lively mix that we never have looked elsewhere. Thirty years later we are firmly settled in Northampton, and I am still working in Easthampton.

I was a resident craftsman at Leeds for five years. The school invited several interesting guest speakers, including Tage Frid and Jere Osgood. Being in the school setting was an opportunity to grow as a craftsman, as well as make friends. I opened my own shop in 1983, but I stayed in the same building, a large old textile mill in the middle of town. The building had been broken up into small spaces where a diverse group of artists and craftspeople rented space. It was a great place to trade ideas and socialize.

Shortly after moving to Massachusetts I found out about the American Craft Enterprises fair that was held every year in Rhinebeck, New York. I visited the fair in 1978 and found it exciting, for craftspeople and visitors alike. Rhinebeck was the premier crafts fair in the country.

It drew from the New York metropolitan area a large audience for whom a trip to the fair was a pleasant day in the country. With both a wholesale and retail component, it was a very attractive venue.

In 1980 I attended Rhinebeck as an exhibitor, primarily showing jewelry boxes (figure 19). I remember also having a coffee table and perhaps a blanket chest. My display was pathetically unsophisticated. It consisted of a folding table with a cloth sheet on top. My lighting was a set of hardware store clamp lamps. Obviously, I hadn't paid much attention during the previous visit to how fancy booths could be. Some had paneled walls, carpeting, and track lighting. I felt like a bit of a bumpkin.

In spite of my naïve approach to marketing, that first Rhinebeck fair was an excellent experience. I sold enough boxes to keep me busy several months into the future. I also sold my furniture pieces to a shop in Honolulu. It was very gratifying that someone so far away was willing to take a chance on my work. In the process I got some worthwhile feedback from other gallery people. I vividly remember talking to Rick Snyderman, who ran the Works Gallery in Philadelphia, one of the oldest craft galleries in America. Rick noted the brass chain that I was using as a stay on the jewelry box lids. He said he liked my boxes, but the chain looked cheap in comparison with the marquetry and the overall quality of the box. He said a higher quality stay wouldn't cost that much, but make the work salable in a gallery like his. It is a lesson that I have tried to keep in mind over the years, that a general sense of excellence should be evident in every aspect of the piece.

One of the things I have always liked about being a craftsman is being part of a group of like-minded people. I felt this in both Rochester and Easthampton. Rhinebeck reinforced the sense of community for me. Most of the exhibitors were around my age and seemed to have joined the craft world for similar motives. They were interested in an alternative lifestyle. It didn't seem to matter what the medium was; the clay people were coming from the same place as the wood people or the glass people.

Emboldened by my experience at Rhinebeck, I approached a gallery owner in Northampton and asked about the possibility of doing a show. He agreed. It was my first chance to see my work displayed in a gallery setting. The memory is still satisfying. The shop owner, Don Muller, and I remain friends to this day.

There were few opportunities to show fine woodwork in a gallery setting. A couple of galleries around the country had shown craft objects as art, but none was devoted to studio furniture. The first to open was the Dick

Kagan Gallery in Philadelphia. Dick was a woodworker himself. He set up a very small showroom in the front of his South Street studio to show the work of others whom he admired. The hours of the Kagan Gallery were limited (as he was trying to get his own work done), but it became a weekend destination for people looking for unique furniture. I went to Philadelphia to see the showroom and asked Dick if he would represent me. He seemed to like my marquetry and we worked out an arrangement for him to display a piece or two. He sold several pieces and introduced my work to a whole new audience of people who were looking at furniture as a collectible. The experience also gave me confidence that my work could succeed in an art-market setting.

I continued to go to Rhinebeck, as well as several other fairs run by American Craft Enterprises, such as the Winter Fair in Baltimore. Every show I would decrease the display of jewelry boxes and increase the furniture. It worked relatively well, as I was finding an audience for the larger pieces. That was my goal, to build art furniture. Then I started making more and more complex objects. With increasing complexity came higher prices. After several years, I priced myself out of the fairs. The furniture was no longer an impulse buy. It seemed like a stable relationship with a gallery would serve me better. Dick Kagan had recently gotten out of the gallery business and I was looking for new ways to show my work.

Even after moving from Rochester to Massachusetts, I stayed in touch with Richard Newman. He had been invited to exhibit with several other furniture makers at Gallery Henoch in New York's Soho neighborhood. He suggested I go to the city and see the show. I could then also talk to the gallery director about representation. Gallery Henoch is primarily a painting gallery. At the time they were representing mostly photo-realists. The director, George Schectman, was reluctant to spend too much energy on furniture. But he did plan on doing at least one more furniture show the following year. After a bit of cajoling he agreed to include me. I was part of a group show in 1985 that included Richard, John Dunnigan, David Ebner, Lee Weitzman, and Dick Wickman. The gallery sold several pieces of mine at the show. Henoch put together another show the following year, and again we sold some pieces. George then offered me a one-man show.

❧

In 1983 someone gave me an article from *Scientific American* about fifteenth-century Italian intarsia, a technique that is a hybrid between marquetry and inlay—

most of the picture parts are put together and glued to a backboard like a jigsaw puzzle (as in marquetry), but many of the smaller parts are inlaid into the picture. The subject of the article was the development of perspective geometry and its use in the wooden panels that decorated the choir stalls in numerous churches of Renaissance Italy. I had seen a few photos of Italian intarsia in Lincoln's *Art and Practice of Marquetry*. One of them was a trompe l'oeil open cupboard from the choir of the cathedral in Siena (figure 53). The book identified the artist as a monk named Fra Giovanni da Verona. That image piqued my interest in Italian work. The *Scientific American* article included excellent color reproductions of several panels, as well as an explanation of the history of the work. I wanted to see more.

The authors of the article, Judith and Alan Tormey, were an academic couple from Maryland. I wrote them to ask how they had learned about these marvelous works. I discovered they were not art history professors but rather philosophy teachers who had fallen in love with intarsia on trips to Italy. Each summer they would go back and visit new sites. During the winters they studied Italian to help with their travel. They told me they were returning to Italy at the end of the academic year and invited me to join them for a week, saying they would show me some highlights. It was too good an opportunity to pass up.

In June of 1984 I flew to Rome and met Judith and Alan. We drove to the small Tuscan hill town of Cetona, where they had arranged to rent an apartment. Each day we set off for a different intarsia destination: Orvieto, Todi, Assisi, Siena, Florence, and Perugia. I know they enjoyed introducing me to these marvelous panels, and I certainly appreciated having them as guides. They took me into dark churches where you had to put coins into a machine to turn the lights on the panels for a few minutes. We visited the Monte Oliveto Maggiore monastery, which is now the home of the Fra Giovanni panel that I had seen in Lincoln's book. We had to be shooed away from the choir by a monk when in our enthusiasm we got too close.

The Tormeys had also made an appointment at the major workshop for the restoration of intarsia. There we saw panels disassembled and in various states of repair. Alan acted as translator for questions about the cutting and construction of intarsia. I much valued gaining a greater understanding of the history of Italian intarsia. These panels were the wellspring of European marquetry. But information was not easy to find. Trips to the university library yielded a few source books about the Italian work and some further insight into how the work was conceived and constructed.

❧

Middle Ages

To understand Italian Renaissance intarsia, one has to look back a little earlier in European history. What were the conditions for the birth of this art form at that particular time and place?

The break-up of the Roman Empire signaled profound changes for the whole European continent. The unified government in Rome had spread a shared culture—reflected in all aspects of design, including furniture—throughout most of Europe, western Asia, and north Africa. With the decline of Rome and the western portion of the empire under siege, the eastern Byzantium Empire began to develop its own aesthetic. Slowly, the unstable western Roman culture withered and was eventually overwhelmed by invaders. The era of western European history that we refer to as the Dark Ages exhibited very little in the way of stylistic development in furniture or architecture. No pieces of furniture survived that we would now point to as seminal. No new techniques or materials advanced woodcraft. In fact, economies had been shattered and the threat of war limited trade between Europe and areas in Asia and Africa. Without trade, societies remained poor, and few exotic materials arrived from afar to inspire craftsmen. At the same time, the aristocracy was in decline, in no position to support high craft as it had been in Roman times.

This isn't to suggest there were no woodworkers in Medieval Europe. But rather than making sophisticated objects, their work was more like carpentry. The tools of these woodworkers were the same as those used by their predecessors in ancient Rome. Iron was used to make cutting tools such as chisels, gouges, planes, and various saws. Unfortunately, very few of these tools have come down to us from the post-Roman era. Perhaps this indicates how great was the decline in European woodworking. Even royal and ecclesiastical furniture during this period was rudimentary.

Only those areas in the West that maintained a connection with the East had some level of sophistication. The Byzantine world, centered in present-day Turkey, kept alive some of the traditions of Rome. The regimes in Constantinople supported craftsmen of talent and skill. A new force driving creativity, the Eastern Church began commissioning important decorative work for the religious buildings being constructed.

One of the most important art forms of Byzantium was mosaic tile (figure 31). Mosaics had been very sophisticated in the Roman Empire. In some ways the aesthetic of mosaics, where contrasting materials are pieced together to make an image, is similar to inlay. Mosaics are done with small pieces of colored tiles pieced together with a grout between the parts. Wall surfaces as well as floors and ceilings were decorated with mosaics. From the many representations of furniture in Byzantine mosaics, it appears that furniture was often elaborately inlaid with metal and jewels. These objects would have been in the tradition of the earlier Roman pieces.

Beginning in the tenth century, when European culture was stagnating, the Arab world played an important role in conserving ideas and learning, as well as in commerce and craft. Science and mathematics flourished in the great cities of the Near East, such as Damascus, Alexandria, and Baghdad. The Arab (and ultimately the whole Muslim) world was unified, powerful, and rich. Muslim Spain had some contact with the rest of western Europe, but the Pyrenees were a barrier that practically stopped the flow of culture. Western Europeans were not inclined to borrow ideas from people they regarded as infidels.

It wasn't until the Crusades began in the twelfth century that Europeans became interested in importing goods and later techniques, styles, and ideas from the Muslim East. Initially it was commodities like spices that attracted European traders. A burgeoning system of fairs facilitated the spread of goods throughout the continent. Byzantine craftsmen came to Europe, particularly Italy, to work, which re-introduced craft skills that had been dormant for hundreds of years. It was not by chance that northern Italian woodworkers were the first to imitate the geometric aesthetic of Muslim decoration. Italian merchants in Venice and Genoa actively pursued trade with the East.

❧

31. SAINT EUDOKIA, EMPRESS OF BYZANTIUM (LATE 10TH- TO EARLY 11TH-CENTURY)
Stone inlay in marble; 25¾ in. h; from the Church of Lips Monastery, now Fenasi Isa Mosque
Archeological Museum, Istanbul;
Photo: Erich Lessing/Art Resource, New York

Islamic Influence

32. WOODEN DOOR PANEL WITH HORSEHEADS AMONG ARABESQUES (11TH CENTURY)
Museum of Islamic Art, Cairo;
Photo: Erich Lessing/ Art Resource, New York

33. SCREEN OF THE CENOTAPH, DETAIL OF INLAY (C.1640)
Taj Mahal, Agra, Uttar Pradesh, India;
Photo: Scala/Art Resource, New York

The earliest Muslims were nomadic people, who had no need for luxurious furniture. They were warriors committed to spreading their faith, and their domain grew rapidly. But these early Muslims from the Arabian peninsula also absorbed the cultures of the people they conquered, inheriting several important traditions: Greek, Byzantine, Persian, and Syrian. Many aspects of design were transposed into something uniquely Muslim. The craft of mosaic decoration that is rooted in the Byzantine world flourished in the hands of Muslims adorning their mosques. A style of ornamentation commonly used in these designs is referred to as *arabesque* (figure 32). Some of the arabesques are reminiscent of the Greek acanthus leaves; other designs appear to owe something to the running pattern known as the Greek key. The Muslims also took these geometries and made them increasingly complex. The forms are designed to repeat and interlock in very complicated ways. Remarkable examples of inlay incorporate a variety of materials. Highly skilled craftsmen, such as those who produced the stunning stone inlay of the Taj Mahal, also used metal, stone, ivory, shell, and exotic woods to decorate architecture and furniture (figure 33).

Many of these decorative patterns reflect an interest in and a deep understanding of geometry, discovered by the Greeks in the sixth century BCE and kept alive in the Arab universities. The mathematician Euclid was first translated into Arabic in the ninth century. These mathematical texts weren't available to western Europeans until a Latin translation was done in the twelfth century.

Some inlaid furniture and architectural parts from Islamic Spain and North Africa have been preserved. A marvelous twelfth-century minbar (a pulpit in a mosque) from Cordoba, Spain, is now in the Badia Palace in Marrakesh, Morocco (figure 34). Hundreds of ebony and ivory parts are inlaid into cedarwood. The geometric

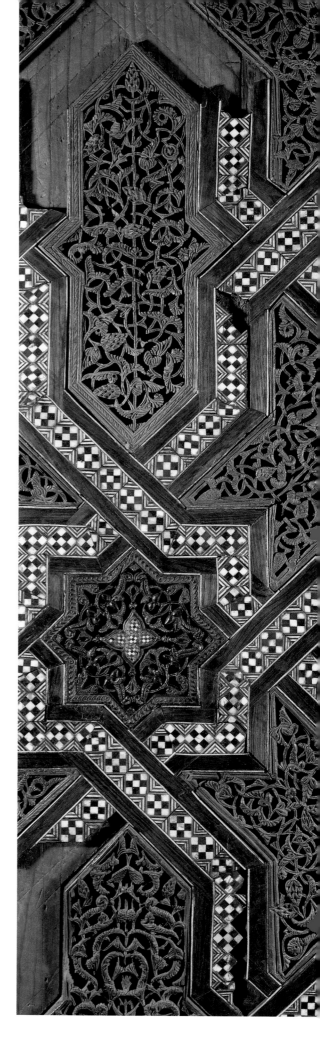

**34. MINBAR FORMERLY IN
THE QUTUBIA MOSQUE
FROM CORDOBA, SPAIN**
(1137)
Cedar wood, ebony, ivory;
150½ in. h
*Badia Palace, Marrakesh,
Morocco; Photo: Erich
Lessing/Art Resource, New York*

composition is complex and typical of
some of the fine work found in Islamic
furniture.

Islam was an important influence
on the Iberian peninsula, until Muslims
were expelled by Ferdinand and Isabella
in 1492. Nevertheless, skill at inlay
remained part of Spanish craftsmanship
and continued to be used in Spanish
furniture. A fine example of geometric
design is a chest from early sixteenth-
century Spain. The surfaces are covered

35. Vargueño Cabinet (c.1520) Spanish
Walnut inlaid with ivory
Victoria and Albert Museum, London, BW1736;
Photo: V&A Images/Victoria and Albert Museum

36. Bishop's Throne (11th century)
Cosmati workshop
Duomo, Anagni (Lazio)
Photo: Alinari/Art Resource, New York

with complex patterns, and the effect is striking (figure 35).

Few medieval European designs can be traced directly to early Roman inlay and mosaic, but there are isolated examples of craftsmen carrying on in Italy with mosaics in stone and glass. A family named Cosmati specialized in the decoration of ecclesiastical furnishings using marbles and semi-precious stones. Their designs were obviously influenced by work from the Islamic world, with an emphasis on geometric designs. (figure 36).

Wood craftsmen of the time were beginning to make simple designs of contrasting species, such as decorative borders on architectural elements. The Museo dell'Opera del Duomo in Orvieto in central Italy has a sample board of borders, the work showing the early influence of geometric pattern. Italian craftsmen of the thirteenth century had long used the various woods and the tools to cut these designs, but had only recently attempted inlaid designs. Polygons can be cut relatively easily using saws and chisels, and then pieced together into bands in the desired pattern, which could then be inlaid into a solid piece of wood. From these simple roots a re-birth of European inlay began.

☙

Italian Intarsia

A Sienese master named Vanni di Tura dell'Ammanato designed the choir stalls for the cathedral in Orvieto in 1331. Vanni also organized the other early woodworking in the cathedral, overseeing a crew of twenty-eight craftsmen. However, the interior work was not completed for another hundred years. As with so many of the great European cathedrals, work proceeded only when money was available. One of the most interesting panels that once decorated the cathedral is the tympanum (now in the Museo dell'Opera in Orvieto). The picture depicts the Coronation of the Virgin (figure 37). The large panel has twenty-four figures, with the faces beautifully executed. The lighter woods of the clothing are broken up by a cross-hatched pattern. Perhaps the intent was to make the pieces look smaller, more like a Byzantine mosaic. The panel also has lighter pegs in the darker walnut surrounding the figures. These pegs would have helped secure the walnut to the baseboard, but they also add an interesting decorative effect.

❧

In the fourteenth century Italian craftsmen began decorating woodwork using gilding and painting. A style of decoration also evolved where the surface was covered with a flat design composed of pieces of colored wax. The work was in the tradition of mosaics, but significantly less costly than something done in stone, glass, or even wood, and therefore more accessible to the new and growing middle class in Italy. Wax "inlay" became very fashion-able. According to Giorgio Vasari, the sixteenth-century chronicler of Italian art, no home was complete without an example of this style of furniture.

The next style of decoration introduced into this milieu is known as *certosina* marquetry, a geometric piecing together of contrasting materials influenced by Islamic art. It took root in the northeast of Italy, the area that, not coincidentally, had the most commerce with the Muslim world. The

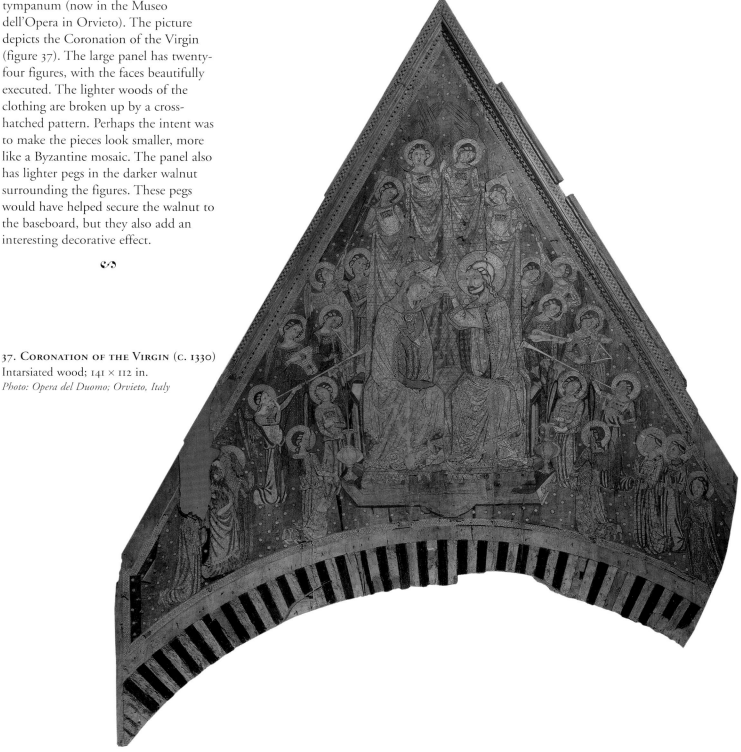

37. CORONATION OF THE VIRGIN (C. 1330)
Intarsiated wood; 141 × 112 in.
Photo: Opera del Duomo; Orvieto, Italy

38. Chest (c. 1500) Northern Italian
Ebony and ivory; 22¼ × 48 × 19½ in.
Rijksmuseum, Amsterdam;
(inv. M-BK-16629-00)

39. Certosina Cabinet
(17th century) Anonymous Italian
Detroit Institute of Arts, Detroit, Mich.;
Gift of Mrs. Russell Alger;
Photo: Detroit Institute of Arts

word certosina comes from Certosa di Pavia, a celebrated Carthusian monastery where this work was done. Very fine certosina used the decorative effect of inlaying the contrasting ivory into solid walnut or cedar. The choir at the Certosa monastery is decorated this way. A beautiful chest in Rijksmuseum in Amsterdam features certosina decoration in ebony and ivory (figure 38). Such chests were a typical format for certosina decoration. A cabinet in the collection of the Detroit Institute of Fine Arts is interesting because the certosina is used on the doors of the taller piece (figure 39).

In the thirteenth and fourteenth centuries the building trades in Italy were closely linked. Architecture, sculpture, and woodwork all shared connections, while the respective guilds ferociously protected their turf. A craftsman had to be a member of a guild to be employed. Tradesmen were secretive of their techniques. Painting did not have the same status that it was accorded a century or two later. Painters were closer to what we might think of as decorators, being paid more for the square footage covered rather than the vision of their art. But it was during this time that individual artists began emerging from anonymity and were lauded for their talent. You can find the names of individuals attached to specific artworks, beginning in the fourteenth century. Contrast this to the great art of the High Gothic era. The sculptures of Chartres Cathedral are among the most celebrated carvings of Western art, yet the names of the sculptors have passed into obscurity. The age we call the Renaissance changed that attitude, as artists found a special place in the culture. The names of wood craftsmen, such as Vanni, first get recorded at this time.

The first important painter of this period is Giotto (c.1276–c.1337), who was also a sculptor and architect. He belonged to the Siena painter's guild, which was founded in 1261. The guild included designers of all sorts: plasterers, molders, stained glass artists, even makers of playing cards. Thirteenth-century Siena had become a very important commercial city and was accumulating the trappings of wealth. A growing merchant class wanted to have luxurious objects for themselves and also to build bold and striking public buildings that would display the sense of importance of the city. Painters such as Giotto were kept busy both in Siena and in area towns and monasteries. Intra-continental trade was thriving, and the European economy could support hundreds of artisans. Italy was the wealthiest part of Europe, with merchants and bankers leading the way. They poured money into their own lifestyles, as well as into building and decorating churches and municipal buildings.

The regional center of Tuscany, Siena became the focal point for the craft of intarsia during the 1300s. It was Sienese craftsmen who had worked on the cathedral in Orvieto. At the beginning of the fifteenth century the reputation of one Sienese *intarsiatoro*, Domenico di Niccolò, spread beyond Tuscany. His style is characterized by a very bold graphic quality. To make his figures jump out of the picture, he set them in black backgrounds, consisting of bog oak. Bog oak comes from an oak tree that has fallen into water and remains submerged. The water reacts with the tannic acid in the wood, turn-

ing the fibers dark. The longer the wood is in the water, the darker it will be. It takes centuries for the oak to fully blacken, but unexposed to air, it won't rot.

Domenico executed the panels for the choir of the Cappella de Signori, in Siena's Palazzo Pubblico (figure 40). His method was to glue bog oak veneer to a backerboard, securing it further with pegs, and then inlaying the picture parts into the oak background. Domenico composed his images using relatively few species: walnut, poplar, cherry, pear, plum, and boxwood. All of

these woods contrast well with the bog oak background, especially the very dark bog oak that Domenico chose. To accentuate details, Domenico also filled incised lines with colored pastes (a technique used in the earlier geometric inlays of northeastern Italy) and occasionally metals, including silver.

In the course of doing the panels for the Cappella, Domenico requested money from the city to teach intarsia to apprentices. The lords of Siena found the craft worthy and saw the value in passing it on to a new generation. One of the young students was

40. The Crucifixion (1415–28) Domenico di Niccolo
Cappella de' Signori, Palazzo Publico, Siena, Italy; Photo: Roberto Testi

Mattia di Nanni. Some of the work attributed to Domenico was probably done by Mattia during his apprenticeship. A few years later, when he was on his own, Mattia did some remarkable pieces that clearly surpass the master (figure 41). Mattia learned from Domenico how to create a strong graphic presentation through contrast, developing the craft further by laminating small pieces of wood into larger shapes. He even took slivers of wood and formed them into veneers that would have a particularly strong veining. In this way he could make the grain in the wood go far in telling the story of his pictorial designs.

Migrant intarsiatori took the skills of inlaying wood to other cities. First to cities in Tuscany, and eventually to towns throughout central Italy, such as Bologna and Verona. One family who learned the craft deserves special recognition: the brothers Lorenzo (1425–1477) and Christoforo (1426–1491) Lendinara, and Cristoforo's son, Bernardino, as well as Lorenzo's son-in-law, Pierantonio. The brothers were apprentices to a master woodworker, Arduino da Baiso, who specialized in the style of inlay called *tarsia a toppo*. (See Appendix 3: Banding.)

Tarsia a toppo is produced by laminating contrasting woods into a "log," so that a cross-section will show a particular pattern. The log can be sliced into individual tiles, and each tile will look exactly the same. A log 2 feet long sliced at about ⅛ inch can produce up to two hundred tiles. These can then be put together to form bandings, or used individually. The greater part of the labor is in carefully constructing the log. The Lendinaras became expert at this technique and produced some astonishing toppo intarsia. Eventually the family added figurative and landscape work to the geometric toppo designs. Their intarsia pictures are pleasing because of their simplicity, which distinguishes them from painting.

In 1460 the Lendinaras were commissioned to build the choir in the cathedral in Modena. Taking five years

41. SCIPIO AFRICANUS (C.1425–1430) MATTIA DI NANNI DI STEFANO, SIENA
Poplar, bog oak, and other wood inlay with tin, bone, and traces of green coloring; 24 × 16¾ in.
The Metropolitan Museum of Art, New York; Purchase: Rogers Fund, Gift of Mrs. Benjamin Moore, by exchange and bequest of George Blumenthal, by exchange, 1997 (1997.26)

to complete, the work brought them renown as masters of the intarsia craft. They next received a commission to decorate the stalls in the Basilica Sant'Antonio in Padua—fifty-two large and thirty-eight small stalls decorated with perspective intarsia (figure 42). The family carried on making fine intarsia panels for several more decades and influenced many who followed.

A common intarsia decoration of the fifteenth century, *commesso di silio*, usually features a lighter wood inlaid directly into a darker ground. The most common combination was a straw-colored species called spindlewood inlayed into walnut. Sometimes the parts are engraved to add to the graphic impact. This attractive form of intarsia was simpler to make than the

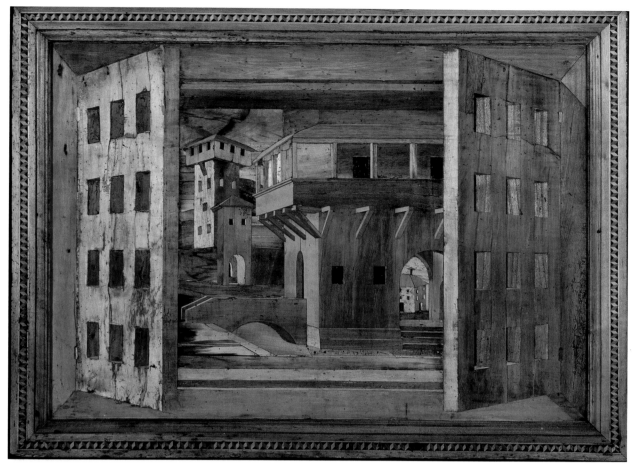

42. City View (c.1462–1469) Lorenzo da Lendinara
Believed to be from Sant'Antonio, Padua, Italy
Museum fur Kunst und Gewerbe, Hamburg, Germany

Detail from Figure 50:
Studiolo from the Ducal Palace of Federigo da Montefeltro at Gubbio

more painterly panels. Occasionally, complex trompe l'oeil panels are juxtaposed with the commesso di silio panels, perhaps as a budget compromise, enabling more resources to be lavished on a smaller number of panels, while still affording decorative woodwork throughout a project (figure 50).

❧

Rivaling Siena for dominance in Tuscany (and even Europe at large) was the nearby city of Florence. Frequently, the hostility between the two erupted into warfare. In the course of the fourteenth and fifteenth centuries Florence became the dominant city, gaining wealth and influence as a center of banking and a focal point of trade throughout Europe. Because of this, Florence attracted talented people from throughout Italy. At the end of the fifteenth and early in the sixteenth centuries an astonishing group of artistic geniuses found their way to the city. Beyond the most celebrated, such as da Vinci, Donatello, and Brunelleschi, a huge workforce of artisans produced a legacy of impressive variety. Intarsia was one of the crafts that found a niche in Florence. In 1478, eighty-four different workshops practiced some form of intarsia. Many of these would have been sole proprietorships, but no doubt some employed a number of people. At the time the city had a population of approximately 150,000, and decorative woodworking was a significant enterprise in the community. These artisans also found patrons for their work in other parts of Italy, and beyond. The intarsia work spanned various levels of complexity, from simple geometric banding to decorative panels produced with a painterly touch.

The fifteenth century was the great period of the discovery of perspective drawing, the accurate depiction of three-dimensional images on a flat surface. Early theories of perspective were put forward by the artists Filippo Brunelleschi (1377–1446) and Leon Battista Alberti (1404–72). The first publication of the theory was Alberti's *Della Pittura* in 1436, in which he explained, "I draw a rectangle, of whatever size I want, which I regard as an open window through which the subject to be painted is seen" (Cecil Grayson's 1972 translation of Alberti's *On Painting and Sculpture*) The approach to perspective became mathematical, as people developed technical understandings for reconstructing reality—as it was thought people see it. Three-dimensional images were elaborately constructed using vanishing points. Other artists, such as Paolo Uccello and Piero della Francesca, carried the theory of perspective into the realm of painting. Della Francesca apparently had an affinity for intarsia, as he designed many panels that were executed by the Lendinaras.

The cityscape was fertile ground for the intarsiatori. Drawings of buildings in perspective captured a great deal of interest. Buildings are geometric constructions to begin with, and so an obvious subject for perspective. Furthermore, the geometry involved in depicting them was already familiar to the intarsiatori, being members of the building trades. The earliest efforts to cut intarsia were the geometric certosina panels. As woodworkers, intarsiatori already knew how to create various shapes and sizes of polygons using straight-backed saws and planes. It was no big stretch to move from the repeated geometric patterns of the early tarsia (such as a checkerboard) to the same design in perspective. The paving on a floor might be that same checkerboard done using a one-point perspective (see figure 54). The design would require cutting trapezoids, rather than squares. Then the parts were put together to make them look as if they are receding in space. Depicting the façade of a building would similarly involve cutting and assembling various polygons.

꽃

Parallel to the development of architectural scenes in intarsia was the creation of trompe l'oeil still lifes (figure 44). Sometimes used to decorate free-standing furniture, these pictures more often appear as iconic and decorative panels in churches and cathedrals. The north sacristy of the Duomo in Florence has what may be the first still-life intarsia panels done in perspective. They date from 1435 to 1445 and were probably drawn by Brunelleschi himself. The intarsiatori were Agnolo di Lazzaro and Antonio Manetti. Meant to look like open cupboards with shelves and objects inside, the designs include doors that are foreshortened. The entire composition has a very pleasing effect, particularly because real cupboards would actually have been constructed of wood.

The aesthetics of Italian intarsia are rooted in the techniques that were used to produce the work. Intarsia parts were assembled out of sawn veneers $1/8$ inch to $1/4$ inch thick and applied to a solid-wood panel (typically poplar boards, glued together edge-to-edge), approximately $3/8$ inch to 1 inch thick. This panel was secured to thicker battens of wood with the grain running at 90 degrees using nails.

The individual pieces of veneer were not shaped with a fretsaw (that type of saw had not yet been invented), but had to be laboriously fitted with knives, chisels, and gouges. Only the straight parts could be sawn. Cutting wood with a knife is difficult, especially if the wood is $1/4$ inch thick. To aid in fitting, the inlay pieces were cut to shape with a slight bevel (about 10 to 14 degrees).

The intarsia design was broken down into composited sections about $1/4$ inch thick, which could be cut and assembled from smaller parts. A section would be as straight-sided as possible, so it could be easily pieced together with other sections. For instance, in the design of an open cupboard, the doors would have been produced as two (or four) sections, and the areas inside the shelves as another section. A border with a design might be another straight-sided element added to the composition. All these parts being simple polygons were relatively easy to fit together using saws and planes.

The sections were glued to the poplar panel. Because the grain in many of the component parts of these sections was at right angles to the backboard, the assembly was subject to cross-grain glue failure. To help secure the parts, the intarsiatoro strategically chose places where he could also add small nails, later covering the nailhead with an inlaid detail.

Once the composited sections were assembled on the panel, smaller elements, such as the objects on a shelf, were cut out and inlaid. The thickness of these parts was about $1/8$ inch, compared to the $1/4$ inch of the initial assembly. Even smaller (and thinner) details could be inlaid into those parts. The process would continue until the finest details, such as lettering, might be incised to a depth of only $1/16$ inch.

꽃

CONSTRUCTION OF A FRA GIOVANNI INTARSIA PANEL

A typical intarsia panel involves the combination of a structural ground, veneer assemblies, inlaid components, and incised details.

A poplar panel with the grain running horizontally is attached to battens using nails clenched over from the rear. Straight-sided parts—the cupboard doors, the shelf, and the background of the cupboard, plus the border—are assembled and glued to the panel.

As shown in the door at the upper left, the diamond shapes at the top and the bottom would have been left as recesses. These allowed holes to be drilled and nails driven all the way through the poplar backboard. These could then be clenched over, thereby securing the door to the poplar. Each of the doors was added in the same manner.

Other elements of the design, such as the skeletal polyhedron, were assembled off the panel. A recess was chiseled into the background, with the edges slightly beveled. The entire assembly was then inlaid and glued into the depression. The books and the urn would have been handled the same way.

The smallest details—the leaf pattern on the urn, for instance—are incised to a depth of about $\frac{1}{16}$ inch.

The last step was to plane the entire panel smooth.

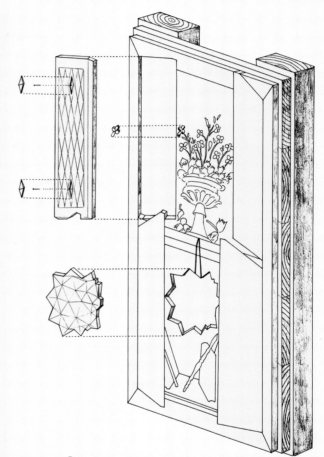

43. INTARSIA PANEL CONSTRUCTION
Horizontal boards are nailed to vertical structural posts. Individual units of the design, assembled separately, are inlaid into this panel and secured with nails. The nail heads are covered with strategically placed inlay that is part of the design. Finally, small parts of the design (such as the flower petals) are shallowly inlaid into the panel.

44. INTARSIA PANEL (C. 1500)
FRA GIOVANNI DA VERONA
37½ × 17 in.
From the choir of Monte Oliveto Maggiore, Italy;
Photo: Scala/Art Resource, New York

Antonio Barili

45. Intarsia panel depicting tools (c. 1490–1500) Antonio Barili
34 × 22 in.; La Collegiata, San Quirico d'Orcia, Italy
Photo: Lensini

O ne of the most important Italian intarsia artists was Antonio Barili, born in Siena in 1453. Siena was Europe's center for intarsia and therefore, not surprisingly, a city that produced great talent. It's not known how Antonio received his training, but by the time he was thirty he was respected enough to receive a significant commission to build nineteen panels for the Cappella di San Giovanni in the Duomo in Siena. The contract stipulated two years to complete the work. Barili had the assistance of his nephew, who was learning the trade.

Fortunately, a record of the contract gives us a sense of how long it would take to complete an intarsia panel of that size, 34 inches high by 22 inches wide. If Barili thought it was realistic for two men to complete the nineteen panels in two years, then each panel would have taken approximately ten man-weeks.

The contract tells us that Barili was to be paid just over 50 florins beyond what he expended. A penalty clause specified that if the work was not completed on time, he was to forfeit twice (100 florins!) what he was being paid. The relative value of a florin is difficult to pin down, as money was just coming into widespread usage in Europe, but it seems that an average worker in the building trades, a mason or a carpenter, in 1500 Florence would earn an annual wage of approximately 10–12 florins. A journeyman, such as Barili's nephew, would earn 8–9 florins. So it appears that the contract of 50 florins was an attractive compensation for an artisan.

In fact, it took Barili almost twenty years to complete the job. His efforts were diverted to many other more important civic projects, including the rebuilding of a bridge in Buonconvento. Two years later he was asked to design a bastion to protect another bridge important to the Sienese people. So he had skills that were valued for their contribution to the defense of the community as well as to the beauty of the cathedral. A true Renaissance man.

The panels made for the Duomo represent some of the most sophisticated intarsia that had been done up to that time. The scenes are varied in subject, ranging from trompe l'oeil open-cupboard still lifes to pictures of saints. Two pictures are of particular interest to the history of intarsia. One is a depiction of the tools of the intarsiatori. The other is a self portrait of Barili at work using those very implements.

The intarsia tools, many of them readily identifiable by today's woodworkers, appear to be in a cupboard with the doors partly open (figure 45). On the upper shelf sits a bow saw and a block plane, with a layout square to

46. Intarsia Self-Portrait (1502) Antonio Barili
Destroyed during World War II
Photo: Oesterreiches Museum, Vienna

knife, supporting its long handle on his shoulder. The length of the tool, and the shoulder support it enables, increases control and power in levering out the chips of wood. Here Barili is working on a tablet that has lettering on it. The words, in Latin, translate, "This work I, Antonio Barili, made with the knife, not the brush, in the year of our Lord 1502."

Several things are worth noticing about this picture. The outline of the sleeve is gently curved. Curved lines can be cut relatively easily with a knife. However, it is difficult to join tight or irregular curves together. So, the contour of the sleeve is rendered as a gentle wave. The darker parts of the tunic are joined together out of several pieces of veneer. This may have been done because of the difficulty of obtaining large pieces of such dark wood. The tighter curves of the fruit in the tree and the parrot were probably inlaid after the basic assembly was complete.

I am speculating about the construction of the panel because unfortunately it was destroyed during World War II. The only record left of this important piece is a black-and-white photograph. Of the original nineteen panels, only seven are known to have survived. In 1655 a Sienese scholar named Alfonso Landi decried the deterioration of the work. He cataloged the entire set and mapped out the way they were arranged in the cathedral. He argued that they were an important part of Sienese culture and should be preserved as a set. Nevertheless, in 1663 the panels were moved from their original setting in an effort to modernize the chapel. Barili's work was scattered, with seven of the panels installed in the small church in San Quirico d'Orcia about twenty-six miles south of Siena. The other twelve, including the self portrait, were dispersed. We can hope that some day some of the others will reappear.

the upper right. On the lower shelf is another plane, pliers, more layout tools, and a glue pot. The tools shown harken back to the tools depicted in the Egyptian tomb of Rekmire (figure 104). The one unfamiliar tool, sticking through the opening in the lower right door panel, is a shoulder knife—the tool Barili, his contemporaries, and his predecessors used to cut intarsia.

We get a chance to see how the shoulder knife was used in Barili's self-portrait (figure 46). The artist is shown at a window, working on a panel that rests on the window sill. The window itself is done in one-point perspective, framing the artist symmetrically. Behind him is a garden with a tree and a rather exotic parrot perched on a branch. Barili is using the shoulder

47. Intarsia panel of a saint (left)
48. Intarsia panel still life (right)
(c.1490-1500) Antonio Barili
Each panel: 34 × 22 in.
La Collegiata, San Quirico d'Orcia, Italy;
Photos: Lensini

The Barili panels are interesting for many reasons. One depicts a remarkably three-dimensional representation of a saint (figure 47). The man appears to be leaning out the window, his left forearm on the sill and his right hand at the upper corner of the window opening. He is looking upward. As with the self portrait, the window is drawn in one-point perspective. Layering enhances the three-dimensional effect. Farthest in the background is the landscape with trees that look like Lombardy poplars. A step closer is a wall with an arch in it. Next comes the body of the saint, and finally the window itself. The way the man leans from inside the room to outside the window, as if he's straining from one space to peer around the corner into another, has a commanding effect.

The folds of the tunic are wonderfully rendered by alternating dark and light pieces of wood. The man's hair and beard are made more realistic by incising lines into the larger shapes and then filling them with a contrasting material. Sometimes such lines were filled with slivers of wood, other times with a paste.

Barili does one other thing in these panels that I find inventive, and maybe a little disturbing. He took shards of wood of various species and mixed them with glue and pressed them into what could be thought of as the world's first chipboard. But this chipboard isn't used for construction. Barili took these composites, sawed them thinly, and used them as veneers. They can be seen in the sidewalls of the window frames. It has been suggested that the intent was to simulate marble or alabaster. To my eye it's so foreign to normal wood grain that it just looks out of place, and I wish he had used other regular veneers. However, I salute the bold use of wood.

One more of the Barili panels deserves attention here. Unlike the portrait panels, it is a still life, not one of the open cupboards but a variation on the window theme (figure 48). A simple inkstand and knife rest on the sill.

Outside the window a branch of a fruit tree holds a bird. The same architrave is continued from the other panels, and one can also see the distant landscape through the arch. The composition is notable for its snapshot quality. There appears to be no attempt to create a focal point for the picture, as was the norm for contemporary paintings.

Some of the other figurative panels also show a disregard for the fifteenth-century rules of composition. Scholars have wondered if Barili designed the panels or was simply the technician who used a greater artist's drawings. Art historian Federico Zeri wrote, "It is undeniable that the figure compositions in San Quirico achieve heights of inventive excellence that could scarcely be attributed to a woodcarving artisan, however great he might be." This seems an unfortunate, highly prejudicial statement. The fact that one of the compositions is a self-portrait should lead to the more likely conclusion that this "woodcarving artisan" was capable of inventive excellence in figurative work.

&

Giuliano and Benedetto da Maiano

The north sacristy of the Duomo in Florence and its trompe l'oeil intarsia panels executed by Agnolo di Lazzaro and Antonio Manetti obviously influenced Barili. Those panels had an even stronger impact on a Florentine boy whose father was a carpenter working on the cathedral. Giuliano da Maiano, who was a teenager when he joined his father as a tradesman, would certainly have seen the room being put together and been affected by the admiration that it no doubt engendered. Even at this young age Giuliano evidenced mature woodworking skills and began distinguishing himself as an intarsiatoro. In 1463 Giuliano received the commission to create additional intarsia panels in the north sacristy. Emulating the style of the original panels by di Lazzaro and Manetti, Giuliano's perspectives are excellent and his compositions intensified by incorporating strongly contrasting woods. He also used laminations to enhance the woodiness of the grain, in the manner of the earlier Sienese intarsiatori.

In 1476 Federico da Montefeltro, the Count of Urbino, commissioned the building of a small but elaborate study room, called a *studiolo,* to be a part of the Ducal palace (figure 49). The walls were paneled in wood wainscoting with trompe l'oeil cupboards and shelves. The work was done in Florence, though it is unclear who the master craftsman was. Tradition has it that the studiolo was the work of an intarsiatoro named Baccio Pontelli. One wonders if all the best intarsia artists in Florence weren't involved because it was such a huge undertaking. Recent research suggests that the Urbino studiolo came out of the workshop of Giuliano's younger brother, Benedetto. Primarily a sculptor, Benedetto had no doubt learned intarsia from his father and his brother.

In 1477 Federico commissioned a similar studiolo for his other palace in the eastern Italian hill town of Gubbio. The intarsia, built in the workshop of Giuliano, is now on display in the Metropolitan Museum of Art in New York (figure 50). Completed in 1996,

the restoration of the woodwork was painstakingly done under the direction of Antoine Wilmering of the Met's conservation department. Wilmering also wrote the definitive book on the craft of Italian intarsia. It is because of his efforts that we know so much about this wonderful period of woodcraft.

The Gubbio studiolo is a small, odd-shaped room. As in Urbino, trompe l'oeil intarsia wainscoting runs around all sides. Originally, paintings were displayed above the woodwork, as the walls are quite tall. The only source of natural light is one window, in a little alcove to the right as one enters the room. The trompe l'oeil intarsia panels appear to be latticework cupboards containing objects that have personal and symbolic importance to Federico.

Below the cupboards shelves are depicted, holding other objects. If you seek out the vantage point from which the perspectives were constructed, the illusions are very effective. The shading of the doors and objects is also done in accord with the light coming from the lone window.

It is difficult to know where to begin talking about the nuances of this great woodworking masterpiece. The skill that Giuliano displayed in the Duomo in Florence is brought to full fruition in Gubbio. Any of the individual panels would be worthy of analysis. Let's look at one part of the room.

To the left of the one window a panel depicts an open cupboard containing a cage with a parakeet. Intarsia columns with Corinthian capitals

49. Studiolo in Pallazzo Ducale, Urbino, Italy (c.1476)
Designed by Donato Bramante; Intarsia attributed to Benedetto da Maiano
Photo: Erich Lessing /Art Resource, New York

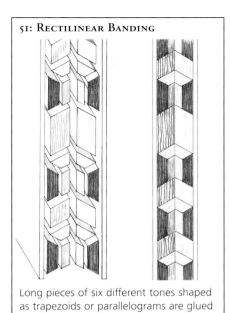

51: RECTILINEAR BANDING

Long pieces of six different tones shaped as trapezoids or parallelograms are glued together, then a flat veneer glued to each side. Pieces are sliced off the assembly.

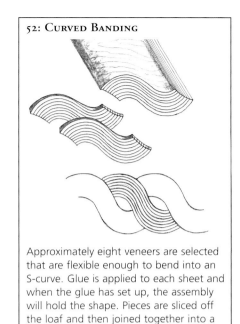

52: CURVED BANDING

Approximately eight veneers are selected that are flexible enough to bend into an S-curve. Glue is applied to each sheet and when the glue has set up, the assembly will hold the shape. Pieces are sliced off the loaf and then joined together into a longer running border.

flank the cupboard. Below the cupboard is a shelf with one section appearing to be hinged and flipped up. The underside of the shelf appears to be decorated with commesso di silio intarsia.

Around the corner from this panel is the next section of wall. The intarsia again is a trompe l'oeil open cupboard. This cupboard displays the Duke's armor and his sword. The next panel again turns a corner and the cupboard here holds musical instruments. Music was a particular passion of the Duke. In all, twelve panels depict open cupboards.

The cupboard with the parakeet deserves special attention. The left lattice door is closed, while the right door appears to be open at about a 45-degree angle. The birdcage is constructed of vertical columns with complicated capitals. The horizontal bars are made up of lighter and darker pieces of wood, which make them look round. The drawing of the cage is interesting because it is rendered as if eye-level is near the middle of the panel, and you can see the bottom of the cage, below, as well as the underside of the top, above. Additionally, note how the cage continues behind the left door, visible through that lattice.

Among the most fascinating parts of the panel are the running borders. On first glance they would appear to be a typical toppo design, with disks connected by a rod. Closer inspection reveals that each disk is individually cut. The perspective is such that the vantage point is close to the left hand edge of the panel. This means that in the group of disks running horizontally above and below the cupboard the disks are flatter as they progress to the right. Similarly the vertical set of disks are flattest just below the middle hinge (the eye level from which the perspective was constructed).

Finally worth noting about this panel is the effect of lighting and cast shadow. The right door is opened toward the window and therefore is made from a lighter wood. A shadow from the door is cast on the frame of the cupboard, and the whole picture is enhanced by very dark bog oak at the rear of the cupboard.

The Gubbio studiolo is a masterwork of perspective intarsia. It is remarkable that the design also includes some simpler toppo designs as well, including toppo banding that looks like a series of cubic forms connected by a square-sectioned rod (figure 51). Above the cupboard is

50. FACING PAGE:
STUDIOLO FROM DUCAL PALACE OF FEDERIGO DA MONTEFELTRO AT GUBBIO (C.1479–82); DESIGNED BY FRANCESCO DI GIORGIO MARTINI (ITALIAN, 1439–1502); EXECUTED BY GIULIANO DA MAIANO (ITALIAN 1432–1490)
Walnut, beech, oak, fruitwoods on walnut base; 15 ft. 9 in. × 16 ft. 9 in. × 28 ft. 9 in.
The Metropolitan Museum of Art, New York; Rogers Fund, 1939 (39.153)

Fra Giovanni da Verona

another toppo border that would have been a little more complicated to make (figure 52). Eight or ten thin pieces of wood are laminated into an S-shape, with darker woods on one side and lighter on the other. This is a slightly more complicated toppo because the parts within the loaf are curved. Much of the room is lined with this toppo. It can be seen surrounding the cupboard with the musical instruments.

The da Maiano brothers achieved fame never before known to those whose chief occupation was woodcraft. The Urbino and Gubbio commissions created reputations for both men. Benedetto is the only intarsiatoro singled out for a complete biography by Giorgio Vasari, the sixteenth-century chronicler of art in his book *The Lives of the Most Eminent Painters, Sculptors and Architects.* Vasari tells an interesting story about Benedetto, who was summoned to the court of Mattias Corvinus of Hungary. He made two coffers decorated with intarsia to present to the king. Part of the trip to Hungary was made aboard ship. When Benedetto arrived and unwrapped the coffers, he discovered to his dismay that the sea voyage had softened the glue, and almost all the pieces of intarsia had fallen off. "Putting the work together as well as he was able, he contrived to leave the King well enough satisfied; but in spite of this he took an aversion to the craft and could no longer endure it through the shame it had brought upon him and he took up carving instead." (Giorgio Vasari, 1550, translated by Gaston deVere, 1913.)

The next time I have technical problems with glue I will think of poor Benedetto (and perhaps take up carving as well, where I won't have to worry about adhesives). At the same time I am reminded that 500 years later Benedetto's fame is based on his intarsia.

૪૭

Most of the intarsia that has survived was produced to decorate churches in central and northern Italy. Much of this decoration was done by monks of the Benedictine order, who were devoted to work. Many fine craftsmen were trained in monasteries. The best of all the monks who were skilled in intarsia was Fra Giovanni da Verona, who was born in 1457 and entered the San Giorgio monastery in 1475. His initial work seems to have been illuminating choir books. The next year he was living at Monte Oliveto Maggiore, a monastery not far from Siena. One of the Benedictines there, Fra Sebastiano da Rovigno, was an accomplished intarsiatoro and Giovanni learned the craft from him. The Monte Oliveto monks were asked to decorate the cupboards of the sacristy and the choir stalls—thirty-four panels depicting the principal cities of the world.

Giovanni's next work was at an abbey near Villanova, where again he turned to book illumination. The versatile Giovanni was a talented fine artist, as well as a consummate craftsman. In 1502 Fra Giovanni was recalled to Monte Oliveto and asked to construct more choir stalls for the church—fifty-two panels in all, completed in three years. In the nineteenth century thirty-eight of the panels were removed and placed in the choir of the Duomo of Siena, where they are now on view.

Giovanni next constructed the choir stalls of another Olivetan monastery near Siena. In 1813 this church was in disrepair, and the order appealed to the hierarchy to allow the panels to be sent to the monastery church in Monte Oliveto. Among the finest ever produced, these intarsia panels can now be seen in the choir there. Trompe l'oeil open-cupboard scenes alternate with "windows," offering distant views of landscapes and cityscapes, all remarkably realistic.

In one panel the theme is music (figure 53). Pictured are two stringed instruments, two flutes, and a sheet of music. The cupboard's four doors, each with ten panels, are all open at different angles. The light, from the right

and above, is shining through the opening in the doors. The two doors on the right are of two slightly different tones, which correspond to their being at different angles to the source of the light. The door on the bottom left is the lightest of all four, while the door on the top left, in the shade, is the darkest. The shadow of the two left doors is cast onto the frame of the cupboard, which required cutting the marquetry border in both light and dark versions. Even the hinges are done in intarsia, those on the left in different tones from those on the right.

It is quite likely that parts of the picture were cut by an assistant. Several of Giovanni's young acolytes went on to achieve fame as intarsia cutters themselves. It would seem that Monte Oliveto was something of a "university for intarsiatori." The border designs and some of the more rectilinear parts of the pictures, such as the doors, would probably have been done by someone other than the master. Even if these doors were cut by someone other than Giovanni, they are still skillfully executed. But it is the working drawing that underlies the picture's real vitality. The doors, for instance, offer a subtle play of light and shadow across four different series of vertical patterns. They add to the graphic interest, as well as the three-dimensional illusion. Through the grate of the upper door at the part closest to the middle, you can see a sliver of the black background. As your eye moves closer to the hinges you can no longer see through the grating. Remember that the point from which the drawing was conceived was directly in front of the middle of the picture. The more your view would go to the right or left, the less you could see through the grate. He made the drawing (and the intarsia) depict that fact. The vanishing point for the drawing was half way up the bottom doors. Notice how little dark triangular shadows are cast on the panels at the point where the vertical frame members meet the horizontal parts of the door.

The inside rear of the cupboard is a very black bog oak. The ceiling of the

shape of the torn sheet music is also realistically rendered using the scorched shading technique. The musical staff and notation are all inlaid.

The lute on the bottom shelf is a tour de force of marquetry art. The rendering is superb, with its extreme foreshortening. The segmented body of the instrument is made with different pieces of wood, the change of grain direction and the glue lines helping to delineate the volume of the shape. Additionally, the left side and the area under the neck are shaded by scorching. The neck of the lute sticks out through the opening of the cupboard, and the tuning head overlaps the border pattern. A shadow is cast on the wall and floor of the cupboard, which again is scorched. The shadow of the neck travels over the floor and down the front of the border inlay, represented by a darker wood. Three of the lute strings are broken and curl into spirals. These were incised and then inlaid with contrasting wood. Notice how one string goes behind the sheet music and another behind the lute, while all these curled strings begin on top of the lute. This layering enhances the three-dimensional representation.

Perspective drawing was important to the success of these pictures, but shading is also a key to getting realistic effects. One older book on marquetry, written by Englishman Hamilton Jackson in 1903, suggested that the scorching was done by dipping the wood in molten lead. While this is possible, it would have been quite difficult to control the shading this way. The Metropolitan Museum's conservationist, Antoine Wilmering, writes it is more likely that Giovanni used the modern method of inserting the veneers in hot sand (see Appendix 6: Sand Shading).

It is certain that some of the woods used by Giovanni and other intarsiatori were altered with dyes. Wood is a fibrous product and can be dyed in a manner similar to fabric. Tuscany, being the center of the cloth trade in Europe during the Renaissance, would have included many people who understood the chemistry of dyeing

cupboard and the underside of the shelf are also bog oak, but not quite so dark. The pieces of wood are carefully selected to go from brown to black as the plane descends into the cabinet.

The musical instruments are outstanding examples of intarsia. On the top is a cithara. The sound hole is very delicate, made with small slivers of

wood to depict the fretwork. The sound board uses three different pieces of wood, from light to dark, as the light falls off and is shadowed on the parts of the instrument that are deepest in the cabinet. The curved side of the cithara is rendered by scorching the wood to create a gradual shading as the side approaches the shelf. The curled

54. INTARSIA PANEL DEPICTING A CITYSCAPE (C. 1500) FRA GIOVANNI DA VERONA
39 × 18 in.
From the choir of S. Maria in Organo, Verona, Italy;
Photo: Erich Lessing/Art Resource, New York

55. INTARSIA PANEL OF GEOMETRIC OBJECTS (C. 1500) FRA GIOVANNI DA VERONA
37½ × 17 in.
From the choir of Monte Oliveto Maggiore, Italy;
Photo: Scala/Art Resource, New York

56. INTARSIA PANEL OF OPEN CUPBOARD WITH OWL (C. 1500) FRA GIOVANNI DA VERONA
39 × 18 in.
From the choir of S. Maria in Organo, Verona, Italy;
Photo: Erich Lessing/Art Resource, New York

and what substances could be used. The fabric industry produced a red by using decoctions of cochineal insects. Indigo yielded blue, and saffron or turmeric could make bright yellows. Chemical baths could generate other colors. For instance, a blue could be obtained by dissolving copper in spirit of nitre, making a substance called aqua fortis, which turned a light wood blue. A fifteenth-century manuscript suggests how to dye an object green, using "strong red vinegar and brass filings mixed together with a little Roman vitriol and stone alum in a glass vessel. When it has stood for a day and the object dipped in it and allowed to stand for a day, the color will be very permanent."

Most of the color in the marquetry panels has faded over the centuries, except for the green tones. Most dyes of the period were not colorfast. But dyes with a base of copper sulphates, such as

the recipes for the blue and the green above, are in fact colorfast. We don't see blue because the pale base wood itself would have yellowed over the years. As we know, when blue and yellow are mixed, you end up with green.

Antoine Wilmering, who restored the Gubbio studiolo, has found one other green in Italian intarsia that has maintained its color. The wood is poplar that has turned green due to a fungal attack. This rare occurrence made the wood highly prized for intarsia. It is found in the work of Giuliano da Maiano, and it is also seen in panels by Giovanni.

Fra Giovanni created many scenes looking through windows to a landscape or cityscape. In the case of the cityscape pictured from the choir of the church of S. Maria in Organo in Verona, the window is an arch with the light coming from the left (figure 54). The columns of the arch are decorated

with commesso di silio intarsia. The view is looking down a street, which is slightly off center. The design is done in a simple one-point perspective. The checkerboard paving recedes in space. All the buildings are constructed using simple shapes. In the far distance are towers and other fortifications in the hilly landscape. The format is very similar to pictures done by the Lendinara brothers (figure 42). Cutting the polygons which make up the buildings that are the pieces of this intarsia could have been executed primarily using simple saws and straight chisels. Here the intarsia is a celebration of the contemporary Italian interest in perspective.

Giovanni also created a panel that is noteworthy for its interest in geometry (figure 55). The format is similar to his panel with the musical instruments—two shelves and four doors open at various angles. In the cupboard are two interesting geometric constructions. On the bottom is an object called a *mazzocchio.* The three-dimensional solid is octagonal in section, with each plane alternating in color. To draw a mazzocchio was a test of a draftsman's ability in perspective art. They are found in the sketchbooks of famous painters, such as Paolo Uccello. A mazzocchio is prominently found in the Gubbio studiolo. On the upper shelf of Giovanni's panel is a fantastical spherical object looking as if it were built from pieces of wood (see also figure 44). All of the planes are accentuated by the choice of wood tone, creating the illusion of three-dimensionality by subtly differentiating how the light strikes each plane. Through this grillwork you can see to the parts beyond.

Hanging from the shelf is a group of layout tools: a square, dividers, straightedge, and triangle. Winding through them is a ribbon. The inlaid inscription reads, "these are the tools of intarsia." Giovanni wanted to make clear that his craft was more than saws and glue pots, but an extension of the contemporary interest in mathematics and learning.

Giovanni was an excellent draftsman. He did some very sensitive intarsia where the subjects were animals. There are lively pictures of birds, a cat, a rabbit, and one delightful panel with an owl in a cupboard (figure 56).

Giovanni's fame spread throughout Italy and his work came to the attention of Pope Julius II, who had him make some panels for the Vatican. These panels decorate the doors of the famous Stanza, a room whose painted decoration was done by Raphael. In Giovanni's later years he returned to Verona, where he died in 1525.

Fra Giovanni's legacy is perhaps best summed up in the writing of Giorgio Vasari, the sixteenth-century artist and historian. He wrote about the intarsia in the S. Maria church in Verona, "And it is certain that in that craft there never was any man more able than Giovanni, either in design or workmanship."

**57. THE FINDING OF MOSES (16TH CENTURY)
JACOPO BAROZZI DA VIGNOLA (ITALIAN, 1507–1573);
INTARSIA BY FRA DAMIANO DA BERGAMO (ITALIAN, 1480–1549)**
35½ × 32 in.
*The Metropolitan Museum of Art, New York; Rogers Fund,
1912 (12.130.2); Photo: Metropolitan Museum of Art*

Fra Damiano da Bergamo (1480–1549) was taught intarsia work by Sebastiano, the same monk who had instructed Giovanni da Verona in the craft. Damiano was twenty-three years younger than Giovanni. Abandoning the perspective geometries of the open cupboards, he concentrated on scenes of the Bible, depicting people in a more sophisticated way than earlier work had. Older intarsiatori, including Barili, had done figurative work, but Damiano's used figures as actors within a larger context. His panels are much more painterly than is typical of earlier intarsia, both in composition and in tonal range.

"The Finding of Moses," is a fine example of Damiano's work (figure 57). The architectural elements are similar to the intarsia of the Lendinaras or Giovanni. But Damiano has peopled the picture not only with the baby Moses, but also with about twenty others, as well as many animals. The composition looks like a theatrical set. People's expressions and body language add to the drama of the picture. Damiano was particularly skillful at choosing wood—in terms of color, tone, and figure—to tell the story. Notice the use of figured wood for some of the architectural elements. Curly wood and burls, which were seldom used in earlier intarsia pictures, find their way into Damiano's palette. His predecessors may have avoided figured wood because of the difficulties in working it. He also used the resawn composite chipboards to simulate marble, as Barili had done decades earlier. The fine detail in his compositions is sometimes achieved by engraving into the individual veneer and then filling it with a small piece of wood or a colored paste. He used sand shading, as well as dyes, to enhance the picture.

There is a wonderful story about Damiano and his extraordinary skill at intarsia. Charles V of the Holy Roman Empire was in the Church of San Domenico in Bologna, which contained a choir decorated by Damiano. Charles thought the work was so beautifully done that it couldn't possibly be made of pieces of wood, as he had been told, but rather that it had been painted. To assuage his curiosity, he took his sword and chopped out a bit of the panel. Confirming that the picture was in fact composed of wood pieces, Charles asked to meet the man who could do such work and was taken to Damiano's studio. Apparently still not sure that the intarsia was not treated with paints, Damiano pulled out a hand plane and passed it over the

panel he was working on, thereby shaving off the top layer of wood. Charles was finally convinced that the picture was all wood.

It is possible that Damaino and the intarsiatori who followed him became too proficient at their craft. In attempting to imitate painting, they came close to the realism that could be achieved with fresco or oils, but then were hampered by the inherent limitations of the craft. Wood tones would always seem muted next to a painting, no matter how skillfully tiny pieces could be put together. In trying to "paint," they strayed too far from the roots that had served intarsia artists like Fra Giovanni so well. Giorgio Vasari acknowledges the talent of many intarsiatori, including Giovanni and Giuliano. But he dismisses the bulk of intarsia as an imitation of painting, and simply "requiring more patience than skill." "And thus it is," he writes, "that though many things have been produced in [intarsia], such as representations of figures, fruit, and animals, some of which are in truth most lifelike, yet it is a work that soon becomes black and does not do more than counterfeit painting, being less than painting, and is short-lived because of worms and fire; it is considered time thrown away in vain to practice it, although it may indeed be both praiseworthy and masterly."

This is a harsh judgment, but perhaps warranting consideration. In later periods the craft of marquetry, whose roots were in the Italian intarsia that Vasari had insulted, found their fullest expression as decorative elements on furniture objects. Perhaps wooden furniture is the best place to use the beauty of marquetry.

‍

58. WRANGELSHRANK (1566); DETAIL OF INSIDE OF DOOR (LEFT)
Made in Augsburg, Germany; 27½ × 39½ × 18 in.
Westfalisches Landesmuseum, Munster, Germany; Inv. K-605 LM

The fame of Italian intarsiatori spread throughout Europe. Some, like Benedetto da Maiano, were invited to work for foreign patrons. In 1532 records show that François I had an Italian in his employ making intarsia panels. Woodworking skills took root in the area of southern Germany centered around Augsburg. Augsburg was important commercially because it was in the middle of trade routes that crossed Europe and Italy's gateway to areas north. By the early sixteenth century the city had become an important banking center, in many ways surpassing Florence. Augsburg was rich and attracted craftsmen who were experimenting with new ideas.

Metalworking was a vital craft in sixteenth-century Augsburg, known for its intricate mechanical devices, such as locks, crossbows, and clocks. Many of the tools used to cut precise metal parts, especially the fine blades needed to cut clock gears, could also be used to cut inlay. While the fretsaw was used in Italy by craftsmen like Fra Damiano, in Augsburg the tool was refined. The same saws that produced state-of-the-art clocks yielded intricate shapes in wood and ivory for decorating furniture.

German workers became renowned for working with ebony. Some furniture was made with carved ebony decoration. Other furniture was inlaid with contrasting woods or, on the most expensive pieces, ivory. Sometimes the ivory was engraved, again this work evolved from a metalworking tradition. Elaborate pieces involved the skills of cabinetmakers, carvers, lapidary workers, and metalsmiths.

One particularly famous cabinet made in Augsburg in 1566 is notable for its marquetry (figure 58). It is called the Wrangelschrank (named for the Swedish commander who took it as booty during the Thirty Years War, 1618–48). The cabinet was built by Lorenz Strohmeir and Bartlmä Weishaupt. The front of the cabinet has two doors, which open to a set of

59. Cupboard (1569)
Pine with cherry, pear, plum, maple,
and limewood
Ulmer Museum, Ulm, Germany (inv. 2124)

ER ER WER VND VON WAN ER WER KOMMEN HER ODER WA

drawers with carved boxwood fronts. The inside of the doors is also decorated with marquetry. The scenes reflect the interest artists had in Roman antiquity: scenes of ruins and Roman armor. Note how intricately the picture is rendered. It is much more complex than anything that had been made in Italy. The key is the use of the finer fretsaw, which allowed the marquetry cutter greater freedom in cutting small shapes with tight curves.

German cabinetmakers developed a unique style, emphasizing marquetry pictures of architectural scenes and Roman themes, like those of the Wrangelschrank. In 1567 an artist named Lorenz Stoer printed a book of designs for marquetry called *Geometria et Perspectiva,* a reflection of how important marquetry-decorated woodwork and furniture had become.

One major difference between the German and Italian work is that the former decorates freestanding furniture, while the latter is applied to architectural elements. The freestanding furniture, objects ranging from small boxes

to large cupboards, could be exported (figure 59). Chests and cabinets were exported throughout Europe, to such an extent that some homegrown craftsmen in other countries suffered. To protect Spanish craftsmen, Phillip III of Spain banned the import of furniture from Augsburg.

Nevertheless, craftsmen throughout Europe got a chance to see marquetry, and they realized the demand for furniture decorated with pictures in wood. It wasn't long before these skills took root in other countries.

☙

Two things about the Italian intarsia compositions particularly impressed me during my trip in 1984. I loved the trompe l'oeil open cupboards, and I found the portraits remarkable. I had never tried anything other than floral patterns in marquetry, and I wondered if I could expand my vocabulary into new areas. When I got home, I was eager to try cutting something different. My first foray from the world of flowers was a picture of hands holding a woodworking plane (figure 60). Perhaps it was a nod to the Barili self portrait.

I then designed a piece of furniture using a face (my own) peeking through what looks to be a woven membrane of wood. I titled it *1498–1984* (figure 61). The piece is a cabinet with a marquetry door and drawers below. To make the marquetry I started with a checkerboard pattern out of straight-grained oak, turning every other piece at right angles to its neighbor. I scorched the end-grain edges of each piece in hot sand to simulate shading, so that the assembled panel looks woven. I further wanted the weave to look as if it was cut open with several slits. The surface would then appear to be curled away from the opening and protruding from the picture plane, like the doors in an Italian intarsia cupboard. To create the effect of a light source from the left, I needed two other woods that would be similar in grain to the white oak, but lighter and darker. I used ash for the areas facing the light source and English brown oak for the surfaces appearing to be in shade. Along with the scorching, these three woods create the illusion of a three-dimensional picture plane.

The portrait appears behind the oak weaving. To add to the illusion I had the fingers of the right hand protruding through the picture plane similar to the way Giovanni and Barili composed their pictures. Each of the Italian designers would use the device of having parts (human or otherwise) sticking through the picture plane (see figures 45, 47, 53). This layering is something that makes the Italian compositions so compelling.

Also contributing to the illusion of perspective is the placement of the detailed part of the marquetry picture at eye level. The furniture becomes the functional frame for the marquetry, and the focal point is quite literally at eye level, where the detailing is easiest to appreciate.

I started a series of projects related to the Italian concept of the open cupboard. Unlike the choir stalls, I had the advantage of actually designing a cabinet that would need cupboard doors. I needed to decide about what kind of things might actually be put in the type of cabinet I was designing. In the Italian examples, the subject was often something the patron would have used or liked. Mine were going to be speculative pieces, so on a certain level I could please myself. But perhaps the

60. HANDS ON PLANE (1984) SILAS KOPF
17 × 9½ in.
Photo: David Ryan

61. 1498-1984 (1984) SILAS KOPF
Mahogany, maple, and marquetry;
66 × 24 × 18 in.
Photo: David Ryan

pieces would be more marketable if they had some broader appeal. I enjoy the occasional glass of wine, and know others do as well, so I figured a composition with that theme might work. *Wine Cabinet* depicts a bottle, two glasses, and a corkscrew behind a partially open raised-panel door (figure 62). The cabinet has what I call a pocket to fit the odd shape of the door: room in the curved top and in the marquetry "drawer" below. The light is coming from the left. Therefore the door is in shadow, with the chosen woods having a tone darker than the frame of the maple used in the cabinet. I needed various species to represent the different facets of the raised panel and the drawer. I made a matching cabinet at the same time with a marquetry theme of a tea set.

To aid in the design, I constructed a simple plywood box and attached a piece of cardboard to the front as a hinged door, left ajar. I placed the objects inside and shined light on the whole box, trying several different compositions until I found a grouping of objects and lighting that pleased me. I made a full-scale pencil drawing of this arrangement and from it created the marquetry panel.

An important component in the composition is the use of the cast shadows. They appear on the rear of the cabinet, the floor of the cabinet, and the wine bottle. Additionally, the door itself casts a shadow on the frame of the cabinet. It was particularly challenging to make the glasses in marquetry. They needed to be transparent, yet absorb some of the light. They also needed to produce a refractive effect, distorting things behind them, as well as focusing the light in certain spots. I achieved this effect principally by using very thin slivers of wood to show the outline of the glass. The lines and the distortions inside the outline make it look like glass.

I built several cabinets that had the basic format of *Wine Cabinet.* The cabinet then becomes a frame for the display of the marquetry. I made one of these pieces as if it had a glass door with a tea set inside (figure 63). As with *Wine Cabinet,* I mocked-up a plywood box the size of the cabinet, filled it with real objects, and lit them to develop the composition in the form of a full-size pencil drawing. I do this with all of my trompe l'oeil cabinets (figure 64). Generally I cut the marquetry and then build the cabinet based on the size of the door.

62. WINE CABINET (1986) SILAS KOPF
Maple and marquetry; 52 × 20 × 14 in.
Photos: David Ryan

Often perspective dictates that the door of the cabinet is an odd-shaped trapezoid, which can create some curious problems in building a carcase. In the case of *Tea Cabinet* it was necessary to create a pocket for the door to accommodate the foreshortening that occurs in the perspective of the door.

These early experiments with trompe l'oeil opened up new possibilities for me. The trip to Italy and subsequent study of Renaissance intarsia would prove as inspirational as my survey of French Art Nouveau furniture. Trompe l'oeil cupboard panels are themes I have returned to again and again over the years.

One of my more ambitious pieces based on the Italian open cupboard was a fall-front desk I designed in 1986. The marquetry depicts a white cat lying on two books behind two partly opened doors and a drawer below (figure 65). The primary wood is mahogany. The left door, opened to the light, is primarily maple, with lighter and darker veneers rendering the different planes of the raised panel. The door away from the light source is principally walnut, to suggest its being in shadow. These are the same devices used in *Wine Cabinet.* In this case, the cabinet-

63. Tea Cabinet (1985) Silas Kopf
Cherry, madrone burl, and marquetry; 53 × 20 × 14 in.
Photo: David Ryan

64. Mock-up for trompe l'oeil cabinet
Plywood box filled with real objects and lit to develop working drawing.

65. Fall Front Desk with Cat (1986) Silas Kopf
Mahogany and marquetry; 52 × 30 × 18 in.
Photo: David Ryan

66. TROMPE L'OEIL DESK WITH VIOLIN (1988) SILAS KOPF
Mahogany, rosewood, and marquetry; 46 × 35 × 18 in.
Photo: David Ryan

67. AQUARIUM FALL FRONT CABINET (1989) SILAS KOPF
Mahogany, amboyna burl, and marquetry; 52 × 49 × 18 in.
Photo: David Ryan

work itself was a little more challenging. It is important that the marquetry composition be carefully integrated with the furniture design. I always hope that the furniture object is satisfying without the marquetry, and the marquetry is more pleasing because it is used on furniture.

In this composition I again used the device of layering the objects and the shadows they cast. The open doors appear closest to the viewer. A shadow from the right-hand door is cast on the drawer front and follows the curves of the molded edge. The shadow line changes course again at the floor of the cabinet, then traces the curved surfaces of the bindings and pages of the books. I needed many different tones and grains of woods for this effect. The bindings are burls, to simulate leather, and two different yellow tones represent the gilded edges of the pages.

Taking a note from Fra Giovanni (figure 53), the illusion is strengthened by making things stick out of the picture plane. So the cat's foot is draped over the books and the tail comes right out of the cabinet and descends in front of the drawer. I added faceted drop pulls done in marquetry, which also cast shadows. Small details like this help to make for a more interesting illusion.

One final note about the desk. The background veneer depicting the interior of the cabinet is African wenge, which is quite dark and has a prominent grain. The dark ground makes the white cat stand out as if in

relief. I needed a variety of tones for the cat, ranging from holly to ebony, to ensure that her body does not look flat.

Fall Front Desk with Cat led to a commission for a similar piece (figure 66). This time the trompe l'oeil effect simulates an open cupboard with glass doors and objects of the client's choice inside.

Some animals work nicely in wood marquetry. I had done a number of birds and insects, too. In 1987 we built a drop-front liquor cabinet that looked like an aquarium, using dyed woods for the bright tropical fish, as well as the plants in the water (figure 67). The hood of the aquarium was difficult to build. We bent curved plywood panels at a 4-inch radius and then veneered them with a highly figured burl. We also veneered a flat, rectangular panel in the same burl, mitered the curved plywood parts, and joined them to the flat panel. Because the veneer is thin, there was little margin for error in flushing off the joints to make the whole smooth. I was fortunate to have someone with Tim Faner's skills to execute this design.

ᛒ

68. Iris Coffee Table (c. 1990)
Silas Kopf
Machiche and marquetry with
mother-of-pearl inlay; 17 × 52 × 19 in.
Photo: David Ryan

On my return from Italy I went back to floral work
with new eyes. I realized that getting more detail in the
marquetry could produce terrific results. Some of the
success of the Italian work could be attributed to the
small, differently colored pieces that blend together from a
distance to create painterly effects. Sometimes tiny pieces
can be used as highlights to great effect. French Art
Nouveau marquetry is generally composed of larger pieces
for a simpler, bolder look. I started making flowers more
like the Italians did their realistic still lifes and portraits.
For instance, a coffee table I made features irises on top
(figure 68). I had made irises in the past on boxes or
blanket chests. In the earlier work an individual flower
might have twelve or fifteen pieces in it. The flowers in
this table have fifty to a hundred pieces per flower. This
complex of subtly differentiated tones blend together to
make a more interesting, more realistic image.

I made several cabinets with the more elaborate floral
forms based on an early American piece of furniture
called a Hadley chest, which often featured a lifting top
and drawers below and was decorated with chip carving
and paint. I thought it might be interesting to update this
important style of American furniture. Additionally, it
intrigued me that the town after which this style of chest
is named, Hadley, is a neighbor of Northampton, where
I live.

I used the format of the lifting top and one or two
drawers, decorating the main part of the chest with
elaborate marquetry. The first chest has tulips on a
rosewood background (figure 5). The area at the bottom,

where the drawers are, looks deep enough to contain the
soil in which the flowers are growing. The whole chest can
be thought of as a planter box. Another chest was very
similar, featuring the branches of an apple tree with ripe
fruit (figure 69).

One of the early pieces I designed with elaborate floral
marquetry is a tall chest with azalea branches on the doors,
totally veneered in Australian jarrah and bordered with
⅛-inch ebony (figure 70). This was a complicated piece
to veneer, as many of the parts are curved. Such shapes
normally require building two-part forms to press the
veneers. (See Wood in Appendix 1: Marquetry.) The usual
construction is to make the panel and then frame it with
solid wood. But because the veneer here is comprehensive
and the sides are curved on the outside and flat on the
inside, this piece required a new strategy. The outside
curve was bent out of several layers of ⅛-inch plywood
and connected with struts to the inside, a piece of ½-inch
plywood, creating a torsion box. Next, the legs were glued
on and shaped to fit the outside curve. Then the whole
side was put in the veneer press to add the jarrah burl.
This way, the veneer ran right out to the edges. Finally, the
⅛-inch corner was routed away and a piece of ebony was
glued in place. I usually have a piece of solid wood on a
corner because it is the most fragile part of furniture, and
the solid wood wears better and is easier to repair in case
of damage.

A complicated sideboard followed this piece. *Cardinal
Sideboard,* which features a very highly figured Cuban
mahogany and marquetry panels depicting tree branches
and two pairs of cardinals, also involved adding the
veneers after parts were already assembled (Figure 71). The
legs are shaped in gentle compound curves, and the
veneers that cover them and the whole cabinet frame are
pieced together to make diagonal patterns.

69. Hadley Chest with Apples (2000) Silas Kopf
Narra, madrone burl, rosewood, and marquetry; 33 × 44 × 22 in.
Photo: Kevin Downey

70. Azalea Cabinet (1987) Silas Kopf
Jarrah burl, ebony, and marquetry; 61 × 22 × 16 in.
Photo: David Ryan

71. Cardinal Cabinet (1992) Silas Kopf
Cuban mahogany, maple, ebony, and marquetry; 34 × 73 × 20 in.
Photo: Kevin Downey

72. GARDEN CABINET (1998) SILAS KOPF
Narra, amboyna burl, and marquetry; 36½ × 98½ × 25 in.
Photo: David Ryan

I hope that the furniture objects can stand alone satisfactorily without the marquetry decoration. I think this is true of *Cardinal Sideboard*. But it certainly wouldn't be successful if the quality of the craftsmanship weren't of the highest caliber. None of these pieces is produced without the skilled craftsman's touch. In 1984 I began a relationship with Tim Faner, who added significantly to my furniture and craft vocabulary. Tim and I met when he was a student at the Leeds Workshops. He liked my work, and I had seen what a talented and exacting craftsman he was. Tim would find clever solutions to thorny problems and his work was always superb. He was particularly inventive in adding secret compartments to pieces. Our collaboration lasted eight years. I have subsequently been ably assisted by Tom Coughlin. Both Tim and Tom proved to be better

technicians than I, and it has been a great opportunity to exploit their skills. As a designer I am able to bring an understanding of woodcraft to the process and then utilize the talents of others, like Tim and Tom. I believe that designs are often better if the person who drafts the object has an understanding of how things are constructed. When that isn't the case, implausible ideas struggle to get turned into concrete objects. When we look at great objects of furniture craft, like those of Chippendale or Boulle, we see pieces where the designer understood intimately how things are put together. This sensitivity to process cannot help but come through in the final design.

The next piece in the evolution of my elaborate floral designs was a large, low bedroom cabinet, about 8 feet long and neo-classically styled (figure 72). The client suggested a garden scene with mixed flowers, which required a density of marquetry that I had never before attempted. Beside the flowers sits a birdbath and several birds and butterflies. The front of the cabinet is slightly bowed. Behind two pairs of doors are eight drawers. The marquetry panels total about 4½ feet wide and over 2 feet high. The plain veneer panels are amboyna burl, and the solid wood is narra. Carved pilasters flank each of the side doors. Because the marquetry picture is so large, it was necessary to break it up into sections in order to have parts that could fit on my saw for bevel cutting. Each of the

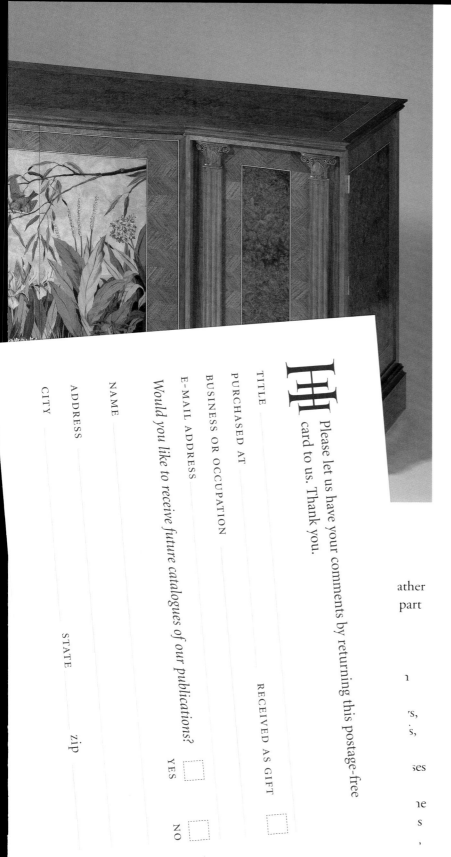

ather
part

's,
s,

ses

ne
s

g ... the glaze. For the larger vase I used tight-grained maple as the predominant wood with some holly highlights. It was a particular challenge to simulate the glass vases. I used the same technique I had used in *Wine Cabinet* (figure 62) to make the glass work like a lens, with shiny highlights and changes of tonality as one looks through the layers of glass and water.

73. COLLECTOR'S CABINET (1999) SILAS KOPF
Sassafras and marquetry; 40 × 65 × 29½ in.
Photo: David Ryan

74. Floral Cabinet (1695–1710) Jan van Mekeren
Oak veneered with rosewood, olivewood, ebony, holly, boxwood, tulipwood, and kingwood; 58 × 43 × 23 in.
Rijksmuseum, Amsterdam; (inv. M-BK-1964-12-15)

75. CABINET ON STAND (C.1700–01) JAN VAN MEKEREN
Oak veneered with rosewood, olivewood, ebony, holly,
kingwood, tulipwood, and partly green stained marquetry woods;
70¼ × 54 × 22½ in.
Metropolitan Museum of Art, New York;
Ruth and Victoria Blumka Fund, 1995 (1995.371ab)

The bouquets on the Amsterdam cabinet are in vases
rather than tied with ribbons. The sides are also decorated
with marquetry flowers, and there is a matching console
table. A painstaking study by the conservators at the
Rijksmuseum revealed that among the 676 flowers on the
cabinet and the table, 157 are repeated, some of them as
many as five times. The pictures are so busy with petals
that it is difficult to find the duplicates. Identical cutting
appears cleverly in mirror image, to disguise the
duplication. It would be interesting to know if the same
flowers are also "cross-pollinated" between the Amsterdam
and New York chests. Using the technique of *peinture en
bois*, which was the common way of cutting marquetry at
the time, also produced off-cuts, some of which could be
assembled into other flowers elsewhere. Van Mekeren was
a clever craftsman who knew how to work efficiently.

☙

Perhaps no piece better illustrates the synergy between
technique and design than my *Typewriter Desk* (figure 76).
The piece is another trompe l'oeil concept, this time
without the open doors. I took objects that would be used
at a desk—a typewriter, books, a pencil holder—and
arranged them in the space. I wanted to mount the
marquetry on a tambour that would slide off to the left and
out of sight. The interior of the desk behind the tambour
would then have drawers and pigeon holes. I wasn't sure if
the marquetry would be successful on the tambour. I was
also apprehensive that the tambour would run smoothly. I
leaned heavily on Tim to work out the details of tracking
the slats and making everything work well.

The most challenging part of the marquetry was
making the typewriter itself. I had to simulate the shiny
metal parts, as well as produce all the individual keys.
Each of the keys comprises fourteen tiny pieces of wood.
These little disk forms are similar to those in the toppo
intarsia of the Gubbio studiolo (figure 50), and I made
them using a similar stack-and-slice technique (figure 77).
I put together long strips with five or six different woods
running from light to dark at the sides. These were to be
the metallic edges of the keys. I cut the stack at an angle to
produce an elliptical shape that would be the flat part of
the key. I then turned the packet around and used the
other side of the ellipse to surround the flat part of the
key. This way, making the forty-two different keys was
manageable.

To build the tambour, we made a frame to hold the
individual slats tightly together, so this panel could be
pressed in the traditional manner. Each slat was about
½-inch square and 15 inches long. We applied a light coat
of lacquer to the edges that would touch in the frame,

My client's interest in Dutch flower painting paid
other dividends for me because I became aware of the
classic use of flowers in marquetry, which was
contemporary with the paintings I was looking at. Floral
marquetry reached its height in Holland in the late
seventeenth century, at the time of Tulipmania, when
flower bulbs became a precious commodity. One
cabinetmaker, Jan van Mekeren, became famous for
decorating furniture with flowers. His cabinet-on-stand in
the Metropolitan Museum is a celebration of marquetry
(figure 75). Stripped of its decoration, this would be a very
plain piece indeed. The structure itself is rigidly
symmetrical and architectural, but the two marquetry
vases add a lively, natural energy to the piece. Flowers also
decorate the frieze at the top, the aprons, the legs, and
even the stretcher at the bottom.

A second, slightly larger but almost identical cabinet
in the Rijksmuseum in Amsterdam also has flowers on the
horizontal friezes, the legs, and the stretcher (figure 74).

76. TYPEWRITER DESK (1987) SILAS KOPF
Mahogany, satinwood, and marquetry;
46½ × 41 × 23 in.
Photos: David Ryan

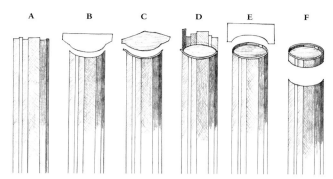

77. PRODUCING MULTIPLE TYPEWRITER KEYS
  A. Strips of different tones of veneer are pieced together.
  B. Curved piece of veneer is added at the "rim" of the key.
  C. Veneer is added for the "pad" of the key.
  D. Strips are added to the top with reverse shading.
  E. Curve is added to the top of the rim.
  F. Individual key is cut off.

then waxed them to prevent glue from adhering the slats to each other. In the frame, the slats could be squeezed together, creating a flat surface that was broken by only a hairline every half inch. We cut and taped together the marquetry picture like any other picture then glued the assembled veneer sheet to these slats in place of the normal corestock. Once the glue set, I was able to crack the lines open from the back. At this point the individual slats are hinged by the veneer itself. To separate the slats, I carefully sliced through the veneer (the marquetry) with a knife from the backside. Because we had aligned most of the grain in the marquetry vertically, in the same grain direction as the slats, slicing was cleaner and easier. We then lightly cleaned each edge and put the slats back in the frame, this time gluing a piece of canvas on the backside to create the tambour, in the traditional way. The track for the tambour has a slight concave curve across the face of the desk. This helps to push the front edges tightly together.

❧

Italian intarsia has influenced my figurative work in several ways. I did a life-size marquetry picture of my daughter, Sasha, sitting to one side of a window seat, holding a book and looking out to a street scene (figure 78). In the relationship between figure and window, and the architectural scene outside, the composition is inspired by Barili (see pp. 38–40). Given its size, I needed a way to divide the picture into sections that would be small enough to cut on the scroll saw. The individual panes of glass, which occupy most of the composition, afforded this opportunity. I was able to construct the sixteen individual panes, plus the rectangles of the windowseat, separately, then assemble them into the large panel. Sasha was also put together out of smaller parts: the right leg, the left leg and part of the dress, the book and fingers, and the left

78. SASHA (1987) SILAS KOPF
Marquetry panel of various woods; 87 × 49 in.
Photo: David Ryan

arm and upper body. These were assembled first and then laid on the window construction to be cut in using an X-ACTO knife. This technique of compositing a complex image, from large areas to small details, proceeds in much the same way Renaissance intarsiatori created their designs (see pp. 36–37).

Also inspired by Barili (and also featuring a member of my family) is the marquetry picture that is the focal point of a tall cabinet I did in solid padauk (figure 79). The upper portion of the cabinet has a trompe l'oeil open cupboard door, out of which my wife, Linda, is leaning as if to glance around the corner. Her pose is directly related to the Barili panel with the saint leaning

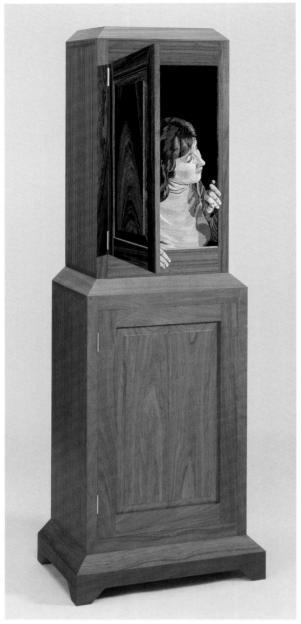

79. Linda (1985) Silas Kopf
Padauk and marquetry; 75 × 23 × 17 in.
Photo: David Ryan

80. Dad (1990) Silas Kopf
Shedua, marquetry, and mirror; 52 × 21 in.
Photo: David Ryan

on the window sill (figure 47). I used the positioning of her hands as a way of layering the composition and developing a realistic perspective.

I used my father as a model for a marquetry panel, posing him as if he were adjusting his tie in a mirror (figure 80). The marquetry was cut with a plain wood background surrounding the figure, then glued onto a piece of ¼-inch plywood. After sanding, we finished it with lacquer. At this point the picture was a simple rectangle. I purchased a mirror of the same height and width, and scraped the silver off the back of the glass in all the area corresponding to the marquetry figure. When the glass was laid on top of the marquetry panel,

the negative space in the silver matched the outline of the wood portrait. Because the silver layer on the back of the glass is so thin, it appears as if the wood is inlaid in the silver. A frame keeps the mirror and the marquetry panel together.

My daughter Sasha has appeared in several pieces besides the life-size portrait. The first was when she was young enough to be playing with Lego blocks (figure 81). I posed her as if she were building with giant toy blocks from the inside of the cabinet. I used colorful dyed veneers for the blocks. At the top we added painted dowels to the unfinished construction to make it look like the Lego building process was still going on.

I used marquetry hands in a number of pieces in the mid-1980s. We built a small mantle clock that depicted a hand holding a magnifying glass in front of the clock face's number three (figure 82). The rim of the magnifier casts a shadow on the dial, and the numeral, seen through the lens, is enlarged.

The theme of the second piece I did using hands, *Enthralled* is a little dark (figure 83). It shows a grill of straight bars through which the fingers of a pair of hands protrude, as if someone were at the bottom of the cabinet grasping at the door to get out. To make the drawing, I took a photograph of a friend holding a piece of architectural lattice, and worked from that. Then I cut oak veneer into parquetry pieces, with English oak for the parts that would be in shadow, and added the hands, using seven or eight different species, from holly at the lighter end of the scale to ebony at the darkest.

One of the most complicated portrait pieces we built was a cabinet for music lovers to house their stereo system and compact-disc collection (figure 1). I thought it would be appropriate to have a musician as the marquetry subject, and asked a professor who teaches violin at Smith College to pose for me. The cabinet has three openings. Instead of doors, we built tambours. The lower tambours have herringbone patterns in English brown oak. The marquetry of the violinist was mounted on slats for the tambour, the way we did *Typewriter Desk* (figure 76). The case is veneered in a herringbone pattern throughout, including on the octagonal corner posts and the curved moldings at the top and bottom.

❦

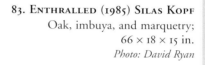

83. ENTHRALLED (1985) SILAS KOPF
Oak, imbuya, and marquetry;
66 × 18 × 15 in.
Photo: David Ryan

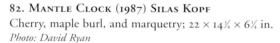

82. MANTLE CLOCK (1987) SILAS KOPF
Cherry, maple burl, and marquetry; 22 × 14¼ × 6¼ in.
Photo: David Ryan

81. LEGO CABINET (1986) SILAS KOPF
Maple, anigre, and marquetry;
72½ × 21¼ × 17½ in.
Photo: David Ryan

DETAIL OF FIGURE 4: PRIMAL WOODWORKING (1985) SILAS KOPF

DETAIL OF FIGURE 86: BRICOLAGE (1989) SILAS KOPF

Self-portraits: I have continued to use myself as a model for marquetry, producing a new piece every year or so. I will occasionally be giving a slide presentation, showing all the self-portrait pieces in sequence, and watch myself get grayer, balder, and fatter. It's a sobering reality check.

Following *1498–1984* I made a coffee table called *Primal Woodworking* (figure 4). The picture is of me gnawing on a branch of a tree. One evening I was in a club listening to some quiet piano music, attempting to eat a carrot stick. Taking a bite out of the carrot was distractingly noisy. So I sat there with the carrot protruding from the side of my mouth while I quietly masticated away. It took so long to consume that I assumed I looked rather foolish with the carrot looking like an orange cigar. In the marquetry picture I turned the carrot into a tree branch and imagined myself as a beaver creating nice scalloped tooth marks on the wood. Teeth, the primal woodworking tool.

The next self-portrait piece was a return to the idea that someone might be inside the cabinet. I posed as if in a telephone booth (figure 84). This marquetry relied on some of Barili's perspective ideas, such as having the elbow protruding through the picture plane. Additionally, the cast shadows on the back wall enhance the three-dimensional effect. The cabinet itself is very simple. The parts are square with easily routed molded edges. We did use some exotic Brazilian imbuya for the solid construction, as well as a highly figured oak burl for the panels. But the basic idea behind the design was to have the focus on the marquetry and keep the cabinetwork simple.

This first *Telephone Cabinet* led to a second one a few years later (figure 85). This time, the cabinet is intended to look like a glass-fronted phone booth, with me standing inside talking on the phone and fishing in the coin return for loose change.

The next cabinet that had me in it, called *Bricolage* (figure 86), evolved from *Lego Cabinet*. This time the entire surface looks like it was built from bricks. I had a narra veneer from Indonesia with a nice brick color. I used curly maple for the mortar. The upper door appears to have me inside holding a trowel and brick, apparently closing in the opening. I used a very strong light to accentuate the contrasts in the picture. The black interior of the cabinet helps make the figure jump out. The jagged profile of the brick also casts a strong shadow on the shirt. The arm is delineated simply with a very thin lighter line between the two black parts.

Bricolage is the French word for handyman-work. At the time I was designing the cabinet I had a young Frenchman visiting my shop and working as an intern. I was working on the marquetry for another piece,

84. PHONE CABINET ONE (1989) SILAS KOPF
Imbuya, oak burl, marquetry; 74 × 20 × 17½ in.
Photo: David Ryan

85. PHONE CABINET TWO (1993) SILAS KOPF
Maple and marquetry; 84 × 29 × 20 in.
Photo: David Ryan

where a mistake needed correction using an X-ACTO knife. I was showing the fellow this particular operation and he looked at me and said, "in France the teacher says that using the knife for marquetry is little more than bricolage." I was trying to show him something that might offer a new way of working, but he clearly would have none of it. In my irritation I decided that I would memorialize the moment by naming the next cabinet *Bricolage*.

In 2000 I had an interesting opportunity to participate in an exhibition sponsored by Wilsonart and the Furniture Society. Wilsonart manufactures plastic laminate, and they were launching a new product, allowing clients to design their own laminate pattern. You could give the company a digitized representation of something you wanted to see printed in the plastic and they would make it for you. Some of the examples they offered as possibilities were photo representations. Others were graphics generated on a computer with an art program. I was one of several craftsmen asked to design a piece using the product.

I was pleased to have an opportunity to develop my own graphic for a laminate, but I had also thought for a long time that it would be fun to create a marquetry design with the regular line of laminates. I rarely used laminates and therefore had never assembled enough to make a decent picture, but I loved all the colors. From scraps of Formica I had on hand, I discovered they worked nicely using the same blades I use to cut wood veneer. The colors that are available in the Wilsonart line are bright and engaging. I asked if they could send me some small sheets in twenty or thirty colors.

The design of my Wilsonart piece involved doing another self portrait (figure 9). I would be looking in a mirror and brushing my teeth (it seems that's the way I most frequently see my own image). Every portrait I do, I start with the eyes because they have the most detail. I used a variety of colors inside the frames of the glasses, then switched to gray tones for the rest of the figure, as if the lenses have a magical quality, exposing a different, colorful reality. The only other part of the picture that deviates from the gray tones is the toothbrush.

Plastic laminate is nice to work with, requiring no extra finishing. Because the pieces are all the same thickness they end up on the same level. I scraped silver off the back side of a mirror, matching the shape of the marquetry figure in the same way I had with the picture of my father (figure 80). Putting the glass in front of the laminate marquetry was an added bit of security, ensuring that none of the pieces could ever come loose and fall out.

My custom Wilsonart laminate was a graphic I created with my limited computer skills. I decided to used the

86. Bricolage (1989) Silas Kopf
Narra, maple, and marquetry; 76 × 23 × 16 in.
Photo: David Ryan

word processor to repeat a phase over and over across the surface in 18-point type in two pastel colors. Small enough to be illegible from a distance, the lines of print appear as diagonals of red and green on a gray ground. The self-effacing phrase repeated thousands of times on the cabinet surface is "what a knucklehead." As a final touch, the door pulls are actual toothbrushes.

From the time I made my first clock, I was interested in doing a cuckoo. I had seen mechanisms in wood-working catalogs, but I couldn't be sure of the quality of the movement. I didn't want to be selling something that would break down, particularly having to repair something

DETAIL OF FIGURE 9: WHAT A KNUCKLEHEAD (1999) SILAS KOPF

87. CUCKOO CLOCK (1993) SILAS KOPF
Maple burl, ebonized ash, and marquetry; 21½ × 14 × 6 in.
Photo: Kevin Downey

that I know very little about. I decided that the only client I could safely make a clock for, without fear of complaints, was myself. So one of the few marquetry pieces I have built with the idea that I would be the end user was *Cuckoo Clock* (figure 87). And since I was the client, I could also pose for the drawing with no complaints from anyone (but my family).

The case for *Cuckoo Clock* is very simple. The portrait is life-size and done on a black background. The clock's dial is a simple series of ebony dots laid into the pale color in the chest area. And, of course, instead of a bird popping out of a little door to announce the quarter hour, it's a pink tongue.

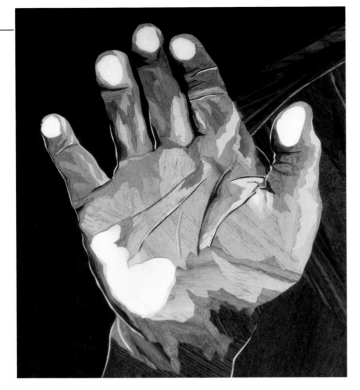

88. Pondering Floyd Collins Blanket Chest (2002) Silas Kopf
Padauk and marquetry; 17 × 38½ × 20½ in.
Photos: David Ryan

In 2002 we built a blanket chest with a self portrait on the top (figure 88). To create the image I pressed my face and hands against a piece of glass and took a photograph. The places where the flesh touches the glass appear as very white shapes. The background is black, as if the figure is trapped in the box. The title, *Pondering Floyd Collins*, refers to the cave explorer who was trapped underground in Kentucky in the 1920s. I am claustrophobic and can't imagine crawling through small passages in a cave, let alone how I'd react to becoming trapped.

In 2003 the Smith College Museum of Art commissioned furniture makers to build benches for museum-goers. I was given the opportunity to make one, and I worked with the staff to come up with a theme. We decided on the four arts that they teach at the college: painting, sculpture, photography, and architecture (figure 89). The design was actually two settees back to back, meant to go in the middle of a gallery where people could face in either direction, comfortably seating four patrons. Two marquetry pictures occupy either side, depicting hands in the act of creating: painting a canvas, carving wood, shooting a photograph with a large large-format camera, and drafting with a compass and ruler. The subject on the canvas is a partially finished picture of myself.

℘

89. Four Arts (2003) Silas Kopf
Ash and marquetry; 38 × 50 × 42 in.
Photos: Jim Gipe

90. Baseball Cabinet (1988) Silas Kopf
Walnut, East Indian laurel, and marquetry; 75 × 20 × 17 in.
Gladstone Collection; Photo: David Ryan

91. Trompe L'Oeil Collector's Cabinet (1998) Silas Kopf
Mahogany and marquetry; 82 × 40 × 19 in.
Photo: David Ryan

Commissions open all kinds of unexpected subject areas for marquetry. A couple who collect baseball memorabilia asked me to build a cabinet for their collection. I love the game and was happy to consult with them to find a concept that would work. We decided to make a trompe l'oeil cabinet that appeared to have objects inside that they owned (figure 90). They were Brooklyn Dodger fans, and their collection included a jersey that had been worn by Jackie Robinson and a glove that belonged to Pee Wee Reese. The composition also includes a bat, a bronze sculpture, and a baseball.

More recently, I was commissioned to build a cabinet that was directly related to the open cupboards of the Gubbio studiolo (figure 50). The client liked the grillwork of the studiolo, and this became a design component for her piece (figure 91). Also, in order to personalize this piece, I wanted to include objects in the cabinet that were of interest to her. She told me she and her husband

enjoyed wine and books. She was a graduate of Mount Holyoke College and her husband worked for Exxon. I worked these elements into the marquetry. The cabinet was to be a traditionally styled object with moldings and rich mahogany veneers. The doors looked partly open, therefore requiring pockets (similar to my *Tea Cabinet*, figure 62) to accommodate the trompe l'oeil effect. The marquetry in between the two doors is attached to the door on the right side. Instead of having handles or pulls, the doors open with touch latches.

I have done several coffee tables that use the trompe l'oeil concept. The challenge with a table is that the marquetry can be viewed from a number of vantage points. Unlike marquetry on a cabinet door, which can involve pronounced three-dimensional effects because it is typically viewed from only one place in front of the cabinet, marquetry on a coffee table must depict objects or scenes that are relatively flat, or the perspective will

92. Magazine Coffee Table (1990) **Silas Kopf**
Eucalyptus and marquetry; 17 × 52 × 20 in.
Photo: David Ryan

seem distorted from many angles of view. (Imagine trying to show a wine glass positioned in front of other objects; the composition would work from only one point of view.) I thought that magazines might be a credible choice of subject on a table. After the marquetry depicting a magazine cover is assembled, it can easily be cut into the background of the tabletop. Slight cast shadows can be added to enhance the illusion.

The first table I did with magazines was speculative and afforded me the opportunity to make a casual composition of magazines, the three publications likely to be found on my own living room coffee table: *The New Yorker, Smithsonian,* and *National Enquirer* (figure 92).

I received a commission to build another table with magazines (figure 93). I asked the clients for some of the publications that they subscribed to. They sent me *Audubon, American Craft,* and *Sierra.* The three magazines are stacked randomly on one another so you can see the

93. Coffee Table for Ann and Joel (1990) **Silas Kopf**
Imbuya, oak burl, and marquetry; 17 × 38 × 38 in.
Photo: David Ryan

title of each. I thought this might be the only opportunity I would have to see my work on the cover of *American Craft,* so I used the picture of the recently completed trompe l'oeil desk in the marquetry. I also asked the clients to write me a note that would be turned into marquetry and look as if it were sitting on the table. The marquetry top is pieced together with the magazines, a set of keys, and the note paper (an unfigured piece of holly). The handwriting was added as an inlay, using an X-ACTO knife to cut a slight groove in the surface which was then filled with slivers of black wood to simulate the pencil line. I added this after glue-up because incorporating it before glue-up, the veneer assembly would have been much too fragile. This is how the Renaissance intarsiatori added the very fine details to their pictures, such as the broken string on Fra Giovanni's lute (figure 53).

‹›

Before Italy, all my marquetry motifs had been simple floral patterns that mimicked the French Art Nouveau. My first forays outside that comfort zone had led me to still lifes and portraits. This proved stimulating as well as fruitful, and I started to look at other possibilities. The oldest and simplest marquetry decoration was geometric. I had read in *The Art and Practice of Marquetry* about cutting parquetry (see Appendix 2: Parquetry). I had used the technique to make the oak squares for *1498–1984* (figure 61). Before I actually worked on the piece, I practiced making a few more simple checkerboards using a veneer saw. I next moved on to a practice panel with three species, and a design called the Louis cube. The Louis cube is an illusionary pattern where three rhombuses are put together in a hexagon, which appears to be a cube. The hexagons can then be pieced together to form a larger repeated pattern.

The key to good parquetry is establishing a way to accurately duplicate parts over and over. The idea is to cut straight and parallel lines so that the pieces can be reconfigured and resliced on a new axis, thereby making smaller, more complex pieces. A good, sharp veneer saw can produce remarkably straight, smooth lines.

We built a carriage to more quickly produce parquetry parts on a tablesaw. We exploited this ability on a little book stand, consisting of a maple frame with a parquetry pattern on all four sides and the top (figure 94). The graphic design, executed in several thousand rhombuses, is a take-off on the Louis cube. Twelve species of wood span a tonal range of very light to very dark, from holly to ebony. From an array of bowls, one for each species of veneer chips, we chose pieces randomly, resulting in an intriguing abstract pattern.

94. Parquetry Bookstand One (1987) Silas Kopf
Maple and parquetry;
42 × 21 × 15 in.
Photo: David Ryan

95. Parquetry Bookstand Two (1988) Silas Kopf
Padauk and parquetry;
42 × 21 × 16 in.
Photo: David Ryan

We set about making a second similar book stand, this time with a curved rear panel, curved top, and shaped legs, so the woodworking is more complex (figure 95). The parquetry pattern is also a little more controlled, with the veneers graduating from dark to light, from bottom to top. When similar tones border each other they tend to blend together. Blending species is an effect that I was using in the more complex marquetry pictures I was making, such as the portraits.

In 2005 I was invited to participate in the exhibition *Inspired By China* at the Peabody Essex Museum in Salem,

Massachusetts. The museum has an outstanding collection of Asian decorative objects and was a natural venue for the show. Early on, we participants were invited to a seminar on Chinese furniture. I was introduced to a decorative motif that recurs in Chinese art called "cracked ice," in which the surface is marked by randomly shaped and sized polygons. The museum's collection includes a wonderful example of this motif on an antique table. Another furniture form that attracted me was the "puzzle table," polygonal tables that could be put together in various configurations. I decided my exhibition piece would combine the two concepts (figure 96). The hand-cut oak veneers were shaped into random polygons and delineated by a pinstripe of rosewood. The veneer sheets were then glued on to the polygonal table tops and sides.

The marquetry on the rectangular table included a trompe l'oeil piece of paper and an ink brush. It was positioned casually on the table's surface, as if a note had been written. The Chinese characters read, "The artfulness of the cracked ice table, shatters to pieces the uncarved block." The couplet makes reference to the ancient philosopher Lao-Tzu, who uses the metaphor of the uncarved block to suggest a state of purity before man's ego intrudes.

96. Cracked Ice Tables (2006) Silas Kopf
Oak, rosewood, and marquetry; 30 in. h; tables based on 15-in. modules
Photos: Dean Powell

The method of cutting geometric parts was turned into a decorative design on a small cabinet (figure 97). We used a very straight-grain zebrawood veneer and cut dozens of parquetry squares. Every piece is perpendicular to its horizontal neighbor. The top row has pieces ½ inch square. As the rows descend, the pieces increase in size until the bottom row, in which the pieces are over 3 inches square. The wood is so striped as to make the cabinet look oddly woven.

☙

97. PANTHERS (2004) SILAS KOPF
Zebrawood, oak, ebony, brass, and granite; 32 × 26 × 17 in.
Photos: David Ryan

Ancient Egypt

I am forever indebted to William Lincoln for his wonderful book, *The Art and Practice of Marquetry.* Not only did he open the door to the basics of marquetry technique, but the handful of black and white pictures in the book became the foundation for my exploration of the history of the craft. The first photo in the book illustrates a fragment of an Egyptian box that is 5,000 years old (figure 98). Decorated with a series of faience triangles, this is the oldest surviving example of parquetry or marquetry.

My interest in the history of marquetry inevitably led to my research into the beginnings of woodcraft. How did ancient peoples go about building complicated wooden objects? Lincoln's book had only three pictures of Egyptian pieces. I believe that knowing about the process is key to understanding the aesthetic. You can't really appreciate the look of an object without some understanding of how it was made. My trip to Italy marked the beginning of my serious attention to the origins of my craft. In some ways, the history of marquetry is the same as the story of woodworking. The key to the advancement of the craft is the state of development of the tools.

It is no coincidence that civilizations grew on the banks of rivers. All of the important early civilizations—Egypt, Mesopotamia, India, China—developed on major waterways. The rivers were the highways that allowed people easily to move themselves as well as goods in trade. Boat building required sophisticated woodworking to fashion timbers. The interaction with other peoples changed societies; with the infusion of new goods came new ideas and new ways of doing things. Agrarian cultures, where everyone had been involved with the production of food, now included new groups of people pursuing other endeavors. These early civilizations accumulated the wealth that could support craftsmen who developed unique skills.

Woodcraft requires tools. The more sophisticated the woodworking, the more sophisticated the tools need to

98. Fragment of wooden box (c.3100-2890 BCE) First Dynasty Egypt
Wood with faience inlay and a carved basket-weave border
Ashmolean Museum, Oxford, England (inv.: AN1896-1908, E138-1255)

be. The most important tool in the development of woodworking was the saw. The concept dates to Neolithic times, when a piece of flint with a serrated edge was likely used with a back-and-forth motion to cut through a piece of wood. Copper tools made their first appearance in the fifth millennium BCE. The discovery that metal ore could be smelted and turned into useful objects was a huge technological leap. However, how to make copper hard enough to be able to cut through a piece of wood also had to be learned. By heating it and beating it, soft copper gradually transforms into a metal that can cut wood. Unfortunately, the process also makes the metal very brittle. Knives and chisels would have broken easily. Tools would have required repeated heating and beating to form new edges. It must have been frustrating, but it certainly was better than cutting wood with flint.

The addition of tin to copper makes bronze, which is much harder than pure copper. Bronze tools first appear around 4000 BCE. This technological advance led to the ability to fabricate more sophisticated woodworking tools. About as hard as soft steel, bronze can make a decent cutting edge. Bronze chisels were hard enough to cut not only ebony but also granite sculptures now found in numerous museums around the world. To cut wood, the

edge would have had to be reworked frequently to keep it sharp enough to cut satisfactorily. The amount of labor to produce a crafted object in wood or stone must have been immense. One has to be in awe of the challenges that confronted these early workers.

A limited number of tree species grow in the Nile Valley. Local woods used by the ancient Egyptians included acacia, almond, carob, fig, date palm, persea, sidder, sycamore fig, tamarisk, willow, and poplar. Craftsmen learned the working properties of various woods and used timbers accordingly. The trees of Egypt were generally of small diameter, and from early times larger timbers were brought in from other areas. One of the principle reasons for Egyptian military forays across the Sinai Desert was to gain control of the forests growing in the area now occupied by Lebanon and Syria.

We know woods were imported because many of the species that have been found in tombs are not indigenous to the Nile Valley. The list includes ash, beech, boxwood, cedar, elm, juniper, lime, maple, oak, pine, plum, and yew. Perhaps the most important imported wood for decorative work was ebony from Sudan. No other wood offers the rich black color that proved so enticing to Egyptian craftsmen. Ebony still enchants us today. Another material that seduced

99. Depiction of ships preparing to return from Punt with ivory and ebony (c. 1460 BCE)
Wall relief; Mortuary temple of Queen Hatshepsut at Deir el-Bahari
Drawing: Edouard Naville, courtesy Egypt Exploration Society, London

**100. Carpenter's tools (c. 1450 BCE)
eighteenth dynasty Egypt**
Including saws and adzes
British Museum, London; Photo: British Museum

these early artisans was ivory. Like ebony, ivory had to be imported from further south in Africa. Egyptian woodwork, particularly that of the later dynasties, found an aesthetic touchstone in the contrast between the black of ebony and the white of ivory. By the time of the New Kingdom

(1540–1070 BCE) the importation of exotic materials to build furniture was important enough to be depicted in a mural on the mortuary temple of Queen Hatshepsut (figure 99).

Polished ebony and ivory are extremely beautiful. Both these materials are very hard and dense—a challenge

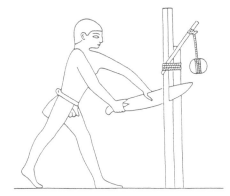

101. Sawing a log, from the tomb of Rekmire (c.1475 BCE)
Drawing: N. de G.Davies, New York, 1943

for craftsmen to work, especially in ancient Egypt, given the primitive nature of the tools. The key to working with these hard, dense materials was having a saw that could cut accurately. A sawblade could be fabricated by repeatedly beating a lump of metal until flat. Further hammering would eventually fray the edge into points that functioned as the teeth of the blade. Teeth of an Egyptian saw were also bent slightly to point toward the tang, so the tool was used on the pull stroke. Neither copper nor bronze blades are stiff enough to hold up to pushing, the way modern western saws are used. Curiously, all the teeth were also set to one side, and not alternately like a modern saw. This convention must have made the tool difficult to control. Saws are depicted on Egyptian tombs as early as 2100 BCE. Egyptian saws that date from 1490 BCE are on display at the British Museum (figure 100).

The ancient Egyptian woodworker sawed veneer from a log by lashing it to an upright post and then proceeding down the log from the top (figure 101). The saw cut in two ways: the metal sheared the wood fibers in the conventional way, but the tool also abraded the wood. Hard quartz sand was sprinkled on the kerf line to aid in the cutting. A British archeologist, Flinders Petrie, mentions finding a piece of hardwood in a tomb still bearing the marks of the saw, showing how the workman started his cut from all four corners of the block in turn. Petrie

102. Coffer from Tutankhamen's tomb (1332–1323 BCE) eighteenth dynasty Egypt
Ivory, Ebony, and faience
Egyptian Museum, Cairo; Photo: Scala/Art Resource, New York

says, "it must have taken him hours, if not days, sawing away under the hot Egyptian sun. Looking at the photograph of this lump of wood, one cannot help but feel a pang of sympathy for this poor fellow, although he has been dead and forgotten these 5,000 years." (W. M. F. Petrie, *Arts and Crafts of Ancient Egypt*, 1910) Remember this lump of wood the next time you are feeling sorry for yourself about some wearisome task in the context of your modern electrically equipped shop.

Dimensional lumber was produced using a tool like an adze. The surface of a piece of wood was chopped to get it close to flat, removing a relatively large

hunk of wood with each blow. This was certainly easier than sawing, although it was wasteful of material. With an adze, a limb or small tree could produce only one board, leaving a pile of chips. Some materials, such as ebony and ivory, were just too precious to work this way. They had been brought to Egypt at great expense, and the artisan had to maximize the yield of each log or tusk. So these materials were sawn. And not only were they sawn but they were sawn thinly—too thin to use structurally. They needed to be glued on to other pieces of wood that were less precious. Thus the first veneered objects were produced.

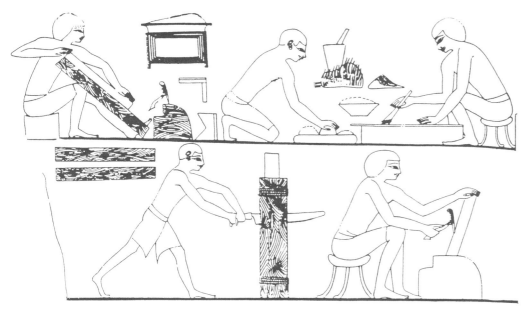

103. FURNITUREMAKING FROM THE TOMB OF REKMIRE (C.1475 BCE)
Drawing: N. de G.Davies, "Tomb of Rekh-mi-ré at Thebes," New York, 1943

Egyptian veneers were approximately ¼ inch thick. After gluing, the wood was polished by abrading it with sandstone. Egyptian furniture is of remarkable quality, given the technologies available. The craftsmen had a sophisticated understanding of how to put wood together, employing fine mortise-and-tenon joints and dovetails. Holes were bored and pieces secured with dowels. All joints were cut with bronze tools. Many of the techniques that furniture makers use today, originated in ancient Egypt.

In the earliest times glues were not used in building furniture. The Egyptian craftsman could get modest sticking force using vegetable gums and resins. But these are not true glues. By 3000 BCE there are several examples of parts actually being glued in place. The earliest glues are hide glues, which were made by boiling skin and bones (parts of an animal that wouldn't be eaten). This protein soup has remarkable adhesive qualities, and early craftsmen learned they could use it to stick wooden parts together. This glue was strong enough to construct furniture joints, as well as to veneer thin pieces to thicker parts.

The primary Egyptian furniture wood was date palm, which grows plentifully in the harsh heat of the Nile

Valley. Date palm wood was often used as a substrate upon which the ebony and ivory veneers were glued. Often the materials were pieced together to form a geometric design. The antecedent of this style would be the Oxford fragment (figure 98). The border, consisting of small triangles of faience, confirms that geometric parts would have been easy to make in a uniform size, and then assembled in a running pattern not unlike the way patterns are traditionally made in modern marquetry borders. Several different colors of faience, as well as wood and ivory, have been found in Egyptian artifacts.

Relatively few wooden objects have survived from the ancient civilizations in Mesopotamia, the Indus Valley, or China. Glass, ceramic, and metal can be found from all those early cultures. Because wood rots and glues don't last, not much furniture has survived several thousand of years of harsh humidity changes. Fortunately, the Egyptian climate is dry enough to stem wood's deterioration. In the confines of an Egyptian tomb humidity stayed basically the same. Therefore the wood didn't change dimensionally, which alleviated the stress joints incur during seasonal changes in a temperate climate. A wealth of wooden Egyptian objects have come down to us. None

are more spectacular than the furnishings of the tomb of Tutankhamen, Pharaoh from 1361 to 1352 BCE. The Egyptians believed in a life after death where one's worldly goods could be enjoyed. The pharaohs were buried with objects commensurate with their station in life. In 1922 Howard Carter, an English archeologist, discovered Tutankhamen's tomb. Most of the pyramids in the Valley of the Kings had been plundered in earlier centuries. Fortunately, this tomb was intact, and the world was given a unique opportunity to study Egyptian culture through the effects of royalty.

One of the objects from the tomb is a box with decorative elements (figure 102). It is of particular interest because the surfaces are all veneered with precious materials: ivory, ebony, and faience. Small rectangles of ebony and ivory alternate to form stringing. This box is the descendant of the Oxford fragment. The corners are made of larger pieces of ivory that had been sawn into veneer and glued onto native Egyptian wood.

The Egyptians were meticulous in illustrating their way of life, including that of craftsmen, on the walls of tombs. A wonderfully informative representation in the tomb of a nobleman named Rekmire dates from 1475 BCE (less than a hundred years before Tutankhamen). In the upper left of the graphic is a casket very similar to the one from Tutankhamen's tomb. On the bottom left a workman is sawing veneer. The log is strapped to a post and he is sawing down the length. Two pieces of veneer are depicted behind him, over his shoulder. The worker on the lower right is using a handheld adze to do the preliminary flattening on a piece of wood. The workman on the upper left is flattening a board by grinding it with an already flattened stone. The two men on the upper right are veneering. A fire heats the glue pot, and one man is brushing on the glue while the other is rubbing and pressing the veneer with a stone to make it adhere.

Ivory and ebony are used to decorate several pieces of Tutankhamen's

104. Golden Throne from Tutankhamen's tomb (1332–1323 BCE) eighteenth dynasty Egypt
Ivory, ebony, and faience
Egyptian Museum, Cairo;
Photo: Scala/Art Resource, New York

furniture. The contrast between the black and the white is a recurring theme. Carter describes one such piece, the Ceremonial Chair (figure 105): "fashioned of ebony and ivory, partially plated with thin sheets of gold inlaid with natural stones, glaze, and polychrome glass…the seat made of ebony and inlaid with irregular shaped pieces of ivory to imitate the blotchy markings of a hide like that of a Nubian goat. The central part of the seat is ornamented with a series of small panels of ivory, stained to imitate various piebald hides." (H. Carter, *The Tomb of Tutankhamen,* 1923) The chair is remarkable for the amount of decoration glued on the surface, the black ebony structure setting off all the other materials. This is a very opulent piece, announcing to anyone who should see it that it is the possession of someone very special (and wealthy).

Another chair from Tutankhamen's tomb is known as the Golden Throne (figure 104). Lavishly carved, this chair features a significant amount of inlay as well. The back is overlaid with gold, and color is added by inlaying faience, colored glass, lapis lazuli, and translucent calcite.

These two chairs are both decorated with contrasting materials, but the style is quite different. They are structurally similar to most chairs, having a seat, a back, and an understructure that stabilizes the legs. The Golden Throne also has arms. The decorative elements were added after the chairs were constructed. The Ceremonial Chair was built from local woods, after which the ebony, ivory, and red faience were glued to the surfaces. Hundreds of small geometric shapes were pieced together in patterns that cover the surface. The patterns have the vitality they do because of the contrast between the black and the white. Although both the ebony and ivory are relatively hard, it would not have been difficult to cut these polygonal shapes with the saws and chisels that were available to Egyptian craftsmen. Rather than inlay the ivory into the ebony structure, it was simpler to create separate bandings, composed of both materials, and apply them to the chair.

Howard Carter found one box in Tutankhamen's tomb and suggested that there are no fewer than 45,000 individual pieces on the surface. One wonders if anyone has ever actually counted them. However many there are, it is certainly an awesome number of tiny pieces. I would love to know how many men were put to work making a box like this, and how many man-hours it required.

One of the keys to successful woodworking is having an understanding of the way wood moves with changes in its moisture content. When a tree is freshly felled, a huge percentage of its weight is water in and around the cells of the wood fiber. When cut, it immediately starts to lose moisture to the air. Once the moisture content gets down to around 30 percent, the wood begins

to shrink, mainly across the grain; shrinkage along the grain is negligible. If left to dry in a temperate climate, wood will reach a moisture content of approximately 15 percent, depending on seasonal relative humidity. In moving from 30 to 15 percent, a wood such as maple will shrink 4.8 percent tangentially to the growth rings; radial shrinkage of maple is about 2.4 percent. The successful craftsman is aware of wood shrinkage and also seasonal expansion and contraction, as moisture content changes with relative humidity. In the consistently dry, hot climate of Egypt wood will quickly reach a point of stability. The Egyptian woodworker took care to work with properly cured materials, or the ancient pieces would not have survived the centuries.

The Egyptians even understood the advantage of plywood. Archeologists discovered the lid of a coffin in the Step Pyramid complex at Saqqara. It was built of six layers of wood, each layer perpendicular to its neighbor. The layers are not glued but fixed together with pegs. This construction is stronger than a single layer of wood because wood is stronger along the grain than across the grain, and the differing grain directions complement each other. This is the earliest known example of plywood construction. Was it the lone inspiration of a single woodworker who saw the potential to reduce weight and gain strength? We'll never know (unless other examples are found), but the concept of plywood is fundamental to much of modern design.

The Egyptians took several thousand years to learn various craft skills. Other societies traded with Egypt and no doubt admired their arts. These ideas were adopted in various places around the Mediterranean. By 500 BCE Greek craftsmen were producing marvelous objects in wood, and the links with modern-day techniques were only just beginning (see Appendix 1: Wood in Marquetry).

☙

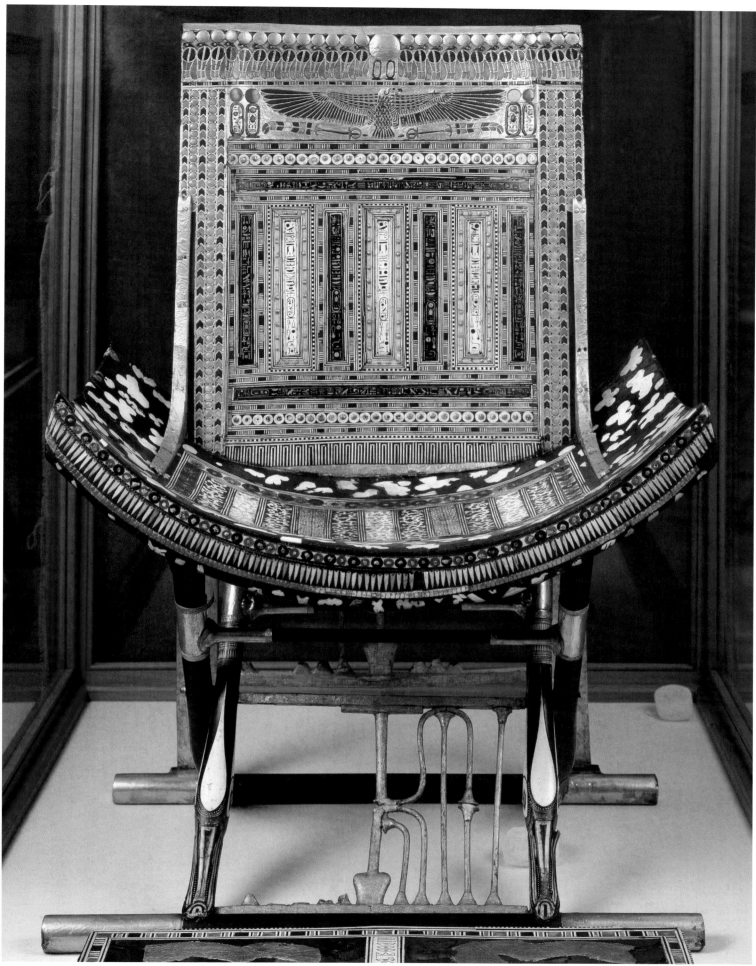

105. CEREMONIAL CHAIR FROM TUTANKHAMEN'S TOMB (1332–1323 BCE) EIGHTEENTH DYNASTY EGYPT
Ivory, ebony, and faience; Egyptian Museum, Cairo
Photo: Scala/Art Resource, New York

Greece and Rome

Archeological evidence shows that Egypt traded with Mesopotamia and Crete from very early times. Influences can be traced through surviving artifacts, such as pottery and glass. Undoubtedly, woodworking and tool making also cross-fertilized. Greece became the heir of Egyptian culture. Unfortunately, conditions in Greece were not as favorable for the preservation of wood as they were in the Egyptian desert, and no wooden furniture remains from the early Greek era. All we have are representations of furniture in painting and the descriptions of writers of the era.

The Mycenean culture, which was roughly contemporaneous with the late Egyptian dynasties, produced furniture that was described on clay tablets found on Crete at the ancient city of Minos: "chair, ebony, with the back inlaid with ivory...worked with a pair of stag's heads and figures of men. Footstool, ebony, inlaid with figures of men and lions." Such a description makes it clear that the Minoans had significant contact with Egyptians. As in Egypt, decoration in black and white was favored. The use of ebony is particularly noteworthy, as this rare wood must have come through Egypt (from further south in Africa). With supplies, surely tools and skills were transferred as well.

By the time of classical Greece, around 500 BCE, an important technological change—the introduction of iron tools—advanced the making and availability of furniture. Significantly harder than bronze, iron tools can hold an edge longer, thus reducing the amount of labor it took to build a piece of furniture. Increased productivity meant that not only less expensive but better, more refined objects were more widely accessible throughout the society. Inlaid furniture, for instance, was now available to more than just royalty. Yet woodworking techniques remained about the same. Compare the depiction of a woodworker on a plate from approximately 500 BCE (figure 107) to the earlier representations of craftsmen on Egyptian murals (figure 103). The wood is still being flattened with an adze. The plane was not to be invented until Roman times.

The Greeks respected skillfully made furniture and objects of wood. They prized beauty in the figure of the wood and had also learned the art of inlay from their neighbors in the ancient world. In *The Odyssey* Odysseus describes a bed he made for his bride Penelope: "Beginning from this headpost, I wrought at the bedstead till I had finished it, and made it fair with inlaid work of gold, and of silver, and of ivory" (*The Odyssey,* Book 23, trans. S. H. Butler). Quite a fellow, this Odysseus, warrior-king and woodworker extraordinaire. Wield the sword, captain the ship, and still have time to practice high-quality woodcraft.

Another revealing description of woodworking comes from the ancient Greek writer Pausanias, who describes the box of Kypselos, in the temple of Hera at Olympia, as being "made of cedar wood and adorned with mythological representations, partly carved in the wood and partly inlaid with gold and ivory, in five strips which encircled the box one above the other." Clearly, the Greeks were taken with the luxuriousness of inlaid work. It is also reasonable to assume, given the high degree of refinement in all the decorative arts, that many craftsmen were capable of doing fine inlay in wood. Some of the important woods written about by the Greeks were ebony, cypress, cedar, oak, sinila, yew, willow, lotus, and thuya.

The Romans greatly admired much of Greek culture and incorporated its aesthetic into their own culture. Roman artists became skilled at imitating Greek sculpture and architecture. Roman furniture also has roots in Greece. The Latin word for mosaic wood decoration on furniture is *xylotarsia,* which is divided into two types: *sectile* and *pictorial.* In sectile tarsia polygons of contrasting woods were inserted into another wood (our definition of inlay). This work obviously references ancient Egyptian faience work (figure 98). Pictorial tarsia consisted of different species of veneer cut out and pieced together as a jigsaw puzzle and overlaid onto another wooden surface (our definition of marquetry). A remarkably detailed description of woodworking during the Roman era is found in the writings of Pliny (62–113 BCE):

"The best woods for cutting into layers and employing as a veneer for covering others are the citrus, the terebinth, the different varieties of the maple, the box, the palm, the holly, the holm oak, the root of the elder, and the poplar. The alder furnishes, also, a kind of tuberosity [burl], which is cut into layers like those of the citrus and the maple. In all other trees, the tuberosities are of no value whatever. It is the central part of the tree which is the most variegated, and the nearer we approach to the root the smaller are the spots and the more wavy. It was in this appearance that originated that requirement of luxury which displays itself in covering one tree with another, and bestowing upon the more common woods a bark of a higher price. In order to

106. COUCH (1–200 CE) ROMAN
Wood with bone carving and glass inlays
Metropolitan Museum of Art, New York (inv. DP 142998);
Photo: Metropolitan Museum of Art

107. VASE PAINTING (C. 500 BCE) GREEK
British Museum, London; Photo: British Museum

make a single tree sell many times over, laminae of veneer have been devised; but that was not thought sufficient—the horns of animals must next be stained of different colors, and their teeth cut into different sections, in order to decorate wood with ivory, and at a later period, to veneer it all over. Then, after all this, man must go to sea as well! For this purpose he has learned to cut tortoise shell into sections." (Pliny, *Natural History,* Book 16, Ch. 84, trans. H. Rackham)

Romans wrote about the importance of the individual piece of wood and its inherent beauty. Cicero, the Roman orator and statesman, spent a huge sum of money—more than ten times the annual salary of a Roman senator —for a tabletop made from thuya from the Atlas Mountains. Pliny describes the different figure in woods, the most highly prized being undulating marks resembling the eyes of a peacock's tail. Color was also an important

factor in the value of a piece of timber, the most highly prized being a color like "that of wine mixed with honey." You might say that George Nakashima was an inheritor of this tradition.

A respect for the uniqueness of figure and color might well have translated into an enhanced use of inlay as a decorative technique. For instance, the Romans used the wood of the palm cut transversely for its decorative effect. This is a particularly interesting wood when cut this way because the surface takes on the unique appearance of a chocolate-colored ground covered with small black dots. Craftsmen today are known to use palm wood this way.

Roman furniture and woodworking was elevated by the unprecedented wealth of the Empire. Trade was enhanced by the power and reach of the central authority in Rome, and exotic materials became increasingly available in the capitol and some of the other large cities. A growing class of people could afford luxurious objects

Ivory was extremely valued as a veneer and inlay material. Occasionally

bone was used as a substitute. The Romans also used tortoiseshell as a veneer. These materials were often combined with precious metals, jewels, and glass to decorate wood furniture. The eruption of Mount Vesuvius was a disaster for the people of Pompeii, but it preserved some treasures of Roman culture for the modern era. A wonderful couch in the Metropolitan Museum of Art is veneered with bone and has inlays of glass and ivory (figure 106).

Roman craftsmen are responsible for one of the most important developments in the history of woodworking—the invention of the plane. Some clever craftsman realized that an effective tool could be made to flatten boards by fixing a chisel blade in a tool body at a given angle relative to the sole of the tool. Eureka, no more laborious grinding to get wood flat and smooth. Boards could be planed with greater ease and accuracy, and woodcraft would never be the same.

સ∕ s

In 1987 I was awarded a grant from the National Endowment for the Arts for a Craftsman's Fellowship. Recipients were to do something out of the ordinary that would expand their work. Immediately I thought about studying traditional European marquetry. A few years earlier I had purchased a copy of *La Marqueterie* by Pierre Ramond. He was the teacher of marquetry at the prestigious École Boulle in Paris. My copy was in French (the book was subsequently translated into English). I had a hard time slogging through the book with my high school French. Nevertheless, it was obvious that Ramond possessed the knowledge about how marquetry was cut on those magnificent classical French pieces from the seventeenth and eighteenth centuries. I wrote him at the École Boulle and asked if I might pursue a brief course of study there. Pierre replied that he could make the arrangement with the school's administration, adding that, in fact, he was familiar with my work, having seen articles that I had written for *Fine Woodworking*.

My study of historical furniture that used marquetry started with those Art Nouveau books on Gallé and Majorelle. Slowly my familiarity with other decorative styles and eras grew. Trips to the library introduced me to some of the great names of French furniture: Boulle, Riesener, Roentgen. But I hadn't seen many real examples. Nor did the art history books explain how the pieces were made. The marquetry looked so complicated. Pierre's book was different. It was the first book I encountered that discussed the techniques used by the great masters—the things I was interested in learning in Paris. For one, I wanted to know how to cut Boulle work, the technique used by André-Charles Boulle to inlay brass into a dark groundwork, and vice versa. Secondly, I wanted to know more about the technique I had seen in *La Marqueterie* called *élément par élément* (piece by piece).

The Fellowship provided enough money to stay in Paris for about ten weeks. If I could learn about Boulle work and the traditional method of cutting marquetry in that limited time, I would count it a great success.

I found a studio apartment to rent, and I spent the summer taking evening classes in French. My language skills were weak, but at least I could communicate enough to function in a restaurant or find my way to the Metro. When I got to Paris I had a long weekend to explore the city before starting at the school. I acquainted myself with the neighborhood and went to a museum or two. The city is enchanting, and I felt very lucky to be there.

There is no educational institution in the United States like the École Boulle. It is a national vocational school for traditional furniture making. About 700 students pursue all different aspects of the trades, including upholstery, carving, enameling, and finishing. The largest area of

108. FROM THE BOOK *LE MENUISIER ÉBÉNISTE* BY J.A. ROUBO, 1772

study is cabinetmaking (ébénisterie), and the marquetry program is a very small part of that workshop. To gain admission into marquetry, a student must first be certified in cabinetwork. The marquetry program can take up to four years. When I was there in 1987, about twenty students were enrolled at various stages in the program. Those who go for the whole four years are likely to find employment in museum-quality restoration. They will know not only how to cut marquetry, but how to properly replace missing parts in antiques.

The French system differs from the way we pursue craft. American woodworkers tend to be omnivores, trying to do all parts of a piece. We design, we do the cabinetwork, we use a lathe when turning is called for, we finish. In France the focus is on one skill. Probably a holdover from the guild system, the advantages of this approach are obvious. You do one thing, and you can do it well. Here, our attempt to be jack-of-all-trades makes it difficult to master any one aspect of furnituremaking.

My first day at the École Boulle exposed my poor French, as I had difficulty communicating with the other students and even understanding my teacher. Who would imagine that there is a French equivalent of a southern accent! Pierre's home town was in the area of Toulouse (in the south), and I had a particularly hard time following him. But, I wasn't totally lost, as Pierre spoke about as much English as I did French. Some of the vocabulary was challenging; words for things like chisels are not taught in

109. STUDENT EXERCISE: PIECE BY PIECE (1988) SILAS KOPF
Marquetry of various woods; 8 × 11 in.
Photo: Rick Mastelli

110. CHEVALET (1989) BUILT BY TIM FANER
White Oak
Photo: David Ryan

French 101. I would try to say something in French, and when Pierre couldn't understand, he would try English. Back and forth we would go, and eventually the idea was passed along.

The first thing any student in the marquetry program at the École Boulle must do is fabricate his own fretsaw blade. I liked the school's emphasis on traditional skills, but I was unclear what good would come from making my own blade since industrialization. Pierre assured me that you can make a better blade than you can buy. So I threw myself into the task. And a challenge it was! To make a blade, you begin by securing a piece of steel in a vise. Then you file the tiny teeth, one at a time. Next, you set them alternately to the right and left. And finally you sharpen. The initial cutting of the teeth must be exact, or there will be problems with the blade. The scale is so small that it is difficult to see, never mind get right. I would make one attempt after another and take it to Pierre for approval. He would pull his glasses down lower on his nose, hold the blade up to the light, and say, "ees no goood." He couldn't explain why, but clearly it didn't pass muster.

Eureka came on the second day of frustration while watching another student make a blade. It had to do with the rhythm of the filing. A cadence to the movement of the hands led to both an even spacing and an even depth of cut. Finally, success! The concept is similar to the old-timer cutting dovetails by feel, without a lot of layout.

Once I had a satisfactory blade, Pierre assigned me to make a traditional marquetry motif of a bird on the branch of a tree, using the piece-by-piece method (figure 109). The value of the method is that multiple copies can be made from one set of cuttings, something I couldn't do with the bevel-cutting method I had been using on all my work at home (see Appendix 5: Piece by Piece). I was excited about the prospect of learning this alternative. I thought I was finally ready to cut some wood! But first I had to prepare the packets. Paper is glued to all the veneers and then they are squeezed together between two pieces of waste veneer. For a professional, the packet might be up to twenty-four layers of veneer in thickness, about an inch thick. For a novice like me, Pierre suggested only four layers. The work went slowly, but the results were satisfying. I was surprised at the level of detail that could be attained with the piece-by-piece method. Tiny parts could be produced easily, and in multiples.

The marquetry students at the École Boulle are all taught to use the traditional marquetry tool called a *chevalet* (figure 110). The chevalet evolved from a style of bench that was used to cut fretsawn work in the seventeenth century. A 1772 textbook on furniture-making written by J. A. Roubo illustrates a marqueteur seated at a bench with the work held vertically in front of him (figure 108). His foot rests on a piece of wood that is hinged at the rear and attached by a rod to a pivoting arm. When he presses his foot down, the arm is pulled forward, clamping the wood being cut between a plate and a sturdily fixed jaw at the front of the bench. With this device he can hold the wood using his foot, saw with one hand, and use the other hand to reposition the wood as he works. Periodically, he pauses sawing, releases pressure with his foot, repositions the work to accommodate the line of cut, re-clamps, and resumes sawing.

In the nineteenth century a newer version of the chevalet was developed using the same basic concept, but the frame holding the sawblade was hung from a cantilevered arm off to one side. The frame slides on a rod that keeps the blade traveling in an arc centered at that rod. It can't vary from the perpendicular the way a handheld frame inevitably does. This allows more delicate and accurate cutting.

The saw frame of the chevalet pivots on the rod, allowing the sawyer to saw for an inch or so before needing to reposition the packet. At some point in the development of the tool the rod was hung from a cradle, which allows the saw to move not just vertically but also slightly from side to side. This gives added flexibility in cutting. The final development of the chevalet was to make the parts that hold the cradle adjustable, in order to easily set the angle of the sawblade relative to the fixed jaw. One end controls the horizontal axis, the other end the vertical. By carefully tweeking these axes the saw can be made to cut precisely perpendicular to the jaw, thus ensuring that all the pieces in the stack are cut exactly the same shape and size. If the saw is not true, then the packet will be cut at a slight taper. If you sawed a 1-inch circle, for instance, in a stack of sixteen $\frac{1}{16}$-inch veneers, and the saw were set at an angle of 87 degrees to the fixed jaw, the pieces in the packet would vary from the desired 1 inch diameter to about $\frac{7}{8}$ inch at the other end.

With the chevalet, the marqueteur had a tool with which he could make duplicate parts efficiently in what had been a laborious process. It was possible to make the same picture accurately many times, and therefore complex pieces of furniture could also be more easily built in limited production. Or the designer could cover larger surfaces with multiples of the same motif. This is how parquetry was used in the style of Louis XV, where motifs like the rhombuses for the illusionary cubes provided a luxurious visual texture across broad surfaces. Parquetry involved only straight-line cuts, which could be executed with back saws and planes. With the ability to execute curved motifs efficiently in large number, the designer could go beyond these simple geometric patterns.

After I had cut a couple of pictures using the piece-by-piece method, Pierre gave me an exercise in cutting Boulle work (see Appendix 4: Boulle). Boulle work is characterized by having two contrasting materials cut in juxtaposi-

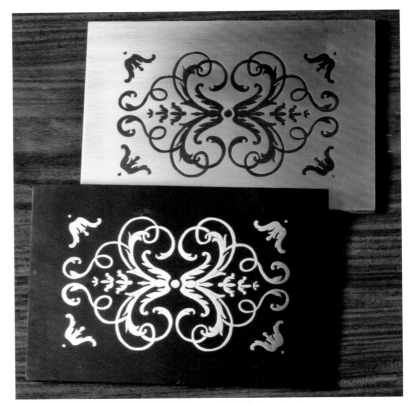

III. STUDENT EXERCISE: BOULLE WORK (1988) SILAS KOPF
Ebonized pearwood and brass; 5 × 8 in.
Photo: Rick Mastelli

tion to one another and then interchanging the parts. The lighter parts are put in the darker background and the darker parts into the lighter background. This way the marqueteur gets two motifs from one cutting.

In this, my first Boulle project at the École Boulle, I learned how much work this entails but also how satisfying are the results (figure III). The order of cuts is critical, so you don't cut free material that needs to be there to support future cuts. After cutting a small panel, I felt I understood the process well enough to go home and confidently do Boulle work. I was also able to visit the museums of Paris and better appreciate some of André-Charles Boulle's masterpieces. Boulle is probably not as well known in America as he should be. We know more about designers and cabinetmakers like Chippendale, Sheraton, and Hepplewhite, men who came out of the English tradition, where we share a language with the makers. But Boulle ought to be included in the pantheon of the great cabinetmakers.

My trip to France was an opportunity to learn more, not only about Boulle, but also about other heroes of classical French cabinetmaking. I got to see their work in the wonderful museums of Paris and to follow the development of the craft through a chain of fascinating personalities, from master to master, each of whom pushed the limits of craft and design as he had inherited them. Studying furniture also proved to be a window on the country's culture and history, as, conversely, that history helped explain how and why furniture changed.

☙

France

By the mid-sixteenth century France was a united country growing secure and wealthy. Resources were coming in from the colonies, particularly North America. Ruled by François I (r. 1515–47), France was ready to participate in the Renaissance in the arts that had begun in Italy. François had immense respect for Italian culture (he was even able to convince Leonardo da Vinci to come and live in France under his patronage). He brought an Italian to Fontainebleau to decorate the royal palace there with intarsia. The sixteenth century saw France, with Paris at its heart, vying to become the center of European culture. By the early seventeenth century, during the reign of Henri IV, France was leading the way. The civil wars between Protestants and Catholics were brought to an end with the Edict of Nantes in 1598. The country was stable and had formed strong alliances through marriage with the Medici family of Florence, as well as the Austrian court. Henri established the Louvre in Paris as the royal palace. He began the work of expanding and embellishing the building. French aristocrats were buying fashionable furniture. Paris became a magnet for craftsmen throughout Europe. A growing middle class of merchants were also becoming customers for fine decorative objects.

Furniture craftsmen trained in other countries made their way to the French capital. These foreign woodworkers settled in the Faubourg St. Antoine, on the eastern side of Paris. The first of these craftsmen came from Holland and Flanders. They were joined by others from Germany and Italy. Marie de Medici invited a talented ex-patriot craftsman named Jean Mace to return to Paris. A Protestant, Mace had been driven from France because of the religious wars. With the peace brought by the Edict of Nantes, Mace felt comfortable returning to his homeland. He had spent his exile in Holland, where he learned the skills of veneering in ebony, as well as the craft of marquetry.

Ebony was one of the most important woods reaching the European market with the expansion of world trade. Though extremely hard and requiring great skill and patience to work, in the right hands this wood could yield very striking results. Ebony became so fashionable that it eventually gave rise to a new category of craftsman, the *ébéniste*. (French developed two words for cabinetmaker: *ébéniste* and *menuisier*. The words go back to the seventeenth century, shortly after the time of Mace, when they signified two different guilds. Originally an ébéniste was a woodworker who worked primarily in ebony, which is to say, veneer. A menuisier worked primarily in solid wood).

Because of a growing demand, the production of veneers became an important industry in seventeenth-century France. From the fourteenth century onward veneers had been sawn by two men holding a saw mounted in a long rectangular frame (figure 112). The technique is similar to a pit saw where larger logs would be sawn into dimensional lumber. In the time of Louis XIV the thickness of veneer was approximately 3mm to 4mm. By the time of Louis XV the sawing technique had improved and veneers were between 2.5mm and 3mm thick. And by the time of Louis XVI the veneers were being cut more accurately at 2.25mm.

Jean Mace's skill as a furnituremaker who could use new and innovative techniques such as marquetry and veneering led him to be given the title *"menuisier et fasieur de cabinets et tableaux en marqueterie de bois"* (joiner and maker of cabinets and wooden marquetry panels). Royal patronage gave Mace significant advantages. He was housed and had his workshops in the Louvre palace. This arrangement conferred prestige and gave him access to many other noble families. His daughter married a turner and joiner named Pierre Boulle, the uncle of André-Charles Boulle.

❧

112. FROM THE BOOK *LE MENUISIER ÉBÉNISTE* BY J.A. ROUBO, 1772

Pierre Golle

One of the early important foreign cabinetmakers to come to Paris in the seventeenth century was Pierre Golle. Born in Holland around 1620, Golle immigrated to Paris as a teenager. He is recorded as having served his apprenticeship with a man named Adrien Garbrant, a *"menuisier en ébène,"* in 1643. Two years later he married Garbrant's daughter, eventually taking over the workshop. Through family connections Pierre began to receive royal commissions. He is described in a document from 1656 as *"maitre menuisier en ébène ordinaire du roi"* (master woodworker to the King).

Initially, Golle worked in the style of his father-in-law, making objects with floral marquetry on ebony grounds. Eventually he developed a reputation for work decorated with materials other than wood—ivory, brass, tortoiseshell, and horn. Golle's primary technique was *peinture en bois* (painting in wood). Peinture en bois is similar to the Boulle technique, where parts are laid out in superposition to one another, and the foreground and background are cut simultaneously. It was primarily used for floral patterns and had the advantage of yielding parts that fit together satisfactorily, even when cut by a marqueteur of modest skills.

A simple flower can be made in peinture en bois by stacking the veneers, one for each color in the flower, and gluing the design to the top veneer. The veneers are sawn as they

113. EBENESTERNA (C. 1775) ELIAS MARTIN
Swedish National Museum, Stockholm

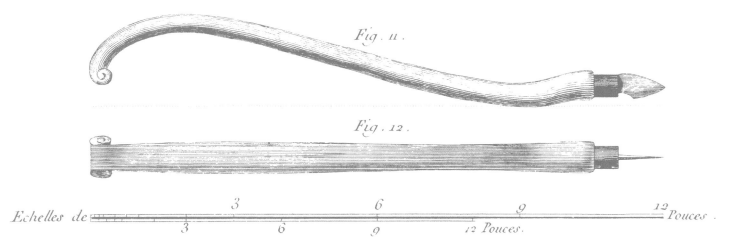

114. FROM THE BOOK *LE MENUISIER ÉBÉNISTE* BY J.A. ROUBO, 1772

A Peinture en Bois Tulip

The tulip is constructed of four different species. The grain of the wood for the center section of the flower runs vertically. The petals to the right and the left have the grain run at an angle to the vertical (figure 115).

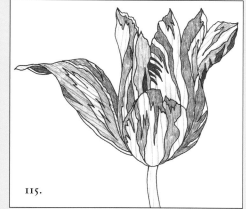

115.

The design is glued to the front of the background. Small holes are drilled through the background to locate the places where the left and right petals and stem join the main body of the flower. The four veneers are spot-glued together and then spot-glued to the background (figure 116). Note that the right-hand petal has only three parts and the stem only the single part.

The dotted line indicates the line of the sawing. After all the parts have been cut, the picture is assembled.

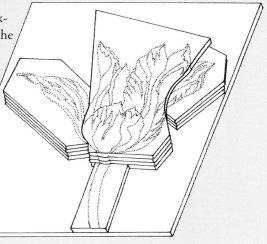

116.

DETAIL OF FIGURE 125: TULIP ON WARDROBE BY ANDRÉ-CHARLES BOULLE

would be in Boulle work, and the parts set aside. The flower parts can be sand-shaded before assembly. The process would leave gaps the thickness of the saw kerf, but usually the parts can be snugged together. This makes the design slightly smaller than the original, but tightening the joints makes the craftsmanship appear better. In Golle's era this flower would then be inlaid into a panel using a knife and chisels. The offcuts can be used for additional flowers in the same way the *contrapartie* is used in Boulle work.

Marqueteurs used a shoulder knife very similar to those used in Renaissance Italy, the only difference being that they would fashion the handle in a curved shape for added leverage (figure 114). Additionally, a short-handled knife was developed to be held with one hand. The blade would be used facing the marqueteur, as with the shoulder knife. With a small mallet the back of the blade would be tapped along the desired line in a manner more akin to chiseling.

A slightly more elaborate example of peinture en bois is the fancy tulip in figures 115 and 116 (similar to the one in figure 125). As indicated, if the design is carefully planned, the grain of the wood can be oriented differently in different parts, to help define the forms. A backing veneer is selected, and the design is glued to the front. On the reverse side oversize shapes of veneer are tacked in place with spots of glue. Each new color necessitates another veneer. The design is cut out from the whole packet at once, and the parts are retrieved and assembled into the background. Because parts are cut at the same time, they will fit with only the narrow kerf of the sawblade left to be filled with glue. Or again, the gap can be reduced by nudging the parts together, which shrinks the design. In Golle's day the outline of this assemblage would be scribed onto a previously veneered

panel with a knife. Then the background would be removed using a shoulder knife and chisels, allowing the flower to be glued in place.

Decorating furniture with marquetry was encouraged by the influx of exotic materials to western Europe. By the sixteenth century Spain, France, England, Holland, and Portugal were all involved in world trade. Ships brought back logs of ebony, satinwood, rosewood, amaranth, and padauk, as well as ivory. The market for materials was competitive, and the major port cities all had active lumber merchants. Craftsmen were encouraged to use woods with beautiful color and grain. The muted tones of local timbers used during the Italian Renaissance were supplanted by an explosion of color and contrast.

Pierre Golle was one of the ébénistes commissioned to provide furnishings for the palace at Versailles. He designed luxurious furniture with stylized marquetry on a ground of ivory. Records preserved in the National Archives list Golle as the only Parisian cabinetmaker specializing in marquetry with ivory. The Victoria and Albert Museum in London has a spectacular piece which has been attributed to Golle (figure 117). The J. Paul Getty Museum in

118. READING AND WRITING TABLE (1670–1675)
MAKER UNKNOWN (ATTRIBUTED TO PIERRE GOLLE)
Oak veneered with ivory, blue-painted horn, ebony,
rosewood, and amaranth; 25 × 19 × 14 in.
The J. Paul Getty Museum, Los Angeles (inv. 83.DA.21)

117. CABINET ON STAND (C. 1660)
ATTRIBUTED TO PIERRE GOLLE
Marquetry on ivory ground
Victoria and Albert Museum, London (inv. W38-1983);
Photo: Victoria and Albert Museum/Art Resource, New York

California owns another little table in ivory and blue-stained horn that has been attributed to Golle (figure 118). The piece was part of a set that was delivered in 1670 to the Trianon de Porcelaine in Versailles. The ivory and horn were chosen to imitate the color of Chinese porcelain. This table is an example of the type of marquetry that subsequently became known as Boulle work. The cutting is much the same as in peinture en bois, but only two materials are used. They are generally in high contrast, like ivory and horn, to create a bold graphic effect. Other materials used this way include brass, pewter, ebony, and tortoiseshell (see Appendix 4: Boulle Work, pp. 201–203).

A table now at the Metropolitan Museum in New York is a wonderful example of how Golle used exotic materials to their best advantage. In fact, it hardly looks like a wooden table. The top is predominantly tortoiseshell and ivory with sprays of inlaid flowers. Golle stained the ivory green to simulate the foliage. The decoration extends to the stretcher near the floor. Flowers on the small-radius cylindrical columns at the bottom of the legs would have been very challenging to veneer. A beautiful and elegant table, this masterful work confirms Golle's preeminence in the field.

The table is noteworthy because cabinetmakers working in wood were competing with another decorative technique imported to France from Italy called *pietre dure* (hard stone). Pietre dure is essentially marquetry in

semi-precious stone. The advantage of the technique is that the maker has a much more colorful palette to work with: bright blues, greens, reds, and golds. Wooden marquetry must have looked drab in comparison. These Italian craftsmen had captured the imagination of the French court and were getting important commissions. Ébénistes such as Golle needed to rekindle attention, and opulent tables with exotic materials like ivory, horn, and tortoiseshell did just that.

Golle has been credited as the inventor of a type of desk known as the *bureau Mazarin,* named after Cardinal Mazarin, France's leading cleric during the seventeenth century (figure 119). The desk has a flat top and a bank of drawers on either side of a narrow cen-

119. TABLE (C. 1660)
PIERRE GOLLE
Oak and fruitwood veneered with tortoise-shell, stained and natural ivory, ebony, and other woods; gilt bronze mounts; 31 × 41 × 27 in.
Metropolitan Museum of Art, New York; Gift of Charles Wrightsman, 1986 (1986.38.1); Photo: Metropolitan Museum of Art

120. DESK: BUREAU "MAZARIN" (AFTER 1692–ABOUT 1700) MAKER UNKNOWN
Oak, fir, cherry, beech, and walnut, veneered with brass, tortoiseshell, mother-of-pearl,
pewter, copper, ebony, and painted and unpainted horn; 27¼ × 35 × 20 in.
The J. Paul Getty Museum, Los Angeles (inv. 87.DA.77)

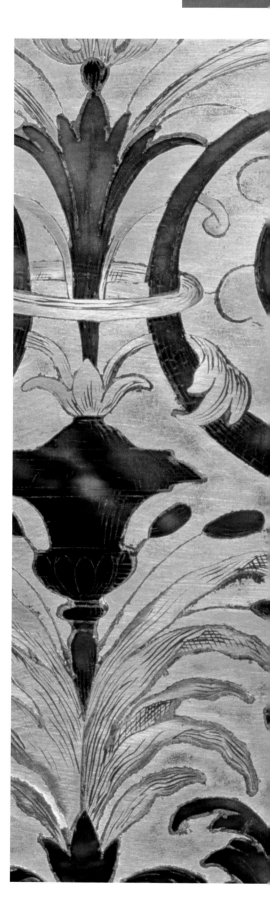

tral kneehole. The carcase was raised off the floor with a set of short legs. Golle made about twenty-five of these desks and some were decorated with spectacular Boulle work of brass and tortoiseshell. A bureau Mazarin was quite fashionable in aristocratic homes.

Golle spent a decade working on the furnishings for Versailles. Royal commissions offered a spectacular opportunity for artisans, particularly foreigners. Working for the royal family allowed them to bypass the punitive levies of the guilds. These commissions also gave them more financial security than they had ever thought possible. In 1679 alone Golle delivered twenty-three tables to the palace.

Historians have been left with an interesting record of the businesses of the ébénistes in Paris. Taxation procedures required complete inventories of the workshops. At Golle's death his workshop contained about 200 pieces, fifteen of which were under construction. The total value of the inventory was listed at approximately 11,000 livres (pounds). To give an idea of the value,

at the time a journeyman cabinetmaker would earn about 400 livres annually. Clearly, Golle had quite a valuable estate. The twenty-three desks in stock each had a value between 40 and 220 livres. Only a few pieces used metal marquetry, and these were listed as the most expensive in the inventory. One such cabinet had a value of 800 livres. Golle's estate had a large stock of ebony on hand (more than three tons), as well as palisander, kingwood, tortoiseshell, and ivory. The workshop employed five cabinetmakers, one lacquerer, and one apprentice.

Golle's son, Corneille, worked in the shop, and he took over after his father's death. However, with revocation of the Edict of Nantes in 1685, Protestants like Golle found the atmosphere in France less welcoming, even risky. Corneille left France, first settling in the Hague and finally in London. This was France's loss. The emigration of many talented Huguenot craftsmen helped spread technical skills and new styles to England.

ↄↄ

André-Charles Boulle

André-Charles Boulle was born into a family of ébénistes in 1642. His uncle Pierre Boulle had married into the family of Jean Mace, one of the first of the great French cabinetmakers. André-Charles wanted to be a painter, but the family insisted that he join the cabinetmaking business. This was financially wise, as Mace and Pierre Boulle had established a working relationship with the royal family. Eventually André-Charles would take over Mace's workshops in the Louvre.

In 1672 André-Charles Boulle was given the warrant *"ébéniste, cisleur, doreur, et sculpteur du roi"* (cabinetmaker, bronzier, gilder, and sculptor to the King). The warrant afforded Boulle great prestige, and the advantage of being exempted from the rules of the guilds. But Boulle was not favored with many commissions from Louis XIV. From the time of the warrant until 1714, when he retired, Boulle made only twenty pieces for the court. Louis evidently preferred the work of the Italian, Domenico Cucci, who specialized in pietre dure. And Louis certainly favored Pierre Golle, to whom he gave important commissions for many years before Boulle was awarded the warrant. But the work that Boulle did do for the court was spectacular and left a remarkable legacy. Among that work is the wainscotting and flooring for the Dauphin's apartments at Versailles. The work took two years to complete and cost nearly 100,000 livres.

Boulle could command very large sums for his work. However, he was bad at managing the money and saw huge swings in his fortunes. He was collecting works of art compulsively, and a huge portion of his wealth was tied up in his collection. The art market is fickle, and at times when he needed liquid assets he would be forced to sell objects at a loss.

The Boulle enterprise was much larger than that of the average Parisian ébéniste. In 1685 at least fifteen men worked for him, including his four sons. By 1720 the workshop had grown to around thirty workers. That year a

121. ENGRAVING DETAIL FROM TRIPOD TABLE (C. 1680) ATTRIBUTED TO PIERRE GOLLE
Brass, pewter, and tortoiseshell
The J. Paul Getty Museum, Los Angeles
(inv. 88.DB.16)

122. MARQUETRY DETAIL FROM CASE CLOCK (C. 1690) ATTRIBUTED TO ANDRÉ-CHARLES BOULLE
Tortoiseshell, brass, and pewter
The J. Paul Getty Museum, Los Angeles
(inv. 88.DB.16)

123. SECRÉTAIRE (C. 1770–1775) PHILIPPE-CLAUDE MONTIGNY
Oak veneered with bloodwood, tortoiseshell, brass, pewter and ebony bandings; 55½ × 33 × 15¼ in.
The J. Paul Getty Museum, Los Angeles
(inv. 85.DA.378)

devastating fire destroyed nearly everything. In this era before insurance Boulle was ruined. Aside from his shop, much of his vast collection of prints and drawings was lost, representing a large portion of his assets. He estimated the damage to be 212,220 livres, a huge fortune.

After the fire Boulle's business was never the same. By the time Boulle died in 1732 the shop had shrunk to only seven benches. His sons took over, but they never came close to achieving the success their father had enjoyed in his prime.

Boulle's legacy is immense. Most memorably, he popularized the technique that now bears his name. Others, like Golle, had juxtaposed metal with other materials, but no one pushed the limits of the aesthetic possibilities the way Boulle did. The graphic impact of the Boulle technique is created through the contrast between figure and ground. The beauty of the process is that in one cutting two panels are produced. It is easy to imagine how the concept developed. A craftsman probably wanted to inlay a piece of brass in a darker wood. He laid the two sheets together and sawed out the design. Hmmm, the off-cuts fit together as well. And they are as interesting in their own way. In Boulle work, the brass motif in a ground is called the *première-partie* (first part). The offcuts are called the *seconde-partie* or *contra-partie.*

The première-partie deserved its name for several reasons. The brass in the ground would have a more delicate look than the reverse relationship. The brass design is smaller by the thickness of a saw kerf. (So is the wood background, but the kerf is filled with wood dust, not metal dust; thus the thickness goes to the wood component, not the metal.) The metal could also be engraved to add detail. The lines in the brass can be filled with a dark mastic, making the whole design more lively. In the panel shown in figure 121, which decorates a little tripod table by Golle, note the way the lines are spaced and used to shade the brass. Extra cross-hatching distinguishes the underside of

leaves. The shading of the ring that surrounds the three vertical elements is particularly effective. Careful inspection also shows that the serpent and the vase form are engraved with scales.

The contra-partie was considered to have less value than the première-partie because the motifs in darker material

appear flatter and less lively. Another reason for the diminished value of the contra-partie is that the brass was harder to glue and would require occasional maintenance. To secure it, the cabinet-makers would sometimes resort to decorative screws. If a cabinet were commissioned only in première-partie, it

124. COFFERS ON STANDS (1684–1689)
ATTRIBUTED TO ANDRÉ-CHARLES BOULLE
Oak, cypress, and walnut veneered with tortoiseshell,
blue-painted horn, ebony, rosewood, pewter, brass;
60½ × 35¼ × 22 in. and 61¼ × 35½ × 22 in.
The J. Paul Getty Museum, Los Angeles
(inv. 82.DA.109.1 and 82.DA.109.2)

was worthwhile for the ébéniste to make the second cabinet in contra-partie because the marquetry would be already cut. However, the second cabinet would have a value typically only about 70 percent of the first.

It made economic sense to use both the contra-partie and the première-partie in a furniture design. Boulle's furniture is distinguished by the particularly effective use of these "secondary" parts. The design challenge that he answered magnificently was to make the contra-partie as interesting as the première-partie. One way he did this was to create designs with equivalent amounts of light and dark (foreground and background). In some of Boulle's work you have to look carefully to determine where a given panel is première-partie or contra-partie. Formal seventeenth-century interior design often called for symmetrical arrangements. Two cabinets balancing one another need not be identical but rather of equal visual weight, without one being obviously more elaborate or luxurious. Featuring an equal amount of brass was one way to accomplish this. In Boulle's designs a première-partie front of a cabinet would be mated with contra-partie sides. And the second cabinet would be the opposite, thus balancing the effect of the pair.

Boulle work can be done with more than two materials. There are a pair of coffers at the Getty Museum where the marquetry was done with three parts: tortoiseshell, brass, and pewter (figure 124). Therefore, three panels are created. Only two of the set of coffers are at the Getty (the third coffer is at Blenheim in England). Interestingly, the design of the bases was altered, presumably because they weren't meant to be a set.

Boulle would sometimes design very large panels for grand cabinets. The size of a Boulle project is limited by the throat of the saw. The curvy Rococo designs would have the marqueteur constantly swinging the packet back and forth around the sawblade. And all this movement has to be accomplished within the confines of the saw frame. The circuitous designs

125. WARDROBE (C. 1700) ANDRÉ-CHARLES BOULLE
Ebony, brass, tortoiseshell, marquetry
Louvre, Paris; Photo: Réunion des Musées Nationaux/Art Resource, New York

entailed a huge amount of cutting. The designs are so busy that smaller parts could be pieced together invisibly to make larger panels. Saw lines could extend to the exterior of the panels. In the première-partie, with their darker grounds, the lines wouldn't show, but even in the contra-partie, a small line in the brass is essentially invisible.

A *secrétaire* by Philippe-Claude Montigny illustrates the way panels can be pieced together (figure 123). The front is symmetrically divided into four parts. The Boulle work is in ebony, brass, and pewter. Within each

of the quadrants the scrolling patterns extend to the edges in numerous places, allowing the pattern to be pieced together in parts that could be cut in manageable portions.

André-Charles Boulle also designed magnificent pieces featuring marquetry without metal. These were produced using the peinture en bois technique. One of his most elaborate marquetry panels is the door of a large cabinet built for Louis XIV (figure 125). It depicts a vase of flowers and a bird and the ground is tortoiseshell. Exquisite work, this is obviously royal furniture,

meant to impress (and perhaps belittle those who could not hope to own something so opulent). The framing wood is ebony. The marquetry panels are not symmetrical, even though this is a very formal cabinet. The vase as a still life subject derives from Dutch painting of the seventeenth century. The flowers are mixed and rather fantastical, as they wouldn't all be blooming at the same time. The tulip at the top is particularly beautiful. The frilly carnation-like flower in the middle, its effect achieved through sand shading, is also wonderfully rich. The parts

126. Box (1675–1680) André-Charles Boulle
Oak, veneered with ebony, boxwood, maple, mahogany, padauk, walnut,
amaranth, cedar, pear, satinwood, brass, horn, and pewter;
16½ × 26 × 17 in.
The J. Paul Getty Museum, Los Angeles (inv. 84.DA.971)

were cut, separated, and then scorched before assembly (see Appendix 6: Sand Shading).

Not all of the work Boulle designed was on a grand scale. The form of a little box at the Getty Museum is simple with straight lines and a slightly curved top (figure 126). Yet the peinture en bois marquetry is exquisite. The floral marquetry is on a ground of ebony that makes the design jump out.

Many of Boulle's pieces feature tortoiseshell, which became popular in the sixteenth century for a variety of decorative objects. It was just one more of the exotic materials being brought to Europe from tropical lands. The shell was taken from one of three different species of sea turtle. The plates of the shell were cut and treated like veneers. Some parts of the shell are translucent; others are mottled. The backside of the shell, which was glued to the groundwork, could be colored with a pigment. Sometimes a colored foil would be glued to the back of the shell for extra reflectivity. The effect can be very rich. Working with tor-

toiseshell is difficult, and it was used on only the most elegant furniture (figure 7).

One of the most remarkable pieces of furniture ever designed features marquetry using natural woods, but some of the accent borders incorporate marquetry with tortoiseshell, brass, horn, and pewter. It is a cabinet on a stand where part of the structure of the stand is figurative sculptures in ivory (figure 127). The sculptures are stunning and used in the architecture of the piece, like caryatids of ancient

127. Cabinet on Stand (1675–80)
Attributed to André-Charles Boulle
Oak veneered with pewter, brass, tortoiseshell, horn, ebony, ivory, and wood marquetry; drawers of snakewood; $90\frac{1}{2} \times 59\frac{1}{2} \times 26\frac{1}{2}$ in.
The J. Paul Getty Museum, Los Angeles
(inv. 77.DA.1)

Greece holding up the plainer form of the cabinet above. The floral marquetry panel in the middle is a masterpiece and is flanked by ten drawers, each of the fronts displaying a unique picture.

André-Charles Boulle established ébénisterie as an art form in the French consciousness. His standard was so high and his objects so luxurious that the aristocracy wanted to own furniture as an expression of their wealth and taste. The cabinetmakers that followed Boulle owe much to the path blazed by this great man.

When I got to the École Boulle I was struck by Pierre Ramond's command of the history of marquetry. He not only has the knowledge but also a passion for the subject, which is infectious. He wants every one of his students to know the roots of the craft. They must have some textbook knowledge, as well as an appreciation for historical work that can come only from seeing a piece of furniture first hand. He made it clear that I should go to as many museums as possible and see the great furniture that is France's heritage.

After my first week at the École Boulle, Pierre and the entire marquetry class made a field trip to Alsace in eastern France. It was a wonderful opportunity for me to get to know Pierre and my new comrades. Our first destination was the city of Nancy, home of Gallé and Majorelle. A major museum there is dedicated to Art Nouveau, displaying many of the inspirational pieces I had seen in books when I was beginning to learn about marquetry. The visit was an absolute delight. It was my first chance to see the work of Majorelle. It is always better to see art work in person. This is particularly true of marquetry, the subtle details of which are never quite captured in a photograph.

Our ultimate destination was Strasbourg, where we were hosted for a traditional Alsatian dinner by the family of one of the students. The dinner was a social ice-breaker for me, as it involved everyone consuming lots of the excellent local beer. The evening ended with drinking songs. When I saw Pierre about ten years later he jokingly asked if I would reprise my performance from that evening.

One of our stops in Alsace was the marquetry workshop of Jean-Charles Spindler. Started by his grandfather, Charles, the atelier was still producing the older marquetry pictures as well as more contemporary designs drawn by Jean-Charles. I had first seen the elder Spindler's work in photos in Lincoln's book, *The Art and Practice of Marquetry*. I was impressed then, and was delighted to see the work in person. We got a look at the inventory of veneers at the shop, some of which probably go back almost 100 years. These are the fantastic burls and figured pieces of wood Spindler used so adeptly.

જી

128. Silas Kopf cutting marquetry using a chevalet at the École Boulle (1988)

129. Silas Kopf cutting marquetry using a chevalet in Easthampton (1989)

Charles Spindler

Eastern France and western Germany have a long tradition of marquetry craftsmanship. This region spawned Abraham and David Roentgen. The École de Nancy in Lorraine used many marqueteurs from neighboring Alsace. Among Alsatian craftsmen Charles Spindler deserves special attention. His workshop was not far from Strasbourg, in the little village of Saint Léonard.

Charles Spindler was born in 1865 in the town of Boersch in Alsace. At the end of the Franco-Prussian War in 1871 the area was annexed by Germany, which turned attention in the province eastward, away from France. When the young Spindler was ready for schooling, he went to Dusseldorf, Munich, and Berlin and studied painting and design. Early on, he was interested in promoting the history and culture of Alsace. Alsace had long been a meeting ground for the French and German cultures. Spindler and many of his contemporary artists were able to meld the two into a unique entity. In 1893 he was accidentally introduced to marquetry.

"Of all the different tasks an artist has to accept" (he is quoted in a 1983 exhibition catalog of his work), "I received an order for the drawing of targets, items of fantasy that transposed mechanically to maple or poplar veneers, were then glued on to cardboard. It was a Strasbourg teacher who had come up with this commercial idea in order to supplement his income…. All I know is that one day I asked him to give me a few scraps of veneer that he had no use for, and that upon my return to Saint Leonard, I cut them into different shapes with my pocket knife and proceeded to compose a tableau according to their different shades. In those days, Grasset and Mucha posters were very much in style and it is in that spirit that, just for my amusement, I did my very first marquetry. It didn't take me long to discover that by carefully choosing the shades and types of wood, one could arrive at tint gradations of infinite softness….I dreamt of making large decorative compositions, in the style of Puvis de Chavannes, in which appeared women of noble gesture, dressed in beautiful draperies against scenic backgrounds."

Spindler's marquetries caught the attention of some in the German art community, and he was invited to participate in the Exposition Universelle in Paris in 1900. At this point he was also learning how to construct furniture. Spindler realized that this was the logical application for his marquetry pictures, and he worked with a local cabinetmaker to build pieces. He had remarkable success at the Paris Fair, winning the Grand Prix. This notoriety led to new commissions for furniture and decorative panels. These initial objects were rather heavy, in a style that was derived from an Arts and Crafts sensibility. His dealer in Strasbourg told him that his marquetry was superior to the work of Gallé, but that his furniture designs were ponderous and not attracting customers. "At the moment," his dealer wrote, "Gallé has a table of which the legs form a dragonfly. The marquetry is nothing extraordinary, but in Strasbourg alone, we have sold six in two weeks. With other shapes, we could sell more than he does since your marquetry is better and newer." Commercial success didn't tempt Spindler to change, and he continued working in his chosen style. Because he had been schooled in Germany, he was aware of the new aesthetic being created in Darmstadt and Vienna. It took several more years for Spindler's vision of furniture design to succeed.

In 1902 Spindler exhibited a dining/smoking room at the Turin International Fair. Again he won a prize, this time silver. International exhibits provided him an opportunity to travel, as well as an introduction to other designers. His travels took him to Darmstadt to visit the famous experimental art colony. In 1904 his work was exhibited at the World's Fair in St. Louis. He was awarded the Grand Prize there for his design of a study.

I believe that the difference between the marquetry work of Spindler and that of Gallé stems from the fact that

130. MUSIC ROOM (1900) DESIGNED BY CHARLES SPINDLER, MADE BY J.J.GRAF
Settle and paneling; marquetry in various woods
Victoria and Albert Museum, London; CT11730

Spindler actually cut the picture. Gallé's operation was so large that the marquetry drawings would have been turned over to a craftsman to execute. Gallé's marqueteur would select the wood based on the code on the drawing itself. For instance, the sky might have been labeled "maple" But obviously there is a great deal of variation possible in an individual piece of maple veneer. It can be flat-cut or quartered, curly or plain, and so on. In the Gallé shop the marqueteur may or may not have brought the requisite artistic understanding to the choice. Because Spindler did his own cutting, his pictures show a great sensitivity in the selection of a particular piece of veneer.

Eventually Spindler's workshop grew, and he employed ten woodworkers to produce his designs. Even with this many workers, Spindler could still maintain a personal touch in the production of pieces. His work continued to reflect his pride in his Alsatian heritage, with many of the marquetry motifs depicting the countryside and people in regional dress.

One of the wall panels from the music room that was exhibited at the 1900 Paris Exposition is preserved in the Victoria and Albert Museum in England (figure 130). In front of the wall panel is an upholstered settee in matching style. The furniture design is not particularly sophisticated. Despite the curving lines, the settee appears quite stiff. But the marquetry is very ambitious. That is probably what caught the judge's eye and led to Spindler's winning the grand prize. The scene depicts St. Odile, patroness of Alsace, draped, in a manner reminiscent of David Roentgen, who produced magnificent furniture decorated with marquetry at the end of the eighteenth century. The white fabric of Spindler's picture jumps out at the viewer, while the tree foliage, rendered using various burls, broods in the background.

In 1903 Spindler built a three-fold screen where the marquetry is paramount (figure 131). Again, the subject is figures in a landscape, though this

131. FOLDING SCREEN (1902) CHARLES SPINDLER
Marquetry of various woods; 73 × 74 in.
Musée d'Art Moderne, Strasbourg, France

landscape is contiguous across the panels. The figured wood used for the sky is lively enough to evoke wispy cirrus clouds. Spindler didn't have pieces of veneer wide enough to fill the whole sky, so he had to join three pieces together. It's done in a book match, which actually accentuates the effect of the clouds. The focus of the piece is a female figure, draped in white. In front of her are a series of swans. The swans to the left are not as white as the ones in the center, which keeps them from throwing the composition off balance. The rich foliage of the trees is cut from

a variety of burls and other figured veneers.

World War I was devastating for the Alsatian economy. Spindler was forced to close his workshop in 1914, and it remained closed until the end of the war. In 1925 he was invited to show at the Exposition des Arts Decoratifs in Paris, the fair that launched the term Art Deco. Even though his work was not considered cutting edge, Spindler was again awarded the Gold Medal. Nevertheless, furniture fashion had passed Charles Spindler. He shifted the focus of his work in the 1930s to mar-

quetry panels rather than furniture pieces. The designs from this era continued to celebrate Alsatian folklore.

Around 1930 Charles Spindler's artistically talented son Paul joined the atelier. Father and son worked together until Charles's death in 1938. Paul continued to produce stunning marquetry panels for another three decades. Now, third-generation Jean-Charles Spindler is at work making marquetry in the Saint Leonard workshops that his grandfather started more than a century earlier.

☙

The regular students at the École Boulle are in the workshops only in the afternoon. Mornings are taken up with more basic academic subjects, such as mathematics and languages. I wasn't taking any of those classes and therefore I had my mornings free. Pierre arranged for me to visit people and workshops around the city. The school stands at one end of the neighborhood called the Faubourg St. Antoine. At the other end is the Place de Bastille, where the ancient prison stood at the time of the 1789 Revolution. Pierre was proud to point out that the rabble who stormed the Bastille, and started the revolt, probably included woodworkers from the Faubourg. ("And not one cabinetmaker lose his head.") The little streets are filled with tiny workshops, as well as suppliers to the industry. There are many shops making reproductions and shops doing restorations, along with a few enterprises producing new work. The spaces are not large, and I was impressed with how organized people are in arranging tools and materials. In America we tend to have extraordinarily large shops compared to those in Paris. Many of us could use a lesson in spatial efficiency.

Pierre's connections included very accomplished craftsmen. For instance, I visited the shop of the man who has literally written the book on *galuchat* (sharkskin). Galuchat was used as a veneer on some remarkable Art Deco furniture. In another shop I saw cabinets built by André-Charles Boulle being restored for the Getty Museum. Pierre also arranged access to the workshop at the Louvre Museum. He suggested many things for me to see, such as small museums off the beaten tourist path. One is a former home, where the décor is as it might have been a hundred years ago. It was in this Musée Nissim da Commando that I first took note of the furniture of Jean-François Oeben and Jean-Henri Riesener, inheritors of the tradition of Boulle (figure 132).

❧

132. Desk (c. 1770) Jean-Henri Riesener
Oak, marquetry of holly, walnut, ebony, boxwood, purpleheart, and mahogany; 54¼ x 76 x 40 in.
The Wallace Collection, London; Photo: The Wallace Collection

Jean-François Oeben

133. WRITING AND TOILET TABLE (C. 1750–55) JEAN-FRANÇOIS OEBEN
28½ × 30½ × 17¼ in.
National Gallery of Art, Washington, D.C.; Widener Collection 1942.9.413.(C-266)

The Regence and the early Louis XV periods continued the tradition of using exotic veneers on furniture. Wood was coming to Paris from around the world, and fashionable, wealthy people demanded the finest materials. The marquetry of this era tended to be more stylized than it had been in the preceding period of Louis XIV. Tropical veneers, such as kingwood, Brazilian rosewood, and tulipwood, took on increased importance in energetic parquetry patterns and borders of contrasting colors.

Jean-François Oeben was one of the many ébénistes who were attracted to Paris from foreign countries. He was born in the German-speaking border town of Heinsberg, near Aix-la-Chappelle in 1721. As with many of the immigrant ébénistes, his first workshop in Paris was in the Faubourg St. Antoine. Oeben took the same route

into the cabinetmaking establishment as had Pierre Golle a hundred years earlier. He married Françoise-Marguerite Vandercruse. She was the daughter of an ébéniste and the sister of Roger Vandercruse, who became a famous furnituremaker in his own right. The Vandercruses were also emigrées. Oeben had come to Paris with the support of an aristocracy looking for quality craftsmanship. At the age of thirty Jean-François began work as an independent craftsman in the atelier of Charles-Joseph Boulle. Charles-Joseph was the youngest son of André-Charles and had taken over his father's workshop in the Louvre, where he ran the business until his death in 1754. Oeben, being an immigrant, could not continue working independently in the Louvre. However, he had clearly established his credentials as an excellent craftsman and at the end of 1755 he was

named *ébéniste du roi*. This prestigious title brought him to the royal Gobelins workshops, and out from under the watchful eye of the guild.

One of the advantages to being at the Gobelins was that after six years a craftsman could become a master and not pay the normal fees. After ten years a foreign artisan could become a citizen, with all the rights thereof. The opportunity to circumvent the usual rules of guilds and citizenship was enormously significant to someone like Oeben.

During the Middle Ages anyone who worked with wood, whether a carpenter, joiner, turner, or carver, was part of the same guild. As workers became more skilled at individual parts of the trade they formed their own organizations to protect their turf. Distinctions were made between carpenters (who built buildings) and

workers in the furniture trades. By the eighteenth century the furniture groups were being subdivided further into menuisiers and ébénistes. The guilds controlled production practices and their statutes were approved by the royal government. The guild would collect dues and re-distribute funds to widows and indigent craftsmen, as well as support the training of newcomers. Those who weren't masters were kept from selling furniture through established marketing channels. At the same time the guilds ensured that the quality of work met a standard. Interestingly, most of the ébénistes were of foreign origin, having learned the trade of working in exotic veneers in their home areas. For a foreigner it was easier to become an ébéniste than a menuisier.

The route to becoming a master began in apprenticeship. This period lasted three years, which was followed by another three years as a journeyman, working in the atelier of a master. At this point the man could produce a *chef d'œurve,* a masterpiece, to show the guild that he was worthy of being called a *maître.* And, of course, money had to change hands. The new master had to pay a fee to join the guild. The amount was based on family and other relationships. If your father was in the guild, the fee to join was less than one quarter the amount a foreign-born worker who had no connection to the guild had to pay. In the mid-eighteenth century the fee for a foreigner was 530 livres, while the son or son-in-law of an adjudicator of the guild would pay only 120 livres. The yearly salary for an assistant journeyman was approximately 400 livres. The financial hurdle of 530 livres was so steep that it prohibited many of the talented foreigners from gaining entry into the system.

Curiously, the area of the Faubourg St. Antoine, and other areas of Paris with religious affiliations, were exempt from the restrictions of the guild from the time of the Middle Ages. The workers in these areas could sell directly to individuals, but they couldn't legally sell subcontracted work to masters (as this would have compromised the master's work and voided the stamp). Some illegal trade did take place, probably involving bribes, because it was cost-effective for a master to buy parts from someone outside the guild and then call it his own. St. Antoine became a magnet for foreign craftsmen, but the guild still made commerce difficult for outsiders. The one legitimate possibility for foreigners to sell their work was to use the *marchand-mercier* (official dealer) as an

est and shows how Oeben pushed the craft to new heights.

The center of the top has a musical motif, created in a delicate and realistic manner. The composition features a violin, several recorders, a drum, a harp, and sheet music. Foliage, with a branch to the right and ferns to the left, fills out the composition. While the eye is drawn to the central motif, the surrounding area is also wonderfully interesting. The design from left to right is varied, complex, and well balanced. Some have pointed to Louis XV furniture as the important antecedent to the French and Belgian Art Nouveau which came 150 years later. Individual areas are separated from one another by sinuous baroque scrolls. Follow any of the white lines that border the scrolls, and your eye will be rewarded. These flowing lines are organic in the way they cross one another, or sometimes miss, or just touch. The craftsmanship is impressive in the cutting of the bold lines, keeping them crisp and parallel where called for. The shapes that are created by the lines are filled with interesting patterns: illusionary cubes, small stylized flowers, or sprays of leaves and blooms.

**134. Writing and Toilette Table (c.1754) Jean-François Oeben
Details: Drawer (below) and Table Top (facing page)**
Oak veneered with kingwood, amaranth, tulipwood, and other marquetry woods;
26 × 31½ × 17 in.
The J. Paul Getty Museum, Los Angeles
(inv. 71.DA.103)

agent. This was the equivalent of a guild, with its own regulations to control sales. In all, the system was rigged for the benefit of French citizens and to the detriment of outsiders.

As a young man Oeben supplied work to the most influential marchand-mercier in Paris. This relationship brought his work to the attention of Madame de Pompadour, the mistress of Louis XV. He built many pieces for her, including a wonderful dressing table that is now at the National Gallery in Washington (figure 133). The table has all the characteristics we associate with Louis XV furniture, such as compound curves, cabriole legs, and ormolu mounts. It is the marquetry that holds special inter-

Another table from the same era has many of the same characteristics (figure 134). The marquetry on the top focuses on a basket of flowers. Surrounding this central motif are stylized architectural elements, a trellis supporting a vine of roses supported by curving columns. At first glance the top looks symmetrical, but closer inspection reveals the left and right to be unique.

turing sliding tops and other transformative components that would allow for multiple uses. A writing table could convert into a dressing table. Oeben also was a master at designing and building locking mechanisms. On this secrétaire, one turn of a key locks not only the top but all the drawers.

Many of the panels on the desk are compound curves with marquetry (or parquetry) covering the surfaces. Louis

shaped like cones, would replace the flat paddles that normally hold the wood for cutting marquetry on the sawyer's chevalet. The single-point of contact would not force the thin veneer shell flat the way the flat jaws would, so the hole could be sawn for the marquetry inlay without crushing or cracking the shell.

The Louis XV desk has ormolu mounts on all the edges, which termi-

The aprons of the table are decorated with a parquetry pattern of flowers inside a grillwork. Oeben added to the luxury of the piece by including the parquetry on the drawer sides. Was this embellishment meant to elicit surprise when the drawer was opened? Perhaps it was simply a statement that this was a piece of furniture without boundaries, catering to a clientele who could afford luxury in the extreme.

In 1760 Oeben received the most important commission of his career, a roll-top desk for King Louis XV (figure 135). Jean-François had gained renown for his mechanical tables, fea-

XV furniture is known for its compound curves. Wood wants to bend in only one direction at a time. It is difficult, at best, to veneer compound curves. In this case the marquetry decoration is part of the solution, because it divides the surface into individual pieces of veneer small enough to conform to the shape of the core. These illusionary parquetry cubes would have been laid on a previously shaped compound-curved core. Paper or cloth would be glued to the veneer sheet and when the glue dried, the parquetry would hold the shape of the core—in the form of a thin shell. Special jaws,

nate at the top in candle stands. The cylinder is designed to roll back and expose the writing surface. The tolerances for operating the cylinder are very tight. Everything needed to be built with great mechanical precision. One of the most complex pieces of furniture ever built, this national treasure is now on display in the palace at Versailles.

Unfortunately, Oeben did not live to see the desk completed. He died in 1763 when the project was just beginning. It was completed in 1769 by one of his assistants, Jean-Henri Riesener. The desk is signed, in the marquetry, with Riesener's name, but the genius behind the design was Oeben's.

As with other ébénistes, fame and important commissions did not bring Oeben lasting financial success. At the time of his death Oeben's estate couldn't pay his debts, and his widow was forced into bankruptcy. The workshop had a dozen workers. Even with an operation that large, and a well-heeled clientele, income was not adequate to provide security. The average workshop of the time would have had three or four workers, producing thirty or forty pieces a year. Oeben's shop, with three times as many workers, was making no more than seventy pieces, though admittedly some of them, like the royal desk, were very complex. Like Boulle before him, Oeben had designed and built fabulous furniture for the wealthiest people in French society, yet at the end of his life he was struggling to make ends meet.

❧

135. BUREAU DU ROI (1769) JEAN-FRANÇOIS OEBEN AND JEAN-HENRI RIESENER
Chateau de Versailles, France; Photo: Réunion des Musées Nationaux/Art Resource, New York

136. Mechanical table (c. 1780–1791)
Jean-Henri Riesener
Oak veneered with mahogany and
marquetry; 28½ × 30¼ ×19 in.
Metropolitan Museum of Art, New York;
The Jules Bache Collection, 1949 (49.7.117);
Photo: Metropolitan Museum of Art

Jean-Henri Riesener was another of the immigrants who added much to French furniture history. He was born in the small Westphalian town of Gladbeck in 1734. At about twenty he left Germany, attracted by the greater possibilities of making a living in France. He became a worker in Oeben's atelier. By the time Oeben died in 1763 Riesener was one of the best men at the bench. Oeben's workshop also employed another talented cabinetmaker and marqueteur, Jean-François Leleu. Leleu was five years older than Riesener, and he thought that taking over the workshop upon the death of the master should fall to him. But Riesener had an inside track. He was soon to marry Oeben's widow and become the *maitre de l'atelier*. Leleu never got over the fact that the shop did not come to him and, according to the furniture historian Alexandre Pradère, he remained bitter toward Riesener for the rest of his life.

Riesener lived in Oeben's home and ran the shop at the Arsenal on the banks of the Seine for twenty-nine years. His most important job was to oversee the completion of the king's desk that had been designed and begun by Oeben. It was not finished until 1769, six years after it had been started, but the work brought

Riesener fame as well as more commissions from the royal family. Actually, fame was Riesener's even before the desk was completed. He was commissioned to build a copy of the King's desk by the aristocrat Grimond d'Orsay (figure 132). In 1774 Riesener, like Oeben before him, was named ébéniste du roi. The building projects at the palaces at Versailles were expanding, and Riesener began to produce a prodigious amount of work for the royal family.

Marie Antoinette favored Riesener's furniture and commissioned numerous pieces for her rooms at Versailles. Riesener designed clever mechanical tables (as had Oeben before him) with tops that would slide open to enable other functions. One such table has an interesting marquetry top with a central oval motif featuring an astronomical globe surmounted by a rooster and resting on books and symbols of science (figure 136). This table is a wonderful example of the style of work for

**137. SECRÉTAIRE WITH PICTORIAL AND TRELLIS MARQUETRY (1790)
JEAN-HENRI RIESENER**
Marquetry, ash burl, bloodwood, tulipwood; 45½ × 56½ × 20 in.
Frick Collection, New York; Henry Clay Frick Bequest (1915.5.75); Photo: Frick Collection

**138. PORTRAIT OF JEAN-HENRI RIESENER
(C. 1785) ANTOINE VESTIER**
*Chateau de Versailles et de Traianon, Versailles,
France; Photo: Réunion des Musées Nationaux/Art
Resource, New York*

heart, with a circle at each intersection. The entire effect is rich and refined.

Riesener favored this motif and used it in other work, particularly in pieces made for the Queen. A fall front secrétaire, now in the Frick Museum in New York, again features lozenges with stylized flowers in a matrix of wood tones, all surrounding a unique central marquetry image (figure 137).

It was common for Riesener (and many other ébénistes) to subcontract work. This was one of the advantages of working in Paris, where the Faubourg St. Antoine was full of competent craftsmen. Carvers, turners, bronziers, and of course marqueteurs could be counted on for talented workmanship. The marquetry lozenges in Riesener's work were probably jobbed out to another shop, allowing his own workers to concentrate on producing the one-off marquetry that required more attention.

One other piece of Riesener's is quite unique. It is a cylinder desk made for Marie Antoinette in the 1780s for the palace at Fontainebleau (figure 139). It can still be seen there today. The decoration is very similar to the table at the

which Riesener became so well known. It has all the opulence of Oeben's work: rich woods, ormolu, and uncompromising craftsmanship. Here the cabriole shapes have been straightened, marking a change from the style of Louis XV to that of Louis XVI. Look at what he has done with the marquetry decoration. The panel in the middle of the top features a one-of-a-kind marquetry image, the focal point

of the piece. Surrounding that is a repeated motif of lozenges with a floral design in the middle. The small identical flowers themselves have eight petal parts plus the center. These parts were cut using a fretsaw and then each piece was sand-shaded before assembling in the lozenge. Each lozenge is surrounded by a dark line and then another lighter line of sycamore. The parts are assembled into a grillwork of purple-

Metropolitan Museum and the secré-taire at the Frick Collection, but this time instead of marquetry flowers for the lozenges Riesener used mother-of-pearl. The pearl was a particularly exotic material at that time and using it to cover the entire surface of an object was the height of luxury. This is royal furniture at its most opulent.

In 1776 Riesener's wife died. When he remarried in 1783 it was necessary to record his net worth. The workshop itself had assets of more than 36,000 livres, in both inventory and equipment. Riesener's personal assets amounted to more than 10,000 livres, and his income was over 6,000 livres. Around this time he had his portrait painted, and he certainly doesn't appear to be the workingman, but more the gentleman in his ruffles and silk (figure 138).

In the ten years after he was named ébéniste du roi, Riesener had sold an astonishing 938,000 livres worth of furniture as catalogued by the Garde-Meuble Royal. At that time a journeyman ébéniste was being paid only 400 livres per year. But Riesener's fortunes were soon to change. The royal family began to favor others, such as David Roentgen, with commissions. At the same time revolutionary fervor was in the air. In July of 1789 the Bastille was stormed, and the violent upheaval began.

The Revolution would destroy the market for luxury furniture. Riesener failed to foresee the impact of the new politics. Many of the assets of the crown were sold to raise money for the new government. Riesener was able to buy back many of the pieces he had recently built at a fraction of what he had sold them for. He presumed a favorable business climate would return and that he could make a great profit. But it was not to be. He even tried to bow to public sentiment, by removing the signs of royal patronage such as the fleurs de lys. On the Louis XV desk he removed the royal ciphers and substituted an imitation wedgewood plaque. The profile of Louis was replaced with a picture of Minerva. Months passed

139. Secrétaire (1786) Jean-Henri Riesener
Mother-of-pearl, wood, and bronze; 44 × 42 × 20 in.
Fontainebleau Palace, France; Photo: Réunion des Musées Nationaux/ Art Resource, New York

and things only got worse. Facing bankruptcy, Riesener was forced to advertise the sale of the furniture amidst the Terror of 1794. He had another sale in 1798, again without much success. Prosperity never returned. He died in 1806, having been forced out of his house and into the home of his son, another ébéniste in financial disarray.

The Revolution had one other effect on French furniture. The new social order overthrew the guild system. Those workers in the Faubourg St.

Antoine had found the old ways too restrictive, and they made sure that the new order no longer had a guild of menuisiers. The change opened up new possibilities for production. The era of the small atelier was supplanted by increasingly large workshops employing many more workers. By 1815 the workshop of George Jacob employed 322 workers. The old order of France was dead, and the height of French furniture was over as well.

એ

140. Portrait of Pierre Rosenau (c. 1930) Vassilieffe
12 × 8 in.

Photo: Pierre Costerg (courtesy of Pierre Ramond)

My trip to Paris paid many dividends, the most obvious
being the understanding I gained in how traditional
marquetry was cut. But perhaps the greatest benefit was
being able to look at the historic pieces up close. My
acquaintance with Boulle or Riesener had been only
through pictures in books. I assumed they evidenced
impeccable craftsmanship, beyond the capability of anyone
today. The photographs in the books had impressed, even
intimidated me, although I considered most of the work
of that era to be aesthetically unpleasing. It was overly
sumptuous and reminded me of giant wedding cakes.
Nevertheless, in real life the work was awesome. In the
museums and restoration workshops of Paris I could get
nose to nose with the furniture. That broke the spell. I
recognized these magnificent objects not as matchless
achievements but as the result of patient workmanship.
That level of craft was attainable, given enough time. I
found this very liberating. It allowed me to move along
with what I was doing, less concerned about what I
thought I could never do.

Pierre was aware that I worked primarily using the
bevel method (see Appendix 7: Bevel Cutting). He pointed
out that that was the way marquetry was cut in the David
Roentgen workshop. Pierre considered Roentgen the
greatest marqueteur of all time. He added that the next

best marqueteur was an artist named Vassilieffe, who had
worked in Paris in the 1920s for an atelier specializing in
marquetry. He had been in the employ of Czar Nicolas II
of Russia, where he learned the craft. He left Russia after
the Revolution in 1917 and settled in Paris.

Vassilieffe became the premier artisan in the workshop
of Pierre Rosenau. He worked differently than the other
marqueteurs, using the bevel technique to make
astonishingly detailed portraits. One of the panels he did
was of his employer, M. Rosenau (figure 140). The picture
owes much of its vitality to the extremely small pieces
Vassilieffe blended together to create the image.

One afternoon Pierre had me give a demonstration of
bevel sawing for the other marquetry students at the École
Boulle. It was difficult, because my French was so poor,
but I was honored to be asked. Doing the demonstration
gave me instant credibility with the students, as Pierre had
called me "*l'expert de la methode.*" I had stumbled on bevel
sawing by chance, simply because when I started it seemed
the easiest approach. Now, I thought it might also be the
best. Pierre confirmed that I was on to something when he
also told me that the finest marqueteur of all time had
made his pictures using the bevel method.

David Roentgen

The man whom Pierre considered the finest marqueteur, David Roentgen, is associated not only with exquisite marquetry panels but with intricate and beautiful furniture as well. His furniture can be found in museums around the world. His work is admired for its elaborate designs and superb craftsmanship.

David Roentgen was born in 1743 in the German town of Neuwid on the Rhine River. His father, Abraham, was a successful cabinetmaker who came from a line of furnituremakers estab-lished in the area around Cologne in the seventeenth century. Abraham was born in 1711 and began work in the family woodworking trade. As a twen-ty-year-old he left home to learn from other masters. He spent at least a year and a half in Holland as a journeyman

141. DESK (C. 1760–1765) ABRAHAM ROENTGEN
Oak veneered with various woods;
58 × 43 × 23 in.
Rijksmuseum, Amsterdam

and then in 1733 went to London. According to records, Abraham specialized there in "engraving, making mosaics in wood, and producing mechanical devices." He was sought by master craftsmen to embellish their work with his skills. Just as many German and Flemish woodworkers found a market for their marquetry skills in Paris, Abraham found that being a marqueteur provided opportunities in England.

In 1737 Abraham converted to the sect of Protestants known as the Herrnhuter Brotherhood, and he returned to Germany to live in a Herrnhuter community. The beliefs of the sect played a role in his professional life and later that of his son David. The group was very strict and not inclined toward lavish displays of wealth, which were thought frivolous. But while the Brotherhood thought of luxury furniture as "worldly," it praised manual work. So as a skilled and hardworking craftsman, Abraham was caught in the middle of these two competing forces. The Herrnhuters were also serious missionaries. In fact Abraham was at one point asked to go to North Carolina to help convert native Americans to Christianity. (He was not able to complete the journey when the ship he was traveling on became stranded in Galway, Ireland.) In 1742 Abraham left England and once again set up in a Herrnhuter community in Germany. In 1750 he established himself in the town of Neuwid.

In 1766 Abraham built an elaborate secrétaire (figure 141). The piece was highly crafted with precious materials, such as ivory and mother-of-pearl, plus ormolu mounts. The marquetry panels are very involved, including architectural scenes and landscapes. Compound-curved surfaces are veneered in complicated patterns. This must have been Abraham's masterpiece.

Abraham nevertheless lacked some of the savvy that would have made his business successful. Wealthy clients notwithstanding, he was having a difficult time making ends meet. The Frankfurt Fair did not bring in as much business as it had in earlier years.

Abraham was also losing the support of the Herrnhuters, who didn't approve of speculative enterprises or his luxurious productions. He considered leaving the community and moving the family to London, but a trip there in 1766 dissuaded him from the move. Another option was Russia. Catherine the Great was offering western European craftsmen great opportunities, and while Abraham was tempted, he decided to stay in Germany.

Abraham's son David joined the family enterprise in 1766 when he was twenty-three years old. He had been apprenticed in the Herrnhuter manner in communities away from his family. By the time he was a teenager he returned home and was assisting his father in building furniture. In his early twenties he was playing an important role in the business. He was also determined to make the business a success.

David came up with the idea of staging a lottery to sell some of the valuable furniture that was being built and carried as inventory. Lotteries were used in the period to sell all sorts of things, but it was still a risky venture for the Roentgens. It also went against the grain of the Herrnhuter community.

Held in 1769, the lottery was fabulously successful. One hundred prizes carried a total value of 2,145 ducats. Tickets were 100 ducats each, and 715 sold. Doing the math, it isn't hard to figure out that the Roentgens made out very well indeed. The lottery also proved to be a wonderful advertisement for the skills and production of the workshop. Many German aristocrats became familiar with the name Roentgen through that event. The bold move put the business on firm footing, and David now set his sights on expansion.

The first step was to move from Neuwid to a wealthier city. He looked for court sponsorship and approached Frederick the Great of Prussia. Audacious in his negotiation, David demanded a house (for which he provided plans), moving costs, unrestricted opportunity to trade as he wished (with no interference from the guild), and a commission to build marquetry panel-

ing and furniture for a room in the Prussian palace. Frederick turned him down, though not without purchasing an elaborate secrétaire.

In 1772 David became the legal owner of the family workshop. Abraham stayed in Neuwid and helped for another four years but then left to help another son, Friedrich, establish a workshop in the town of Norden. Abraham became discouraged with what he described as Friedrich's lazy work ethic and returned to Neuwid in 1785. He died in 1793.

Part of David's business genius was to recognize the talents of others. He established profitable relationships with many other artists and craftsmen, such as the clockmaker Peter Kinzing and the painter Januarius Zick. In 1779 Zick produced the designs for some of the most spectacular marquetry Roentgen ever produced. These were eight large panels that decorated a room in the palace of Prince Charles of Lorraine. The panels were almost ten feet square and depicted scenes of Roman history. Prince Charles was the uncle of the French queen, and therefore an extremely important patron to cultivate.

David was no longer thinking of moving the workshop to Prussia or Russia, but instead set his sights on Paris. Paris at the end of the eighteenth century was the center of European culture. A wealthy clientele there already had a taste for fine furniture. Roentgen had worked for Prince Charles and this gave him status among the French nobility. France had long been a place where men from other countries could find work. The guild in Paris was at least open to foreigners, if they paid all the fees involved. Roentgen was successful enough to be able to afford to pay the money that had proved to be such a burden for other foreigners.

Roentgen was not shy in establishing himself in Paris. One of the first pieces he showed in Paris was a very elaborate secrétaire built with Marie Antoinette in mind. It had marquetry panels on the front and sides. The motifs were music, art, and science. Beautifully executed ribbons in mar-

142. BUREAU-CABINET (1779) DAVID ROENTGEN
Fruitwood with marquetry of various woods; 144 × 59¼ × 34¼ in.
Öesterreichisches Museum für Angewandte Kunst, Vienna; Photo: Erich Lessing/Art Resource, New York

quetry tied together various parts. This theme is repeated many times in Roentgen's work over the years. The boldest part of the desk was to inlay the initials "MA" beneath a crown in the cylinder fall of the secrétaire. The gambit worked. The Queen bought the desk. The result was the kind of publicity that would leave other aristocrats clamoring for Roentgen's furniture.

Roentgen's first important commission after introducing his work in Paris was again for Prince Charles. David made several freestanding pieces of furniture, including a bureau-cabinet topped with a clock and a bronze sculpture of Apollo (figure 142). The entire piece is almost 13 feet tall. The marquetry panels in the front were designed by Januarius Zick. The interior is decorated with trompe l'oeil marquetry. Soon after this piece was completed Roentgen built a similar bureau-cabinet for Louis XVI for the astonishing sum of 96,000 livres.

Roentgen's style was unique enough that "Roentgen" marquetry began to show up in work by other cabinetmakers, including Riesener. It is unclear whether the marquetry was commissioned from Roentgen or if others were simply copying the style. Either way, Roentgen's work had taken Paris by storm. Owning a Roentgen was considered the height of fashion.

The collaboration with Zick was obviously fruitful. Roentgen also employed a very skilled marqueteur named Michael Rummer, who was able to execute the designs that Zick provided. The marquetry was cut using the bevel technique. Most Parisian ébénistes at the time were using the traditional method of cutting vertically, which leaves a gap between pieces. Rummer was able to get astonishing detail using bevel cutting. He also used dyes to add detail—not for coloration but to change tonality. Veneers would be cut, one part would be darkened in dye, and then the pieces would be put back together. A close look at the furniture shows areas where the wood has two different tones, yet the grain is continuous across the saw cut. The result is a wonderful three-dimensional effect.

In 1779, two years after building the furniture for Prince Charles, Roentgen was commissioned to make two enormous marquetry panels for Charles's palace. The subjects were taken from Roman history: The Peace Between the Romans and the Sabines and The Peace Between the Romans and the Carthaginians (figure 143). Designed by Zick, the enormous panels were about 11½ feet square. Careful tracings were made of the master drawing and then the paper was glued onto the veneers, individually selected for tone and grain. Because of the size of the panels, the design had to be divided into sections that eventually would be pieced together in the completed composition.

Delightfully, even after more than two hundred years, this work still has great vitality. Wood changes color as it ages; some woods lighten, others darken. Although these panels don't look the same as when they were made, they are still wonderful, which is a testament to the strength of the drawing and the skill of Rummer in selecting the individual pieces of wood.

Transporting the panels to Lorraine presented problems. They were packed in two wood crates weighing 2½ tons. The journey took ten days on difficult roads. Roentgen was paid 1,000 louis d'or (an amount equal to 24,000 livres—this at a time when a carpenter might earn 1½ livre daily and a master craftsman, such as a goldsmith, only twice that). Only fifteen years after they were built, they were sold, with the bureau, to Duke Albert of Saxe-Teschen, who had all the work moved to Austria. They are now displayed in the Museum für Angewandt Kunst in Vienna.

In 1783 Roentgen undertook an arduous trip to St. Petersburg to present his work to Catherine the Great. He had a letter of recommendation from a German baron, who described David as "the best ébéniste-mécanicien of the century." He brought a secrétaire à cylindre. The Empress wanted it, and not only paid the asking price of 20,000 rubles, but gave him an extra

5,000 rubles to show her appreciation. Three years later Catherine commissioned fifty pieces of furniture, with a value of 72,700 rubles.

Roentgen continued to sell his furniture at the fairs in Frankfurt, Hamburg, and Leipzig. This was an extraordinary international business enterprise, especially considering that it had stemmed from a workshop his father had begun using borrowed tools. In 1770 David employed fifteen workers: his father, four brothers, seven journeymen, a mechanic, a clockmaker, and an apprentice. In 1779 there were twenty-four workers, as well as numerous subcontractors. It was an administrative challenge running a far-flung business at this time, given the difficulty of travel. When he went to Russia, for instance, it meant an absence of many months. Shipping fragile pieces with delicate mechanical parts presented other problems. And the supply of essential exotic materials was often uncertain.

At around this time Marie Antoinette commissioned a secrétaire to give to the Pope. Curiously, the marquetry motif is of Chinese people. Europeans were just beginning to take an interest in Asia, a result of growing world trade. A great deal of furniture inspired by Chinese themes was being built in England. The piece for the Pope foreshadowed later work Roentgen did in using pictures presumed to depict Chinese life. One of those pieces is a cylinder desk now in the collection of the Metropolitan Museum (figure 144). The cabinetwork features the mechanical parts (cylinder top and cleverly hinged drawers), for which Roentgen was famous. The cabinetry is in the Louis XVI style that was fashionably European, yet the marquetry decoration is Chinese.

David was a religious man, whose faith would have met a deaf ear with many. Yet proselytizing was an important part of the Herrnhuter sect. He often brought up his beliefs with others, whether they were interested or not. The Empress Catherine complained that "he wanted to Herrnhutize the entire Hermitage. There is too much

143. THE MAGNANIMITY OF SCIPIO (1779) DESIGNED BY JANUARIUS ZICK, MADE BY DAVID ROENTGEN
Marquetry of various woods; 140½ × 147 in.
Austrian Museum of Applied Arts, Vienna; Photo: Georg Mayer/MAK

144. CYLINDER-FALL DESK WITH CABINET TOP (c. 1776–78) DAVID ROENTGEN
Oak and cherry, and marquetry; 53½ × 43½ × 26½ in.
The Metropolitan Museum of Art, New York; Rogers Fund, 1941 (inv. 41.82);
Photo: Metropolitan Museum of Art

sell everything to avoid bankruptcy. The man who was hailed as the finest furniture maker of his age died two years later in relative poverty. However, his influence was felt for years through the numerous workers, dispersed throughout Europe, who had trained in his workshops and continued to build furniture in the Roentgen style.

The work of the father and son should be seen as a whole. The furniture encompasses a great variety of styles. Their careers spanned almost three-quarters of a century, during which time values, including aesthetics, changed radically throughout Europe. Both Abraham and David adapted to whatever was current. David built objects that catered to sophisticated tastes, and also were made with great integrity and attention to detail. Buyers were enamored with his knack for cleaver mechanisms and hidden compartments, as well as his ability to decorate surfaces with skillfully cut marquetry. The marquetry designs ranged from elaborate floral decorations, reminiscent of the

about sheep and lambs in his religion and he failed to arouse our interest in his faith. So he got his payment, gave us the keys, and took away his preaching. With him gone, boredom has gone as well." It seems that Roentgen risked alienating potential clients with his preaching, but his furniture held such allure that customers put up with this disagreeable part of his personality.

The world of French society was turned upside down by the events of 1789 and the ensuing Revolution. Roentgen's sales agent was forced to close his operation in Paris in 1790. In 1791 all of Roentgen's stock was confiscated. Not only was Roentgen's business in France ruined, but the revolution sent shock waves throughout the European economies. France's military expansionism into other parts of Europe forced Roentgen to leave Neuwid in 1795 and seek relative safety further east. He was not able to return until 1802. Business was never the same. In 1805 Roentgen was forced to

145. COMMEDIA DELL'ARTE COMMODE (c.1775–79) DAVID ROENTGEN
Oak, pine, basswood, cherry, and marquetry; 35¼ × 53½ × 27¼ in.
Victoria and Albert Museum, London

work of Oeben or even earlier Dutch work, to motifs in the then popular style known as chinoiserie.

David made brilliant use of figurative elements, such as scenes from the improvisational Italian comedy theater, *Commedia dell'arte* (figure 145). The renderings are simple yet very expressive. Credit must go to Zick for the drawings. He had to know what would be possible for an excellent marqueteur such as Michael Rummer to actually cut. The people are strikingly depicted in two or three tones. The folds in fabric are richly shown, with an equally small number of pieces of wood. Reminiscent of paintings, these woodworks remain true to the character of the medium. The grain in many of the pieces is prominent, for instance in the Romans and Carthaginians panel. The background is a figured cut of veneer. One of the woods Roentgen favored was walnut for the variety of tone and figure available. He used maple for the same reasons. Burls and occasionally exotic woods like rosewood found their way into panels. The fact that Roentgen was also trained in marquetry by his father gave him the sensitivity to design an object that would maximize the decorative aspect of the work.

The decades after the Revolution eroded the fame that had come to Roentgen. Much of the furniture purchased by French aristocrats was dispersed in the desire to raise money. Many of these objects found their way to English and German collections. By 1900 Roentgen's name was largely forgotten. It was only through the work of scholars and connoisseurs that his work began to be catalogued. His stature has been steadily rising since the 1920s. One of the champions of Roentgen was the Modernist Viennese architect Adolf Loos, who said, "David Roentgen has been an idol throughout my life." Now the furniture can be found prominently displayed in museums around the world. These public collections are allowing many thousands of people to encounter the creations of this furniture genius.

ϾϿ

DETAIL OF FIGURE 151: COMMODE (1770–80) ATTRIBUTED TO WILLIAM MOORE OF DUBLIN
Inlaid with satinwood, tulipwood, burr, walnut & holly; probably Irish (Dublin)
Photo: V&A Images/Victoria and Albert Museum

The English Civil Wars, which lasted until 1651, inhibited extravagant investment in the arts. With the end of the conflict, the economy made a strong recovery. Marquetry had come to England in much the same way it had come to France. The craftsmen followed wealth. As English power grew and the country accumulated riches from its empire, skilled workers were attracted from other parts of Europe. In 1688 a Dutchman, William of Orange, acceded to the British throne. This opened the way for many talented Dutch woodworkers to emigrate.

In 1685 the Edict of Nantes was revoked and Catholicism was established as the state religion in France. Celebrated Huguenot cabinetmakers,

such as Daniel Marot, no longer felt welcome in France but were given opportunities in Holland and England. Marot was summoned to London by Queen Mary in 1702, and he brought a group of talented workers with him. Mary gave work to Marot's cousin, Cornelius Golle. Golle was the younger brother of Pierre Golle, who had done such remarkable work for the French aristocracy.

Another of the workers who came to England at the same time and was influenced by Marot, was a young Flemish artisan named Gerritt Jensen. Jensen worked for the London firm of Lawson and Trotter. He added his excellent marquetry to some wonderful pieces that proved influential in later

English design. Jensen was an excellent marqueteur and was skilled at an intricate decoration called *seaweed marquetry*. The look is derived from an equivalently balanced figure/ground relationship, similar to that of the Boulle work becoming popular in France at about the same time. From a cabinetmaker's perspective the major difference is that using wood instead of metal makes the process much easier. At the same time there is no denying the engaging decorative effect of the seaweed marquetry (figure 146).

The Metropolitan Museum in New York has a particularly fine example of a piece decorated with seaweed marquetry (figure 147). It is a cabinet with doors covering a set of small drawers. All of the parts, inside and out, are decorated with seaweed of walnut and holly, with a darker walnut burl used to frame the marquetry. The holly is

accentuated with sand shading. The marquetry on the doors was cut in packs of two pieces of holly and two of walnut, making two complete patterns, which were joined in bookmatched parts. This is distinguished from Boulle work because the counterparts of walnut in holly were not used. Also, these wood veneers were much easier to cut

146. THE LAWSON TROTTER CABINET (C. 1700) POSSIBLY MADE BY JOHN BYFIELD
Walnut veneer, marquetry of burr walnut, sycamore, holly, pine & oak carcase; English (possibly London)
Victoria and Albert Museum, London

than the tortoiseshell and brass of Boulle work.

About the same time the Metropolitan Museum's seaweed cabinet was made a decorative technique of cutting wood "oysters" was imported to England from Holland. To make oysters, a branch of a tree with a heartwood/sapwood contrast is sawn like a loaf of bread into thin veneers (see Appendix 3: Banding). These nearly identical disks are then arranged into a parquetry pattern to decorate a surface. If a limb is cut perpendicular to the growth, the resulting veneers are circular. If the limb is cut at an angle, the growth rings are elongated into an elliptical shape. The designer can take advantage of these differences.

Not every species of wood can be successfully used for oysters. The Dutch and English craftsmen settled on a few different kinds, such as walnut, laburnum, and lignum vitae. These woods all exhibit a distinct difference between the heartwood and the sapwood and therefore are graphically attractive. Also, these woods are all relatively stable and can be cut and dried with minimal risk of checking or cracking.

A cabinet in the Rijksmuseum in Amsterdam decorated with oysters (figure 148). is typical of Dutch pieces of the era, with simple shaping of the structural members and big flat panels for the carcase. But the oyster work makes this cabinet unique. The design uses several large, dark round oysters surrounded by lighter elongated oysters. The composition looks like an array of giant sunflowers. The petals of the motifs are lighter because the elongated oysters have more sapwood. The angled cut also produces more side grain, which is lighter than endgrain. Notice the running frieze of circular disks on the apron. Even the cornice molding is veneered with oysters.

These Anglo-Dutch pieces appear subdued compared to the pieces being built for the French court at the same time. This may reflect the Protestant attempt at restraint. Certainly if

147. Cabinet on a stand (c. 1700)
Pine veneered w/ marquetry of walnut, walnut burl, and holly; 62¼ × 45¼ × 21 in.
Metropolitan Museum of Art, New York; From the Marion E. and Leonards Cohn Collection, bequest of Marion E. Cohn, 1966 (inv. 66.64.15); Photo: Metropolitan Museum of Art

stripped of the oysters, the pieces are very plain. Perhaps this was a conservative way for the cabinetmaker to add interest to and personalize the piece. It is also reasonable to assume that cabinetmakers saw the oysters as an economical way to enrich a project, pleasing the client without extraordinary effort.

In America we think of Thomas Chippendale as the most important furniture designer. His pattern books helped generate designs for decades up and down the Atlantic coast. But Chippendale's designs were much broader than the carved mahogany pieces that most commonly spring to the American mind.

148. OYSTER CABINET (1680–1700) MAKER UNKNOWN
Oak, cedar, olivewood; 82½ × 69½ × 24½ in.
Rijksmuseum, Amsterdam; Photo: Rijksmuseum

Diana complete the classical theme. The skin tones are done in ivory, highlighting the figures. When it was made, this was the most expensive piece of furniture ever produced in the Chippendale workshops. The cost was 86 pounds sterling. At the time a skilled worker in the building trades would earn approximately 35 pounds per year.

English designers of the late 1700s followed Chippendale's lead, incorporating marquetry on elegant pieces made for an aristocratic clientele. An influential firm, Mayhew and Ince frequently featured marquetry on their furniture. Around 1770 they built a delightful commode that took inspiration from the continent (figure 150). On first glance it would be difficult to distinguish it from luxurious furniture being built in France. The marquetry is

149. DIANA AND MINERVA COMMODE (1773) THOMAS CHIPPENDALE
Satinwood and marquetry of wood and ivory; 27½ × 86 × 37 in.
Reproduced by kind permission of the Earl and Countess of Harewood and the trustees of the Harewood House Trust

Chippendale was born in 1718 in northern England. When he was thirty, he traveled to London to improve his prospects. Six years after arriving, he published *The Gentleman's and Cabinetmaker's Directory*. The book proved very popular, and the designs were widely emulated throughout England. As his fame grew, he received commissions for furniture, and he was asked to work on the interiors of elegant homes that were designed by celebrated architects, among them, Robert Adam. One of Adam's projects was Harewood House in Yorkshire, built in the early 1770s. Adam contacted Chippendale, who built a stunning dressing commode with very elaborate veneering and marquetry for one of the bedrooms (figure 149).

The furniture fits the neoclassical style of Adam's architecture. The front center of the piece is a complicated concave form with radiating veneers of satinwood. Marquetry ribbons and ties across the drawer fronts are done in a wood dark enough to stand out against the satinwood stand without being distracting. Two marquetry medallions on the side doors picturing Minerva and

150. COMMODE (C. 1770-80) ATTRIBUTED TO JOHN MAYHEW; ATTRIBUTED TO WILLIAM INCE
Pine veneered with satinwood, kingwood, holly, rosewood and other woods, gilt bronze mounts, marble slab; 38 × 54 × 28 in.
The Metropolitan Museum of Art, New York; Gift of Irwin Untermyer, 1964 (inv. 64.101.1145); Photo: Metropolitan Museum of Art

151. COMMODE (1770–80) ATTRIBUTED TO WILLIAM MOORE OF DUBLIN
Inlaid with satinwood, tulipwood, burr, walnut & holly; probably Irish (Dublin)
Victoria and Albert Museum, London; Photo: V&A Images/Victoria and Albert Museum

152. DESK (C. 1780–1790) ENGLISH
Mahogany, satinwood, and marquetry; 36 × 28 × 16½ in.
Metropolitan Museum of Art, New York; Photo: Metropolitan Museum of Art

classical, with Corinthian columns as elements. Garlands and urns and an unusual border frieze run below the marble top.

Mayhew and Ince were instrumental in spreading marquetry within the British Isles. One of the workers trained in marquetry at the firm, William Moore, went on to a successful career in Ireland, where he produced furniture with marquetry in the current styles (figure 151).

Other great English designers, such as George Hepplewhite also called for marquetry in their designs. His work is well regarded for its elegance, and marquetry was a tool he used to accentuate the sophistication. Hepplewhite furniture uses a lot of satinwood. This gorgeous golden wood is a wonderful ground for marquetry. The Hepplewhite pattern book shows various inlaid motifs, such as garlands and ribbons. Some bandings feature darker woods, including kingwood, rosewood, and mahogany.

A lovely example of Hepplewhite furniture that used marquetry is his tamboured writing desk from the 1780s (figure 152). The shape of the piece is restrained, with straight tapered legs veneered and decorated with marquetry bell flowers. A delicate classical urn-and-wreath motif accents the drawer fronts and sides. Within the arch on the side is a mythological representation. Hepplewhite was most interested in producing pieces of light appearance. Using satinwood goes a long way in lightening a piece. The tapered legs, veneered with satinwood, can be made relatively thin. This design gives a nod to the furniture of Louis XVI, but has clearly come into its own as an English style. With the publication of his *Cabinet Maker and Upholsterer's Guide*, Hepplewhite's influence reached throughout Britain and ultimately into America. American furniture of the Federal period obviously draws on Hepplewhite, as simple marquetry motifs like bellflowers and shells became common decorative features.

Returning home from Paris in 1988, I was anxious to try some of the techniques I had learned at the École Boulle, such as marquetry cut piece by piece. I arranged with Gallery Henoch in New York to have a show the following year, which gave me enough time to design some pieces with the methods in mind.

Before I could really do anything with the techniques I had learned, we needed to build a chevalet. I had bought the hardware for the tool in Paris. My associate Tim Faner was excited about building it (figure 110). He followed the plans in the back of Pierre's book, *La Marqueterie.* The tool was every bit as good as those at the École Boulle, and it was fun to use. It felt like having a piece of history, bringing the old world tradition to our shop.

The first piece we did using the piece-by-piece method was a dining room buffet I named *Formication* (figure 153). The marquetry design was simple: a series of ants in silhouette, marching across the front and sides. Using the piece-by-piece cutting method, multiple copies of the same motif could be efficiently produced. In fact, my usual method of bevel cutting would have been disadvantageous in making exact replicate parts. Riesener exploited this characteristic. He designed objects where a small motif could be pieced together to make bigger panels (figures 136 and 137). In the case of *Formication*, I made 108 identical parts, by cutting nine sets of twelve ants each. The background is curly maple and the ants are cut from brazilwood, in both left-facing and right-facing

153. FORMICATION (1991) SILAS KOPF
Maple, brazilwood, and padauk; 45 × 71 × 22 in.
Photo: Dean Powell

154. ARGUS (1992) SILAS KOPF
Walnut, curly maple, curly ash, and marquetry; 73 × 32 × 22 in.
Photo: David Ryan

orientations. In half, the background grain goes vertically; in the other half, the background goes horizontally. Half of the ants are glued to pieces of wood about ⅜ inch thick, then edge-banded with solid maple. These tiles, glued on to the panel, create a checkerboard pattern, with every other rectangle in relief. The piece was further complicated by making the front faceted, the three sets of doors being at a slight angle to one another.

The second piece we did using the chevalet involved slightly more complicated marquetry (figure 154). Named *Argus*, after the Greek god who had a thousand eyes and never slept, the cabinet is designed to watch over a room from a corner. I thought it might be an interesting piece for an ophthalmologist or perhaps a paranoiac who needs to get over being stared at. As with *Formication* the pattern is composed of tiles, pieced together in a checkerboard.

155. Bees and Tulips (2005) Silas Kopf
Machiche, zircote, African beech, thuya burl, and marquetry;
32 × 48 × 18 in.
Photo: David Ryan

Each eye is composed of fifteen pieces, including one not much larger than a grain of rice, used for the highlight on the iris and pupil. There are 120 marquetry images—sixty left eyes and sixty right eyes. The cabinet has ten vertical rows set at nine degrees to one another and coopered to create the quarter circle. The background for the eyes is again curly maple and the plain rectangles are curly ash. The frame wood is walnut.

The piece *Bees and Tulips* is a further evolution of the concepts explored in *Formication* and *Argus* (figure 155). I again used the chevalet to cut marquetry motifs to use as tiles that could cover a larger surface. Here the design was of honeybees laid into a rich thuya burl background. The pictures of the bees were assembled in a checkerboard pattern with plain rectangles of a lighter colored African beechwood. The doors of the cabinet are

156. SCHOOL DESK (1989) SILAS KOPF
Maple, curly maple, walnut, and marquetry; 29½ × 66½ × 34½ in.
Photo: Dean Powell

decorated with a repeated motif along with the one-of-a-kind picture in much the same way Riesener surrounded complex pictures with repeated themes.

Before going to Paris, I had made several pieces with a repeated motif, cut using the bevel method. I designed these pieces trying not to be as painterly as I had been but rather more broadly decorative. The first is a very complicated desk with fish swimming around the skirt and up and over the drawer front (figure 156). Each fish is composed of fourteen pieces of wood. For each body I chose a piece of veneer with a very tight fleck to it, either sycamore or lacewood. The fins are all in straight-grain ash. Because the fish overlap, only a few are visible in their entirety. I felt it made more sense to cut the fish as a bevel project. (Later, I did cut a similar project partially in a packet. I cut out all the fish and assembled them piece by piece, then cut them into the background using the bevel method.) The desk has six legs. This way, the individual panels could be sized to fit on my saw.

At the time I was using a fretsaw with a 24-inch throat. Therefore, in cutting parts into the background nothing can be more than 24 inches to the nearest edge. In

the desk the biggest panel was the one opposite the knee hole, and it was about 26 inches. I was able to cut the fish only at the ends of the panel by starting the cut and going as far as I could. I then stopped, withdrew the saw blade, and went back to the outside again. But before resuming the cut, I tilted the table from the right to the left. This reversal of both direction and tilt produces the same bevel, and the part will fit perfectly. There are several fish at either end that needed this treatment. By the time I had worked my way into the interior of the panel, I was able to complete the whole circumferential cut, and not run into the arm of the saw.

We built a fall front desk with a repeated pattern: twenty-two faces and hands, done in panels placed in juxtaposition to one another (figure 157). The background is a dark rosewood, and the flesh tones are primarily maple, so the figure/ground relationship is very strong.

My intent was to create a regimented look, where the repetition would make a compelling pattern in its own right. Repetition is carried through to the architecture of the desk and the chair. A series of vertical components between the legs creates a rhythm similar to that of the marquetry. Horizontal bands of geometric parquetry border the figurative elements, appearing also on the chair at seat level. We didn't make this banding. It was made in France by a company that specialized in these decorative elements prior to World War II. They had gone out of business, and the entire inventory was purchased by Lee Valley Tools in Canada. Lee Valley wanted to publicize these unusual old bandings, and they asked me to incorporate some in a design. This desk, with its repeated marquetry motif, seemed like an ideal candidate. The banding was made in the traditional way, using side grain rather than end grain (see Appendix 3: Banding). The

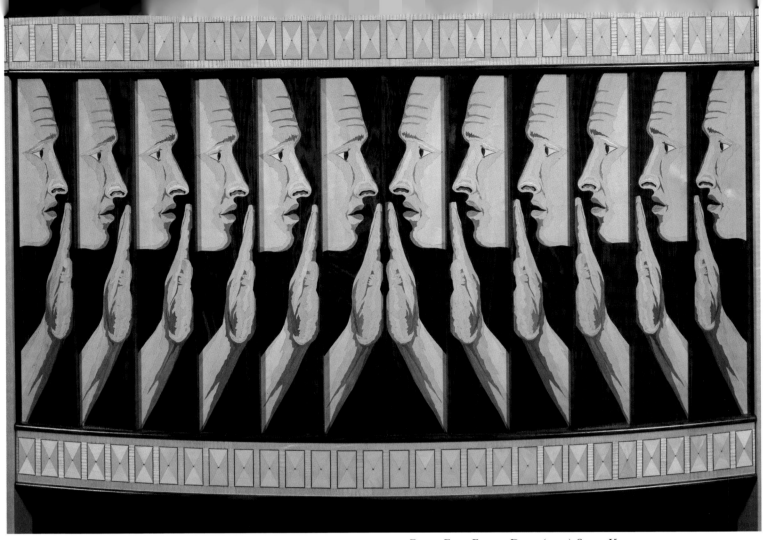

157. FACES FALL FRONT DESK (1991) SILAS KOPF
Maple, parquetry, and marquetry; 48 × 48 × 20 in.
Photos: Dean Powell

technique goes back to the Italian *toppo a tarsia*. This particular banding was made in both a lighter and a darker version. I chose the one that used maple.

Piece-by-piece and toppo marquetry both efficiently yield multiples of a marquetry design. One of the most interesting evolutions of the ancient toppo method for making multiple motifs was developed in England in the area around Tunbridge Wells. In Tunbridgeware geometric designs are created by gluing together longer sticks of contrasting material to produce a pattern in the end grain. This is similar to Italian toppo but more intricate. Parts of a Tunbridge loaf could be as small as $\frac{1}{32}$ inch in section. The effect is a pointillist picture, all the tiny parts blending together when viewed from a distance (figure 158).

Tunbridgeware first appeared in the late 1600s. The initial designs were simple checkerboard patterns made with large square sections. Sometimes the components would be glued up into blocks that were turned on a lathe, making the geometric design into a bowl. By the 1800s the designs were being made more and more intricate. Given the huge effort involved in preparing the block, it only made sense to re-cut the loaf into veneers to maximize the square footage.

The finest Tunbridgeware would start with a drawing larger than the finished picture was to be. The design would be graphed into squares. If the final squares were to be $\frac{1}{32}$ inch and the picture was to be 6 inches by 6 inches, then the total would be an astonishing 36,864 tiny squares: 192 squares across the width and 192 squares along the height of the picture. Each square is assigned a species (or color). Pieces of $\frac{1}{32}$-inch veneer, about 18 inches long and 1 inch wide, are cut in the various woods to be used. The stack of 192 veneer is glued together in the scheme for one row. That block, about one inch thick, is sawn in the other direction, creating a $\frac{1}{32}$-inch veneer six inches wide, with a sequence of stripes running the entire length. The

To gain real-world experience, the teaching program of the École Boulle has each student be an apprentice in a working shop before graduating. One of the French students I met during my stay in Paris inquired about the possibility of spending two months with me toward the end of his time at the school. I remembered him as a talented marqueteur. We had the chevalet, and the young man would at least feel at home with the tools, if not the style of working. I designed a chest of drawers with a traditional parquetry pattern called *fish scale* (figure 159). I wanted strong-grained woods, and chose oak and ash. We cut half the pieces in each species horizontally, the other half vertically. This way the neighboring parts of the same

158. TABLE DESK OR WRITING BOX (1830–70)
Rosewood, with marquetry of various woods
Tunbridge ware; English (Tunbridge Wells, Kent)
V&A Images/Victoria and Albert Museum

subsequent rows are all created in the same way. These rows are then carefully glued together into ten identical blocks. The 18-inch loafs could then be sawn into veneers, with each slice yielding the same picture. An 18-inch loaf might yield 180 pictures, and therefore the entire process could produce about 1,800 pictures, each one 6 inches square. The description of the process sounds tremendously laborious, but when you consider the final yield, it's worth the effort.

ৎ৩

species would be distinguished from one another. We assembled the parts in a chevron pattern with the V meeting in the middle. The pattern repeats, running over all the drawer fronts as well as the sides.

Too often, drawer handles and knobs are afterthoughts on handmade furniture, and they look it. I had a local metalworker fabricate the drawer pulls out of brass in the shape of a fish scale. We then made an ebony piece slightly bigger to go behind the metal. These were then mounted in places directly on top of one of the wooden parquetry

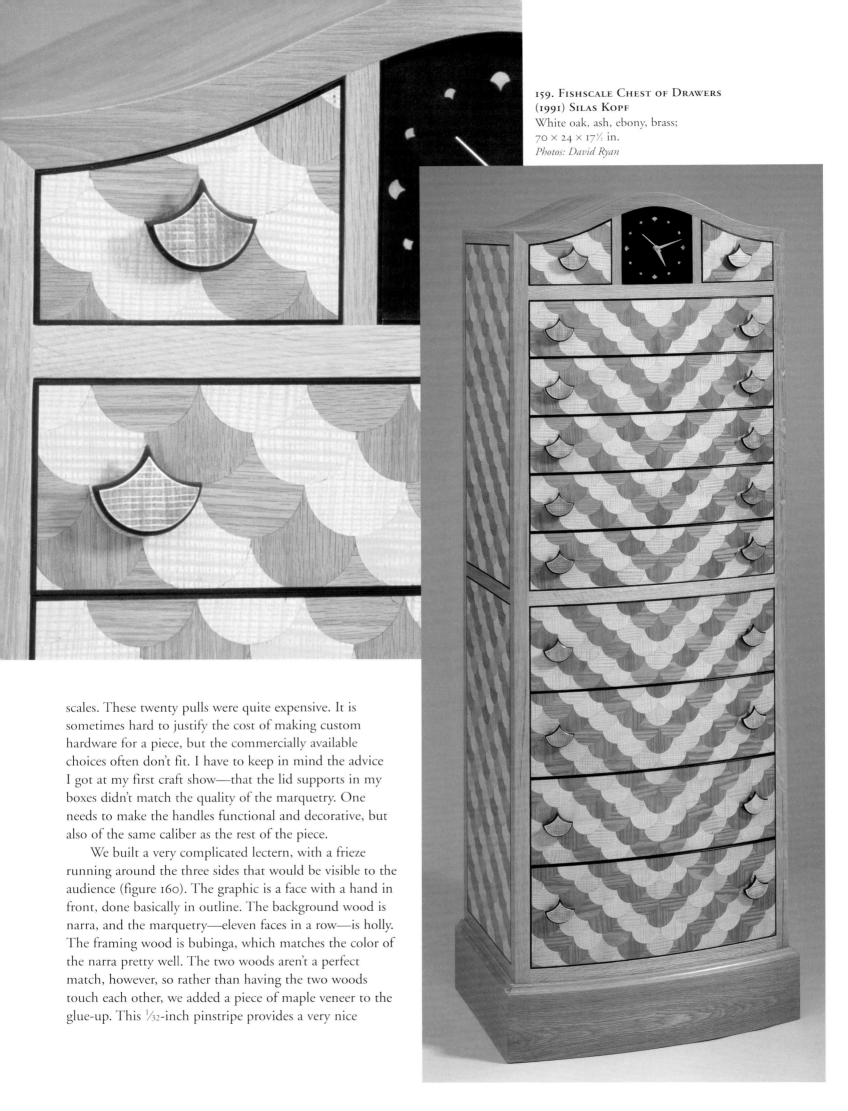

159. FISHSCALE CHEST OF DRAWERS
(1991) SILAS KOPF
White oak, ash, ebony, brass;
70 × 24 × 17½ in.
Photos: David Ryan

scales. These twenty pulls were quite expensive. It is sometimes hard to justify the cost of making custom hardware for a piece, but the commercially available choices often don't fit. I have to keep in mind the advice I got at my first craft show—that the lid supports in my boxes didn't match the quality of the marquetry. One needs to make the handles functional and decorative, but also of the same caliber as the rest of the piece.

We built a very complicated lectern, with a frieze running around the three sides that would be visible to the audience (figure 160). The graphic is a face with a hand in front, done basically in outline. The background wood is narra, and the marquetry—eleven faces in a row—is holly. The framing wood is bubinga, which matches the color of the narra pretty well. The two woods aren't a perfect match, however, so rather than having the two woods touch each other, we added a piece of maple veneer to the glue-up. This ⅟₃₂-inch pinstripe provides a very nice decorative element. The casual observer might wonder, "How did they rout that little line?" It's a technique that I have returned to again and again. A line the thickness of veneer looks very delicate (and difficult to do if it is inlaid). This easier alternative sets off a panel from its frame by adding a subtle extra border between parts.

Boulle work generally uses two contrasting materials; the marquetry of the lectern played off the contrast of holly and narra. *Urban Theme (Life Is A Rat Race)* also uses two veneers (figure 161). The ebony creates a bold graphic pattern on the golden avodire. The intent was to make the black look like ink-brush calligraphy, in a repeated motif of rats running up an incline.

We built several pieces using a very different graphic approach to the marquetry. The method was to have a base wood and then make it look cracked with fine black lines cut into it. The first of these pieces was *Parabola*

160. **LECTERN WITH FACES (1991) SILAS KOPF**
Padauk, bubinga, holly; 47 × 25 × 17 in.
Photo: David Ryan

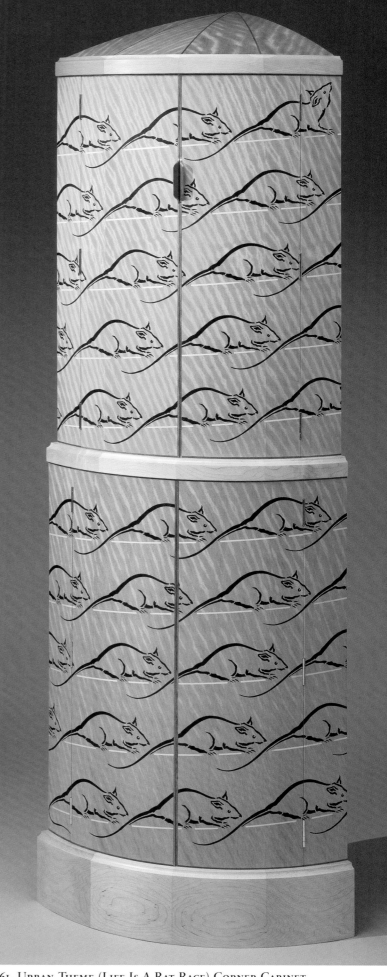

161. **URBAN THEME (LIFE IS A RAT RACE) CORNER CABINET (1995) SILAS KOPF**
Avodire, dyed pearwood, holly; 74 × 19 × 19 in.
Photo: Dean Powell

(figure 163). We built a mold to bend each of the sides. The core was ⅛-inch poplar plywood, which bends nicely and also glues well. It was a problem bending the wood at the very top where the curve is the tightest, but we were able to get the two parts bent. I then laid out a sheet of satinwood veneer and drew random lines on the surface where the cracks would be. It was to look as if the satinwood had shrunk, like the crackled glaze that ceramicists get when a top coat shrinks and reveals the underglaze. The pieces of satinwood (between the cracks) are largest at the bottom, decreasing in size toward the top. They're most dense in the upper right of the front,

163. PARABOLA (1992) SILAS KOPF
Satinwood and ebonized maple; 64 × 34 × 14 in.
Photo: Kevin Downey

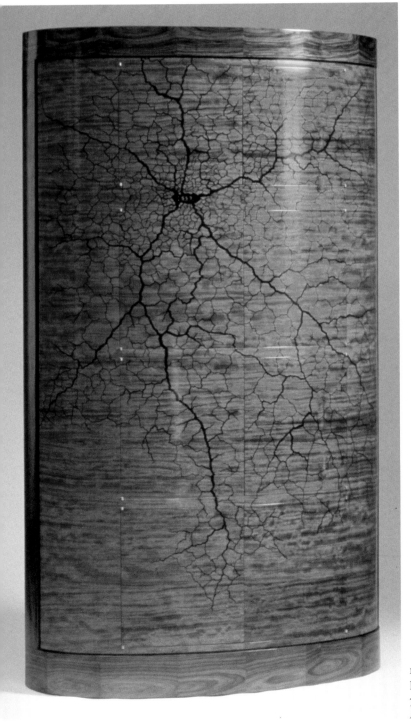

162. CRACKED (1994) SILAS KOPF
Bubinga, ebonized maple, and chechen;
77 × 40 × 15 in.
Photo: Kevin Downey

where they narrow to a black hole. Inside the hole is a digital clock. The framing material is ebonized walnut.

Parabola spurred another piece, called *Cracked* (figure 162). Here the intent was to have the wood look not as if it had shrunk but rather shattered, as if a bullet had struck the surface and radiated cracks from that point. For the veneer I chose a spectacular bubinga. The surfaces are much larger than those of *Parabola*. I wanted the piece to be a celebration of the wood as much as anything, so it needed a particularly striking wood. The bubinga fit the bill perfectly. *Cracked* was also inspired by a cabinet designed by Jacques-Émile Ruhlmann in the 1920s (figure 174). This piece had an abstract marquetry decoration consisting of a series of interlocking circles. I admired the simplicity of the concept, while I also found Ruhlmann's result very satisfying. I was hoping for a similar result with my use of the black pattern on the bubinga.

❧

Some time in the 1970s I read an article in a science magazine about the destruction of the rainforests. Despite their lush look, it turns out, these tropical lands are not very fertile. The nutrients of the ecosystem are tied up in the canopy of trees. The heat and moisture break down any vegetation that falls to the forest floor, and the food to keep the vegetation growing is quickly sucked back up for further growth. If (or when) the trees are removed, the earth quickly becomes barren. Large tracts of land that are de-forested for agriculture become useless for growing anything after only a few years. Then the farmer is forced to clear new land. The article painted a frightening picture of a future without rainforests, without the wealth of species (plant and animal) that exist only in that environment.

The article was an eye-opener for me, more than thirty years ago, when the environmental movement was just beginning to grow. Ideas that now have widespread acceptance were then somewhat revolutionary.

The blame for rainforest destruction was pointed at agriculture, but logging made a significant contribution to the problem. Logging roads often would be the first incursion into the forest, allowing agricultural opportunists to exploit areas otherwise inaccessible.

Marquetry requires the use of a wide variety of species, with a diversity of color and grain. Tropical woods are an important part of the palette. I started to wonder what my complicity was in the destruction of rainforests, by using and celebrating tropical woods. I became concerned that some tropical woods might become as endangered as ivory (which also had a long, storied use in furniture making). The 1970s saw a lot of publicity about the declining elephant population. Poaching for tusks became a serious concern and led to a boycott of ivory. I could imagine a similar client reaction to tropical woods.

Some people felt that furniture craftsmen should boycott tropical wood. I had hoped for a middle ground, where we could find sources for exotic lumber that would not be a part of the deforestation problem. How much more would I be willing to pay for lumber that was ecologically harvested? The model is the organic produce market. If you're willing, you can buy carrots grown without chemical fertilizer and pesticides, but you will have to pay a premium. The goal was forest sustainability. Only enough timber should be extracted to allow the forest to sustain itself indefinitely. At the same time, there was no existing market in sustainably harvested lumber.

I was not the end user of the tropical wood but a middle man in the process. Would I lose customers by not using a species with a proven appeal? I thought the choice should be my client's.

Even if I could find sustainably harvested wood, I wondered if my clients would be willing to pay the premium. With no such wood currently on the market, I decided that closest I could come would be to "tax" the use of tropical wood and then make a donation to forest preservation. I suppose my dream was to have a preserve supported by the contributions of American woodworkers. The model is the Children's Rainforest in Costa Rica. Land was being purchased through donations by American schoolchildren to be set aside as a reserve. It was to be like a privatized national park. Perhaps there could be a Cabinetmaker's Rainforest somewhere. I printed up some simple flyers to hand out to clients. It informed them of the problem in the tropical forests and engaged them in a possible solution: if they wanted a piece in tropical wood, a surcharge would go toward conservation. The name I chose to put on the flyer was Woodworkers Against Rainforest Destruction (WARD).

A trade publication, *Woodshop News,* publicized the idea. Not long after, I was contacted by Scott Landis, who had written an article for *Fine Woodworking* about a forestry project in Peru. The thrust of that effort was to find use for lesser known species as a way of relieving pressure on the forest. In extracting a timber like mahogany, which had a ready market in the developed world, many logs of other species were damaged or felled and left to rot because they couldn't be sold. These timbers were unknown in lumber yards in the U.S. The hope was to create a demand for them, and thereby use less of the valued wood. Interestingly, this effort was being spurred in California by a woodworker, John Shipstad, whom I had met years earlier when he had been a student at the Leeds Design Workshops.

Scott wanted to assemble a group of people interested in forest ecology, and see if there was any possibility of joining forces. We got together in New York City for an all-day meeting. John Shipstad came from California, along with the lumber dealer who was going to sell the wood from Peru. Also attending was a wood dealer from Canada, representatives from the World Wildlife Fund and from the Rainforest Alliance, a tool dealer from Canada, and a forest biologist from the University of Maine.

As the day progressed, it became apparent that information available about tropical forest ecology was limited, and conflicting. The group could not make a decision on how to be proactive. We first needed to get on the same page about the situation in the forests. We decided to hold a conference and bring together experts in the field to address various issues.

The group needed a name. The debate was long, and people had strong opinions on all sides. Many felt that Woodworkers Against Rainforest Destruction was too negative. Ultimately, we agreed on Woodworkers Alliance for Rainforest Protection (WARP).

The WARP conference needed to be on either the east or west coast to attract the broadest group of presenters and audience. We needed a venue and some money to stage the event. I looked into staging the conference at the University of Massachusetts, just up the road from my home. I had no expertise in forestry, but I could make a contribution handling the logistics of the event.

The conference was held at U Mass about a year and a half after the initial meeting. The most important thing to come out of the conference was to agree that there should be criteria established to define sustainability. Lumber companies that adhered to these criteria would be certified and thereby able to market their product as sustainable. Different groups might define the word differently. There needed to be an overarching group that would certify the certifiers in the forest. This was the seed of an organization that became the Forest Stewardship Council.

WARP would continue to focus on the role of the woodworking community. A newsletter was planned that would tackle issues of sustainable forestry and other subjects of specific interest to furniture makers. The board of directors decided to sponsor an exhibition of furniture with an ecological component, as a way of drawing attention to the issues. Entitled *Conservation By Design,* the exhibition opened in 1993 at the Rhode Island School of Design Museum and subsequently traveled to three other venues.

I built a desk for the show (figure 164). The previous summer a hurricane had come through New England, immediately after which I received a phone call from a man in a neighboring town, wondering if I wanted to salvage the lumber from a large walnut tree of his, lost to the storm. I told him that the trunk was a little more than I was ready to tackle, but I would like to get some of the limbs. I had seen photos of antique furniture that used oysters and wanted to try making something with the technique. This looked like an ideal opportunity.

Walnut is an ideal wood for oysters. It has a strong heartwood/sapwood contrast, which emphasizes the growth rings of the tree when cut cross-grain. Walnut is also a relatively stable wood. The limb is cut into pieces to a thickness a little less than $\frac{1}{16}$ inch. Then they have to be stickered and dried. In drying, the discs will distort like potato chips but not crack. Then they have to be flattened, in much the same manner as a burl.

When veneers are cut, they are flat but saturated with moisture. In drying, the wood shrinks, mainly across the grain. In highly figured woods, such as a burl, the grain is often multidirectional. This means that the veneer shrinks unevenly. This uneven shrinkage leads to warping and buckling. The buckled pieces can be made useful only by flattening them. To accomplish this, moisture must be re-introduced. Spritzing the veneer with a solution of water and hide glue will soften it. Then the wood can be squeezed flat, slowly (in a press or under weight), until the wood fibers relax back into a flat sheet. Paper placed on both sides of the moistened veneer will wick away some of the water. The glue will help lock the fibers in the flattened state, allowing the veneer to be glued into a panel. The oysters can be worked exactly this way.

I found oysters particularly appropriate for the *Conservation By Design* show. The branches were of such a small diameter that they would have been useful for little more than firewood. I cut some of the limbs at an angle, which lengthens the concentric growth rings into an elliptical shape. I used these on the skirt of the desk. Directly above them on the top I laid out oysters cut perpendicular to the growth, which makes a circular pattern. In effect, it looks as if the perimeter of the desk top were constructed from a series of blocks about 3 inches square and 7 inches long. Technically this would be impossible to do successfully in solid wood, as the blocks would inevitably crack in drying. But with oyster veneers the effect is achievable.

The top of the desk is veneered in bog oak. I thought this was another appropriate wood for the theme of *Conservation by Design*. Bog oak is not tropical, but it is exotic. The tree died naturally so long ago that nothing is taken from the living forest in harvesting it. The drawer knobs are made of tagua nut, which is quite hard and can be worked like wood. It looks very much like ivory, even displaying a similar grain. Tagua is harvested like an agricultural product and is sustainable.

164. Oyster Desk (1992) Silas Kopf
Walnut, bog oak, maple, dyed maple, and tagua nut; 30 × 62 × 25½
Photo: David Ryan

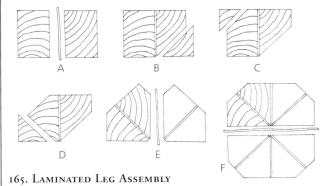

165. Laminated Leg Assembly
A. Glue veneer between 2 pieces of solid stock (repeat 4 times).
B, C, D. Cut 45-degree angles on 3 sides of each assembly.
E. Glue a piece of veneer between 2 pairs of the assemblies.
F. Carefully plane the face back to the point where the 3 veneers meet on both assemblies. Glue a piece of veneer between.

The legs were made by laminating pieces of maple veneer into the parts of the octagon (figure 165). We took two pieces of maple and glued the veneer in the middle. Then we cut a 45-degree angle on the pieces, starting at the veneer. Gluing these two pieces together and another piece of veneer in the middle made four pieces of walnut at 45 degrees to one another, with three pieces of maple veneer separating the solid wood. Finally, two of these

166. Fall Front Desk with Sasha (1994) Silas Kopf
Pucté, ebony, honey locust, and marquetry; $47 \times 29 \times 16\frac{1}{2}$ in.
Photos: David Ryan

parts were glued together, again with a piece of maple veneer between. This made all eight parts; the $\frac{1}{32}$-inch maple lines radiate from the center. We then shaped the parts into octagons and turned the lower section on a lathe. The legs thus look as though they are decorated with very delicate inlays, but in fact no tiny parts were ever cut or assembled.

Over the years the focus of WARP changed. The role of promoting trade in certified wood was taken by a new organization, the Certified Forest Products Council. The program that was of the most interest to those of us on the board was called the GreenWood/MaderaVerde Project in Honduras. The idea behind GreenWood was to have North American woodworkers train local people to build low-technology furniture from certified green wood of lesser known species. The chairs and tables would be a value-added product, leading communities to take an active role in resource preservation. The first training sessions were conducted with the help of two of the board members, Brian Boggs and Curtis Buchanan, professional chair makers from Kentucky and Tennessee, respectively. Brian and Curtis traveled to Honduras and selected species that they thought would be appropriate for greenwood chair making. This work has been going on for a more than a decade now, and the program continues to expand. I am proud to have been a part of this fine effort over the years.

❧

Wood is a precious material that needs to be conserved. The invention of the veneer slicer about 100 years ago forever changed the way that furniture is made industrially. Sliced veneer can be made into large panels of matched material. When I started working in 1973 the standard thickness for veneer in this country was $\frac{1}{28}$ inch. Every few years the standard shrinks. Now, three decades later, a "thick" commercial veneer is $\frac{1}{40}$ inch. Furniture factories are equipped to work with even thinner material. It is difficult for the craftsman to successfully work such material by hand. Marquetry, consisting of various veneers at odd angles that need to be scraped and then sanded, is even more temperamental than thin-veneered cabinetwork. On curved surfaces it is particularly difficult to control the leveling process.

Some species of wood are no longer commercially available. Several of the great cabinet woods of earlier days—Brazilian rosewood, certain ebonies, lignum vitae—are on the CITES (Convention on Trade in Endangered Species) list and are banned from trade. Even mahogany is listed as threatened. It should be a wake-up call to everyone in the woodworking field. We have an obligation to take better care of our resources.

Recently, I have begun sawing my own veneers for marquetry. I regret the necessity of taking this step. Fabricating veneer is time-consuming and wasteful (more than half the wood ends up as sawdust). But the resulting material is superior to the commercially available product. The process of slicing veneers affects the way the wood works. I suspect it's partly because the wood has to be cooked first, and then it is distorted in the peeling process. Sawn veneer has much more integrity than sliced. It doesn't shatter the way some of the sliced sheets do. One disadvantage is that many species can't be found in solid wood for sawing. Certainly there are figures, such as burls, that are hard to find as lumber, and harder still to successfully saw into veneer. It would be a relief if a veneer company supplied thicker material specifically for the craftsman market.

I have come to feel that I make better furniture using thicker veneers. Shouldn't we make objects that are at least as good as those from the past? Does anyone think the commercially available veneers (at $\frac{1}{42}$ inch thick) are as good as the veneers sawn historically? A hundred years ago the standard thickness of veneer (it was sawn, not sliced) was $\frac{1}{20}$ inch, a thickness of material you could actually plane. When I started working in the mid-1970s, most veneer was sliced, and the standard was $\frac{1}{28}$ inch (old-timers complained that it was no longer the previous standard of $\frac{1}{24}$ inch). Over the last thirty years veneer has gotten thinner and thinner. When it reached $\frac{1}{40}$ inch, I finally said, Enough. (It's now $\frac{1}{42}$ inch, and heading thinner.) I find myself now using only older stock that I have hoarded.

I also try to take advantage of found wood. In 1994 I was cutting down a weed tree behind my garage. It was honey locust. I noticed that the heartwood and the sapwood were distinctive and I decided to take the log (which was about five inches in diameter) down to the shop and cut it into oysters. I cut part of it perpendicular to the growth and part of it at about a 45-degree angle. Happily, the veneers dried successfully. As with the walnut oysters used on the *Conservation By Design* desk (figure 164), it was satisfying to save wood that was destined for the firewood pile.

The following year we made a little fall front desk and chair using the honey locust as a border around ebony panels (figure 166). The solid framing members are a lesser-known Mexican wood called pucté. Inside the desk are a pair of doors with a marquetry picture of my daughter, Sasha, posed as if she were sitting at the desk.

Pruning a lilac shrub in my yard led to another discovery. I culled a piece of the lilac about an inch and a half in diameter, and when I looked at the end grain, I thought that the cherrywood-colored heartwood and creamy

167. GAME TABLE FOR CHESS AND GO (1992) SILAS KOPF
Cherry, cherry burl, holly, ebony, and lilac; 30 × 36 × 26 in.
Photo: David Ryan

sapwood might make interesting oysters. Whether they would dry properly was another question. Obviously lilac is too small a diameter to have any use to most furniture-makers. But the effort to cut the oysters wasn't too great and to my delight they dried nicely. The next year I used them on the border of a game table (figure 167).

❧

Many furnituremakers in the 1980s were interested in Art Deco designs. In the late 1970s Wendell Castle did a whole gallery show that paid homage to the great French furniture designer, Jacques-Émile Ruhlmann. The French Art Deco style is particularly beautiful when executed in richly figured wood. Crucial to many of the Art Deco designs is skill at veneering. I had made veneer work the cornerstone of my career. And I, too, was drawn to Art Deco styling.

Although it was sculptural carving that got me interested in furniture, I had put aside my interest in carving and had been doing veneer work for decades. In shifting to more Deco-inspired designs, I put even less emphasis on shaping solid wood parts. I aimed at shaping parts simply and giving more importance to decorative details in the case work.

The first pieces I did with a Deco look have marquetry pictures that are similar to those I did for the earlier Art Nouveau pieces. *Half-Round Cabinet* is a typical example (figure 168). The cabinet has a marquetry door featuring an elaborate picture of a mother bird and a nest in a tree. The carcase itself is a fluted half-column meant to fit against a wall. The bottom section is created by coopering concave plywood panels into a semi-circle: eight pieces, with the middle four forming two doors. The upper case features the centered marquetry door, flanked by two fluted segments on either side. The top is formed by gluing pre-formed plywood wedges into a dome shape. The Deco style is reflected in the rich pommele sapele veneers on the flutes and on the top. Bordering each section is a thin accent line of maple.

Birds have proven to be wonderful subjects for marquetry. I have used them many times as subjects for pictures. In 1996 we built a chest of drawers with another nest and babies (figure 169). I wanted to make the marquetry dense with lots of leaves, hiding the birds. The marquetry decorates a pair of doors placed at eye level, in a manner similar to the Majorelle cabinet (figure 27).

At about the same time we built a sideboard with a Deco-styled carcase (figure 170). Again we used rich veneers, in this case mahogany. The marquetry decorates three pairs of doors. The front is very subtly faceted, with the middle section protruding about 2 inches more than

168. Half Round Cabinet (1988) Silas Kopf
Mahogany, sapele, satinwood, and marquetry; 76 × 26 × 14 in.
Photo: David Ryan

169, FACING PAGE: NEST OF BIRDS CHEST OF DRAWERS (1995) SILAS KOPF
Ebonized cherry, eucalyptus burl, and marquetry; 76 × 30 × 22 in.
Photo: Kevin Downey

170. FLORAL SIDEBOARD (1988) SILAS KOPF
Mahogany, rosewood, and marquetry; 33 × 72 × 17 in.
Photo: David Ryan

the sides. The legs are all octagonal in section and come
to points at the tops. Again, the marquetry doors are done
in the realistic painterly style that I have been using since
my trip to Italy several years earlier.

This combination of realistic marquetry with the
Deco styling of casework wasn't entirely satisfactory. I
spent some time looking at the original Deco work and
tried to decide what it was that had attracted me in the
first place. It was time to go back to the library and check
out some books on the great designers of the 1920s.

⌘

Art Deco

DETAIL OF FIGURE 185: PYRAMID CHEST (2002) SILAS KOPF

The Crystal Palace Exposition which opened in London in 1851 made marketing fairs an important venue for manufacturers to introduce their products to the public in both Europe and North America. The Exposition Universelle in 1900 provided a major opportunity for French designers, such as Gallé, to show their finest furniture. Starting in 1909 several attempts to hold another major decorative arts show failed for one reason or another. The outbreak of World War I in 1914 shelved any possibility of having a fair. It took several years after the war ended for the economy of France to get back on its feet. The pent-up energy made the next expo, in 1925, an exciting event, with a focus on new trends in design in the post-war period. The intent was to show the optimism of the era and display the creative talent that had blossomed in the preceding ten years.

The 1925 Exposition Internationale des Arts Decoratifs et Industriels has given us the name Art Deco. It was very influential and led to interest in the new style throughout Europe and the United States. The look seemed to be steeped in luxury, with designers indulging in the use of rare and exotic materials. In some ways the timing couldn't have been worse for this style, as it was only a few years later that the international economy plummeted with the Great Depression. The ability to market items of luxury shrank. Many of the acclaimed design firms were forced out of business. The social changes brought by the Depression gave rise to a new architectural style that was in conflict with the opulence of Art Deco. The International Style, which was spare and industrial, became the dominant look in architecture for several decades. Influential architects, such as Le Corbusier and Walter Gropius, had little enthusiasm for decorative arts. Luxury items didn't fit their concept of social engineering through design.

Jacques-Émile Ruhlmann

The man who has had the greatest influence on designer-craftsmen of furniture in the last 100 years is undoubtedly Jacques-Émile Ruhlmann. He stood in a long line of great French decorative artists and led the way with innovative ideas, energetic designs, and uncompromising quality. He was a complete *decorateur*, providing clients with a total look for the interior. He designed not only the furniture, but also the draperies, carpets, and hardware.

Ruhlmann was born in 1879. His family had been in the house painting and decorating business in Paris since 1827. His father had become quite successful, and it was natural that Jacques should go into the decorating trade. He began sketching furniture as a young man and first exhibited some of his designs in 1913. His work was well received, but the real excitement in the design world of the time was being generated by the German artists and companies of the Deutscher Werkbund. The French design industry, rooted in the Art Nouveau style, was threatened by this foreign competition. A plan was hatched to hold an exposition in 1915 that would show only

"modern" work, with no reproductions allowed. The hope was that the exhibit would spur French creativity. Ruhlmann's first furniture pieces had identified him as one of the up-and-coming French decorative artists. He certainly had to be included in the exposition. However, World War I intervened and the event was impossible to hold. The fair didn't happen until 1925. This was the celebrated Art

Deco Exposition and Jacques-Émile Ruhlmann became the star of the show.

Ruhlmann's health kept him out of the army during the war; he worked in the family business through those years. Sales of decorative objects were curtailed, but he persisted in sketching furniture. By the time the fighting ended, Ruhlmann was ready to begin production. He turned over the day-to-day running of the house-painting firm (which employed some 500 people) to a partner. The company thrived financially. Ruhlmann used the business's resources to indulge in making luxurious furniture, knowing that the enterprise might or might not be profitable.

Ruhlmann had turned his back on the work of the École de Nancy and the Art Nouveau designs that had dominated French furniture from the 1890s to 1920. He paid more attention to what designers in Germany and Austria were doing before the war. He found attractive the repeated geometric patterns with clean lines in the work of the Viennese designers Josef Hoffman and Koloman Moser. But he never lost touch with the great French tradition of the eighteenth century.

By 1925 Ruhlmann had attracted a well-heeled clientele willing to pay for his creations. And his furniture could be very expensive. A single bed built in 1924 cost 79,000 francs (approximately $3,150). This was more than anyone

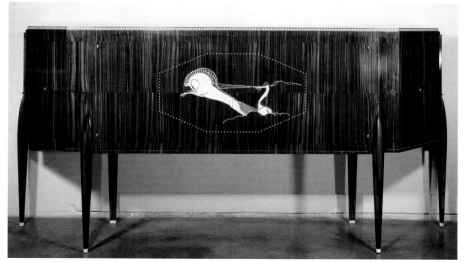

171. SIDEBOARD: MEUBLE DE CHAR (1922) JACQUES-ÉMILE RUHLMANN
Macassar ebony and ivory; 42½ × 89 × 19½ in.
Louvre, Paris; Photo: Réunion des Musées Nationaux/Art Resource, New York

172. CORNER CABINET (1916) JACQUES-ÉMILE RUHLMANN
Rosewood, ivory, and rare woods; 50½ × 33½ × 23¾ in.
Virginia Museum of Fine Arts, Richmond, Va.; Gift of Sydney and Francis Lewis (85.135);
Photo: Katherine Wetzel–Virginia Museum of Fine Arts

Cabinet A (figure 172) is veneered in amboyna burl. The marquetry is a very rich, bold ebony and ivory. Cabinet B (figure 173) is veneered in Macassar ebony, and the vase and flowers are done in ivory and amaranth (purpleheart). The effect of the two cabinets is quite different, simply because of the choice of woods. Each motif has a large area depicting the vase. The spaces between the lines running from bottom to top, demarking the vase segments, are foreshortened at the side. This simple device gives the vase volume. Some of the flowers are mainly in wood, the individual petals depicted by fine lines of ivory. Other flowers are composed oppositely: ivory parts are surrounded by dark lines of ebony or amaranth. The foliage is constructed like the ivory parts of the sideboard. The individual leaf is created by the surrounding dark joints. The marquetry was done not as a Boulle process but piece by piece, to make only one motif. It would be interesting to see what the contra-partie would look like.

These Ruhlmann cabinets were particularly inspiring to me. I liked the stylized design of the flowers and how they were done so beautifully in just a figure/ground relationship. The borders around the parts reminded me of leaded-glass panels. I tried to emulate this effect in a number of my own pieces, finding it particularly apt for Boulle work.

One more Ruhlmann piece is worthy of attention because of its unique marquetry decoration—the Elysée cabinet of 1920 (figure 174). The surfaces are covered with round shapes in ivory on a ground of amboyna burl. The effect is not unlike that of the premiere-partie of Boulle work. The look also resembles the pebbly surface of *galuchat* (shagreen, or sharkskin), which was frequently used in Art Deco design. The circles are of various sizes and look interlocked. They are light and airy and could also be thought of as bubbles rising across the surface. Note the interplay between the small pips of the burl and the large circles of ivory. He used this decoration on a few

was then paying for the finest of the older antiques upon which the French furniture heritage had been built. The pieces were made with luscious materials, such as amboyna burl, Macassar ebony, and tortoiseshell, with accents of ivory. The designs referenced historical French furniture, without being at all imitative. Subtle cabriole legs, for instance, terminate in sleek sabots. The pieces are streamlined, yet luxurious in material and craftsmanship.

A few pieces of Ruhlmann furniture are particularly noteworthy for their floral or figurative marquetry images. During the war Ruhlmann designed a sideboard with an ivory motif of a stylized chariot and female

driver (figure 171). The marquetry is very delicately done. The ivory is pieced together to accentuate the parts of the horses and the woman. Very fine lines of ivory are inlaid into the ebony for the reins and a scarf. Parts are done in outline, such as one of the horse's hooves, the head of the driver, and the horse that is further away. The motif is framed by the series of ivory dots that runs around the image in an octagon.

Ruhlmann's most ambitious marquetry was a series of large vases of flowers used to decorate the doors of six cabinets built over the span of several years. Some of these are triangular corner cabinets with three legs; others have four legs.

173. CORNER CABINET (1923) JACQUES-ÉMILE RUHLMANN
Kingwood, ivory, and ebony; 50 × 32 × 23½ in.
Brooklyn Museum, Brooklyn, N.Y. (71.1501a); Purchased with funds given by Joseph F. McCrindle,
Mrs. Richard M. Palmer, Charles C. Paterson, Raymond Worgelt, and an anonymous donor

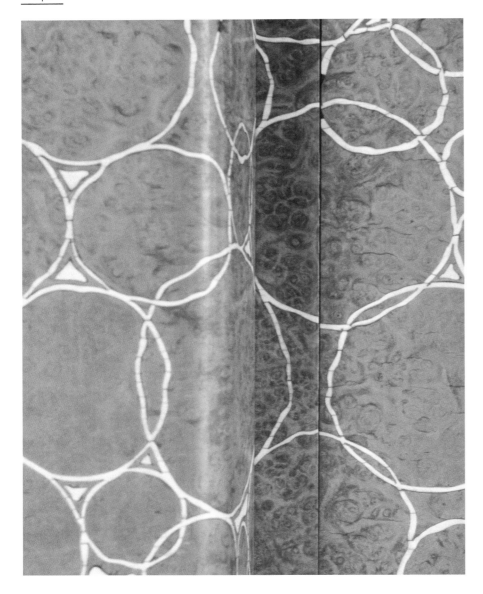

174. MEUBLE D'APPUI CABINET (1927)
JACQUES-ÉMILE RUHLMANN
Amboyna burl and ivory veneered on oak
and poplar; 60½ × 62½ × 20½ in.
Private collection

other pieces, including a similar but slightly smaller version of the cabinet built in 1927.

Ruhlmann was not a cabinetmaker. But he had grown up in the decorative arts and therefore knew many people in the trades. He was able to draw on the wealth of talent in the Faubourg St. Antoine, the same neighborhood that had been home to so many of the great eighteenth-century ébénistes. By 1925 Ruhlmann had enough furniture orders to open his own workshop, rather than rely on subcontractors. He was friends with the director of the École Boulle, already the prestigious school of cabinetmaking in Paris, and was able to get recommendations about the most promising students. He preferred to choose young people for their enthusiasm and the fact that they would

probably be open to new ways of working. Ruhlmann opened two workshops. One had twelve accredited craftsmen, two apprentices, and a machinist. The other had thirteen workers and two machinists. Ruhlmann had no prejudices against using machines. In fact, he wanted to see machine processes used whenever possible, and the workshops were equipped with the most up-to-date equipment. He paid well and was able to attract extremely skilled people. At the beginning of a project an estimate was made for how long the piece should take. The standards were rigorous, but workman were paid a bonus for beating the time estimate.

One of his most skilled cabinetmakers was a man named Jules Deroubaix. Deroubaix kept careful records of the hours it took to build an

individual piece. Occasionally, we also know the price of the furniture and can put the two parts together. For instance, in 1930 a complicated headboard was made with three concentric rings of radiating Macassar veneer, glued to a shaped ground (figure 175). The bed was made for a renowned French actress. Deroubaix worked for 252½ hours (this does not include time spent by his apprentice). He was given a bonus for the speed of his work. His wage rate was 6.25 francs per hour. He would receive up to 12 francs per hour if it was necessary to work on Sunday. The bed sold for 11,375 francs. (A skilled artisan like Deroubaix would earn about 15,000 francs in a year.)

The New York stock market crash in 1929 soon affected the economies of Europe. The early 1930s proved a challenging time to sell luxurious furniture, even for someone of Ruhlmann's reputation. The firm was being hurt by the popularity of the International Style, which eschewed decoration. At the beginning of 1933 he started to lay off employees. At the same time Ruhlmann was facing a serious illness and suspected that he did not have long to live. He drew up a will stipulating that the firm would not continue after his death. He died in November 1933.

Even with the extremely high prices of Ruhlmann pieces, the furniture was never really profitable. In today's parlance it would probably be called a loss leader, attracting customers to the firm for the more profitable decorating services. At the same time, the furniture is what Ruhlmann is remembered for. His work stands shoulder to shoulder with Boulle, Riesener, and the other great cabinetmakers of the French classical tradition. His influence on today's generation of designer-cabinetmakers is ineluctable.

の

DETAIL OF FIGURE 178

175. SUN BED (1930)
JACQUES-ÉMILE RUHLMANN
Macassar ebony, white oak; 77 × 83 × 85 in.
Virginia Museum of Fine Arts, Richmond, Va.;
Gift of Sydney and Francis Lewis (85.130);
Photo: Katherine Wetzel–Virginia Museum of Fine Arts

Louis Süe and André Mare formed one of the important design firms in Art Deco Paris. Their timing for the new movement was perfect. They were young and ambitious when Parisians were looking for innovative work. Süe was the older of the two. Born in 1875 in Bordeaux, Süe's family had been in the wine business, but he gravitated to architecture and painting. He went to Paris as a young man because it was the center of European culture. Around 1910 Süe first became interested in decorative arts. He worked with a friend, Paul Huillard, to design some furniture pieces. These early works were largely derivative of Art Nouveau, but they also showed some of the influence of Josef Hoffman and the Deutscher Werkbund.

André Mare was ten younger than Louis Süe, born in the town of Argenten in Normandy. Initially, he wanted to paint, and he went to Paris to study. Cubist painting was making a bold statement at the time. Mare got involved with the design world through the Salon of 1910, by conceiving of something he called the Cubist House. In truth, it was not a cutting-edge statement, but it put him in touch with people who were primarily working in the world of design. Mare want-

ed to create bold decorating schemes, with bright colors instead of natural wood tones. His designs were a response to the sculptural elements of the French Art Nouveau, using straighter lines and a more logical construction. He looked to ancient ceramics and medieval tapestries for inspiration. He was also enamored of rich, exotic materials. Mare wanted to reject foreign influences and define a purer French design. The Cubist House was roundly criticized, but it brought Mare into the public eye. As is often said, it is more important to be reviewed, even badly, than to be ignored. The Salon put Mare in front of the design profession. Süe was also a part of the 1910 Salon. It was there the seeds were planted for their later collaboration.

One of Mare's early pieces of furniture was a 1913 commode in maple and rosewood with a marquetry bouquet of flowers in purpleheart. The piece is remarkably similar to a dresser designed by Süe from the same year. The marquetry concepts almost look as if one had access to the other's sketchbook. They might have begun a collaboration at that point, but war broke out and any incipient plans had to be delayed.

World War I consumed Europe for four years. Süe and Mare did not form

176. COMMODE (C.1925) SÜE ET MARE - DECORATIVE MOTIF BY MATHURIN MÉHEUT
Ebony, marquetry, marble and gilded wood; 33 × 67½ × 25¼ in.
Private collection

their partnership until 1919. They named their business La Compagnie des Arts Français, specializing in complete interiors. Süe was the artistic director and Mare the technical director. Several others were involved with design work over the ensuing years. In the interest of creating complete interiors, they did not only furniture, but wall coverings, lighting, carpets, and metalwork. Important commissions started to come the firm's way, including work on luxury liners and part of the French embassy in Washington, D.C.

Süe and Mare designed a pair of buildings for the Art Deco Exposition of 1925. They provided the complete interiors as well. The style of their furnishings for the fair was typical of the pieces that they had been doing as a team. The designs often made reference to earlier French furniture, with a par-

ticular fondness for Louis XV. Typically, the legs would distinguish their work—oversized cabriole shapes with carved volutes and tassels.

Several pieces of Süe and Mare furniture are of particular interest from a marquetry standpoint. The pair designed an important commode that stylistically nods to Louis XV furniture (figure 176). It has bulky legs that were carved, then gilded, an imitation ormolu. The top is a patterned marble, also reminiscent of Louis XV. For marquetry, the firm engaged the artist Mathurin Méheut, who designed a fantastic undersea scene with turtles, seashells, coral, and seaweed. A mix of natural and dyed veneers comprises the marquetry. The entire effect is very bold and striking.

Süe and Mare designed several pieces with mother-of-pearl inlay. The

carcases look typical of the firm's designs, yet they are ornamented with elaborate bouquets of flowers in pearl, abalone, and silver. The luminescent shell in an ebony ground, either the solid black Gabon ebony or the stripier Macassar ebony, is lush, indeed. Mare did the art work. Several of the pieces were designed as a set in 1926 for an important client. The set was meant to complement an interior already furnished in Second Empire. The pieces included a commode, a chiffonier, a writing desk and chair, and a fire screen.

The chiffonier is constructed from a very black ebony (figure 177). The marquetry design of a bouquet of flowers is the focal point of the piece.

The writing desk has matching floral decoration also cut from mother-of-pearl (figure 178). The flowers are stylized roses, tulips, and daisies. The

177. CABINET/CHIFFONIER (1927) SÜE ET MARE
Ebony, mother-of-pearl, silver; 62 × 35½ × 15¼ in.
Virginia Museum of Fine Arts, Richmond, Va.; Gift of Sydney and Francis Lewis (85.137);
Photo: Katherine Wetzel–Virginia Museum of Fine Arts

foliage is cut from green abalone shell. The primary part of the abalone shell is called the heart and has a particularly intense grain. The ribbon that holds the bouquets together is inlaid silver that was engraved to enhance the three-dimensional effect.

Mare's preparatory drawings are quite detailed, leaving no doubt as to their intentions. But it is impossible with shell to know with any certainty what you will get in the end; the grain and color of shell can quickly change as you level it. What may appear greenish in the initial cutting can change to rose by removing only a few thousandths of an inch in flushing off the marquetry. The craftsman who executed this marquetry did an outstanding job.

It's a shame that Süe and Mare did so few pieces with marquetry motifs. The decoration works well on the furniture panels. The marquetry coordinates with the stylized carved components. The overall effect is very beautiful.

178. DESK AND CHAIR (C. 1927)
SÜE ET MARE
Macassar ebony, mother-of-pearl, abalone, and silver; 29½ × 46½ × 25 in.
Private collection

179. ANTELOPE CABINET (2004) SILAS KOPF
Cherry and marquetry with wood, brass, and bone;
34 × 52 × 18 in.
Photo: David Ryan

I started combining Deco design of cases with some of the marquetry concepts I had learned in Paris at the École Boulle, such as the repeated motif and Boulle work. Art Deco is a mix of elegance and simplicity. The graphics of Deco marquetry are stylized and easily understood. I was commissioned to design a cabinet that would be the first thing seen upon entering a large living room (figure 179). I used a series of scalloped panels constructed like a fluted column. The wood for the panels is a rich figured cherry veneer. The vertical lines of the individual curved sections create areas of light and shadow, emphasizing the volume of the piece. The marquetry was limited to three small panels using brass for the animals. The shiny metal highlights the smaller details of the pictures.

We built a pair of Boulle commodes with a stylized marquetry motif of grape vines, the leaves broken into sections (figure 180). The individual grapes are done in outline, and the vines are built in parts to suggest the texture of bark. The commodes are demi-lunes in form, the curves made in coopered sections. Eight vertical panels comprise the overall design. This being my first Boulle design, I was reluctant to work on any individual panel that was too complicated. I didn't want to invest too much time in an unsatisfactory result, either technically or artistically. I wanted the fronts to bow, but I knew I wasn't ready to attempt applying Boulle to curved panels. So I made them flat, coopering them to get the curve.

French Art Deco made many references to earlier styles such as Louis XV. Many eighteenth-century pieces have rich stone tops (see figure 150, for instance). I designed these commodes incorporating a beautiful Italian marble with gold veining in a black ground, a color scheme that reflects the brass and ebony of the Boulle work. The carcases are built of bubinga. I have not seen any French pieces with bubinga, but certainly this rich and exotic wood could have fit in with Deco design. Brass sabots on the legs are another nod to Deco.

I very much liked the stylized design of the marquetry grape vines. But I felt I hadn't mixed the brass and the wood as well as the finest Boulle work. One piece was predominantly brass, the other predominantly ebony.

181. BOULLE CABINETS WITH DAFFODILS (1992) SILAS KOPF
Mahogany, maple, brazilwood, zircote, brass, and aluminum;
35 × 48 × 24 in.
Photo: David Ryan

180. GRAPE VINE COMMODES (1990) SILAS KOPF
Bubinga, ebony, and brass; 35 × 40 × 15 in.(each)
Photo: David Ryan

I made a mental note to make the dark and light parts of the next Boulle set we built more equal.

The following year I designed two Deco cabinets, the front of each decorated with stylized daffodils in an oval composition (figure 181). The cabinet wood was the figured sapele pommele that we used on the *Half-Round Cabinet* (figure 168). The dentils at the top and the bottom of each cabinet were made by gluing a thick zircote veneer on a piece of maple and routing through the zircote with a fine fluting bit, thereby exposing the lighter maple below. The Boulle panels were made not with two layers but four: two metals (brass and aluminum) and two woods (zircote and bloodwood). This ultimately yielded four sets of panels. But we used only two for this project. One has an aluminum background with bloodwood flowers and zircote leaves; the other has the zircote background with brass flowers and aluminum leaves.

In 1998 I was commissioned to build a pair of Boulle cabinets in a traditional style. I told the clients that I wasn't interested in doing an exact reproduction, but I would be willing to design something with classical references for their more formal interior. The commission was an opportunity to use Boulle in a way that reflects the finest application of the technique: rich materials and a balance between the premiere-partie and contra-partie that affords them equal visual weight.

I chose maple as the structural wood for the cabinets, topping them with black granite (figure 183). We used bog oak for the dark wood and the traditional brass for the light metal. An egg-and-dart marquetry molding runs along just under the tops. Designed in a stylized Rococo manner, the Boulle panels have numerous parts, making them busy enough for the black and metal to blend. We made the door panels and then framed them with more Boulle work, mixing the première and contra-parties. A primarily black door is framed with primarily brass Boulle work. The sides include wooden panels framed in Boulle work. The cabinet with the première-partie doors have contra-partie molding on the sides and drawer fronts—and vice versa. The overall effect is very satisfying. I love the look of the brass and the black wood together, but using metal is a lot more work than doing marquetry in wood, the techniques for which had become second nature to me. The leveling and polishing of the brass seemed endless in a project with as much surface area as there is in these two cabinets. I used to tell students at workshops that they would rue the day they attempted Boulle.

I was willing to take on this commission, even though the design was a bit outside my normal comfort zone, because it was a chance to stretch my horizons. Shortly after completing the Boulle cabinets, a sideboard in a formal dining room offered similar opportunities. The clients are dog lovers, so we decided that cameos of the family pets would be interesting (figure 182). The cabinet

182. Dog Sideboard (1997) Silas Kopf
Mahogany, brass, ebony, and marquetry; 35 × 77 × 18 in.
Photo: David Ryan

183. TRADITIONAL BOULLE CABINETS (1996) SILAS KOPF
Maple, bog oak, and brass; 36 × 60 × 18 in.
Photo: Kevin Downey

has traditional moldings and pilasters. A Boulle motif frames the door panels, the drawers, and the sides. The contra-partie Boulle decorates the sides. For the veneer, we chose a rich, elegant crotch mahogany. Four different breeds of terrier are depicted in ovals on the fronts.

These traditional pieces made me realize that occasionally the client can lead a design into uncharted territory, yielding interesting results. A man who had purchased several of my pieces over the years approached me about a small chest of drawers for his bedroom. I started on the design and one day he called and told me that he had just seen the type of piece he was interested in. He wanted me to go to the Neue Galerie in New York and look at a chest of drawers. The Neue Galerie is a museum specializing in early twentieth-century German and Austrian art. He said he couldn't remember who had done it, but that it had mother-of-pearl, and I would know it

when I saw it. I was skeptical, but said I would check it out the next time I was in New York.

When I got to the museum I went from room to room looking for the mysterious chest of drawers. Finally, I turned a corner and was confronted by *it*. The chest was constructed as a series of boxes stacked one on top of another, in a sort of pyramid (figure 184). The wood was Macassar ebony with each drawer bordered by a delicate mother-of-pearl inlay. I had seen a similar piece in books, attributed to Josef Hoffman, the great Austrian designer. This piece was said to be designed by Eduard Wimmer-Wisgrill in 1908. When I got home I contacted my client and confirmed that we were talking about the same piece. I told him that I wouldn't do a reproduction, but that I liked the design very much, and would be happy to reconstruct the basic object, with different wood and a new inlay design.

184. Chest of drawers (1908)
Eduard Wimmer-Wisgrill
Ebony and mother-of-pearl; 56¼ × 51 × 21 in.
Private collection on extended loan to Neue Galerie,
New York

185. Pyramid Chest (2002) Silas Kopf
Machiche, thuya burl, bog oak,
mother-of-pearl; 56 × 25 × 19 in.
Photo: David Ryan (also detail photo on p.144)

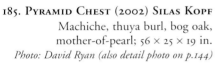

We built a more vertical piece and used a very rich thuya burl for the base wood (figure 185). The inlay consisted of a series of mother-of-pearl triangles, black pin lines, and Mexican machiche wood parallelograms. Echoing the triangular motif, I designed some drop pulls that were fabricated from brass and pearl.

The trip to the Neue Galerie opened up a new area of study for marquetry design. These pieces were done at the time Gallé and Majorelle were developing their Art Nouveau style in Nancy. But the Germanic Art Nouveau took design in a very different direction. Marquetry and inlaid decoration in European furniture was sharply divided stylistically between its use in France and its use in the rest of Europe. The curved line that was so common in French design easily translated into the floral marquetry so prevalent in Nancy. But, late nineteenth–century style looks very different in other places.

☙

England

The craft tradition of the British Isles was very strong in the nineteenth century, fueled by the writings of John Ruskin and William Morris. Each advocated the honesty of craftwork in reaction to the dehumanization of industrialized labor. Morris's company primarily designed wall coverings and fabrics, but the company made the occasional piece of furniture. A very fine escritoire, now in the Virginia Museum of Fine Arts in Richmond, was designed for Morris by a cabinetmaker named George Jack and built around 1895 (figure 186). Marquetry covers the front in a symmetrical design of oak leaves and acorns and a secondary branch with finer leaves. The oak leaves are delicately outlined in gold. Marquetry also decorates the large molding at the top of the stand as well as the legs. The stylized leaves also run around the molding at the top of the cabinet. A wavy line divides the parts in two. The alternating sections have a dark and a light ground. The stylized design of the foliage seems to anticipate the Art Deco marquetry of Ruhlmann.

DETAIL OF FIGURE 186: SECRÉTAIRE CABINET (1893–96) DESIGNER: GEORGE WASHINGTON JACK; MANUFACTURER: MORRIS AND CO.

186. Secrétaire Cabinet (1893–96) Designer: George Washington Jack; Manufacturer: Morris and Co.
Mahogany with marquetry of sycamore, Spanish mahogany, ebony, holly, rosewood; 51¼ × 56 × 27 in.
Virginia Museum of Fine Arts, Richmond, Va.; The Arthur and Margaret Glasgow Fund (2002.528); Photo: Katherine Wetzel–Virginia Museum of Fine Arts

187. Small Cabinet (1904–1912) Ernest Gimson
Walnut with ebony and ivory; 9 × 18 × 9¾ in.
Leicester City Museums, Leicester, England; Photo: Leicester Museums

One of the early advocates of the work philosophy of Morris was Ernest Gimson. Gimson was trained as an architect, but an early encounter with Morris encouraged him to design furniture. Gimson's pieces are often simple, sturdy, well-built objects that deserve to be called honest (figure 187). The level of craftsmanship is superb. He would often decorate surfaces with geometric parquetry. Gimson did not build the pieces himself but was in close touch with the Cotswold craftsmen who did the woodwork. In particular, he employed a Dutch cabinetmaker named Peter van der Waals, who lived nearby. Van der Waals was trained in Holland in marquetry and inlay. Gimson designed many pieces that took advantage of his great talents.

Gimson and three other young architects formed a small enterprise called Kenton and Company. They employed four woodworkers to execute the furniture they designed. Their Modernist styling didn't excite the public, and the venture failed after two years. One of the Gimson projects, typical of their adventurous work, is a cabinet covered with a bold parquetry design that resembles interlocked chain-mail (figure 188). The woods are well chosen: ebony, orangewood, and palmwood, cut to display the end grain. The design is Modernist and at the same time restrained. Difficult to date as a nineteenth-century design, the piece looks very out of character for the era, but would fit comfortably among today's studio furniture.

The work of Gimson that I find most interesting are these cabinets on stands. They are well proportioned pieces, often enhanced with exotic woods. I am particularly taken with one cabinet built in 1908, now in the Leicester Museum and Art Gallery (figure 189). It has fourteen drawers and

188. facing page: Cabinet (c.1891) Ernest Gimson (produced by Kenton and Co.)
Palmwood, ebony, and orangewood; 54½ × 40 × 20 in.
Museé d'Orsay, Paris, France; Photo: Art Resource, New York

189. CABINET ON STAND (C. 1907) DESIGNED BY ERNEST GIMSON, BUILT BY DANEWAY WORKSHOPS
Macassar ebony and ebony inlaid with mother-of-pearl; 46 × 28½ × 13¾ in.
Leicester City Museums, Leicester, England; Photo: Leicester Museums

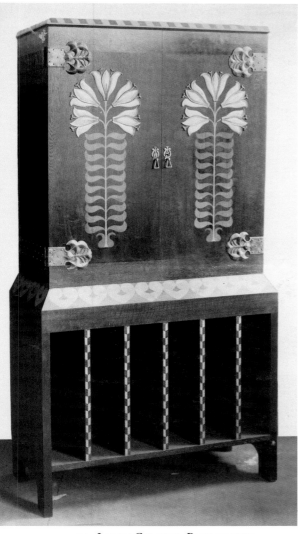

190. Large Cabinet: Part of the Furniture for the Interior of the Grand Duke's Palace at Darmstadt
From an album, one of a set of four albums of photographs of Buildings & Art Objects associated with Charles Robert Ashbee (1863–1942) & The Guild of Handicraft; published by Essex Press; English, c.1908
Photo: V&A Images/Victoria and Albert Museum

two doors in the center. The basic wood is brown ebony. Van der Waals inlaid a stylized floral design in mother-of-pearl on the doors. The design is tied together with mother-of-pearl diamonds on the legs.

In some ways the British designers were more influential on the continent than they were at home. Charles Rennie Mackintosh, the Scottish architect who championed a home-grown style of Art Nouveau, never received major design commissions outside of the Glasgow area. His work elicited more excitement through exhibitions in Germany and Austria than it did in Scotland and England. A group of younger architects looked up to Mackintosh. In 1897 the Grand Duke of Hesse asked several of these English designers to come to Darmstadt to

design furniture for a burgeoning art colony. One of the young men, a talented designer named Hugh Baillie Scott, made tasteful use of marquetry, as in a two-door cabinet reminiscent of Gimson's stylized inlays (figure 190).

Pianos were an important component of home entertainment at the turn of the century, in middle class homes as well as luxury interiors. Scott designed an interesting upright piano, in which the simple rectilinear case disguises the function of the object (figure 191). Two doors are decorated with plaques of shell and pewter. It is only when the doors are opened that the keyboard is revealed. The inside of the doors and the underside of the lid are embellished with a playful marquetry pattern.

&

191. Upright piano: The Manxman (des. c.1896; made c.1902–3) Designed by M. Baille Scott; Piano made by John Broadwood & Sons; Case unsure
Ebonized mahogany with carved wood, pewter and mother-of-pearl decoration, marquetry silver-plated handles and hinges; English (London or Bedford)
Photo: V&A Images/Victoria and Albert Museum

Germany and Austria

One of the most influential architect-designers at the turn of the century was Josef Hoffman from Austria, who was inspired by the English Handicraft Guild and the writings of William Morris. Hoffman's furniture design, particularly in its use of marquetry and inlay, is directly descended from the British Arts and Crafts Movement.

Hoffman was born 1870. When he was twenty-two he went to Vienna to study architecture. He was a student of Otto Wagner's and worked closely with him. Hoffman was part of a broader artistic movement called the Secession (referring to practitioners' "secession" from more conservative approaches to art). The first Secession exhibition was held in Vienna in 1898 and Hoffman

made significant contributions. Originally, Hoffman was inspired by the curvilinear style championed by the Belgian architect, Henri van de Velde. Later, he became more intrigued with the rectilinear designs coming from the British Isles, particularly the work of Mackintosh. In 1902 Mackintosh actually came to Austria and collaborated with Hoffman on the interior of a villa for a wealthy patron. The following year Hoffman and his friend Koloman Moser founded the Weiner Werkstätte, with the idea of transforming Austrian design and infusing industry with the ideas coming from Britain.

Hoffman and Moser attracted an enthusiastic group of young designers to work with them at the Werkstätte. One of those who was particularly

interested in furniture was Eduard Wimmer-Wisgrill, who designed the pyramidal chest of drawers mentioned earlier as being at the Neue Galerie in New York (figure 184). Wimmer-Wisgrill loved geometric designs and exotic materials. He designed another similar chest where the fronts are an optically striking arrangement of concentric black lines on a light ground with ebony shapes in the middle (figure 192). The borders of the tiers are edged with mother-of-pearl.

Hoffman's partner in the Wiener Werkstätte, Koloman Moser, was not trained in architecture. Perhaps this is why his design work focused more on furniture than Hoffman's. At seventeen Moser had begun training in an Austrian art school. He was attracted to

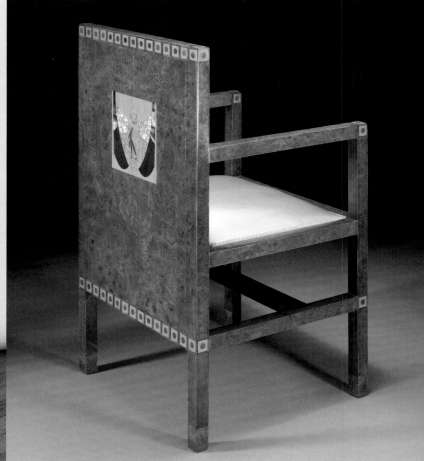

192. Chest of drawers (1908) Eduard Wimmer-Wisgrill
Boxwood, ebony, mother-of-pearl; 56 × 51 × 20½ in.
Austrian Museum of Applied Arts, Vienna (H 2051);
Photo: Georg Mayer/MAK

193. Chair (1904) Koloman Moser
Rosewood, maple, mother-of-pearl; 37½ × 22 × 20½ in.
Virginia Museum of Fine Arts, Richmond, Va.; Gift of Sydney and Francis
Lewis (85.80); Photo: Katherine Wetzel–Virginia Museum of Fine Arts

the ideas of the Viennese Secession, which were making waves throughout the continent, particularly in painting. He joined the movement eagerly. Moser was involved in all the activities and publications for several years.

Moser was particularly influential in his use of pattern to create furniture decoration. In reaction to the florid styles of France and Belgium, he reduced pattern to very simple geometric elements, often in black and white. A chair designed around right angles and square elements, including repetitive square marquetry details, shows how eloquent a simple geometric vocabulary can be (figure 193). The starkness of the form is relieved by the geometrically stylized marquetry image of a bird embellishing the back.

Moser designed another chair, basically a cube with the front cut away to allow a seat to be inserted, along with a fall-front desk, the front of which is also cut away—to receive the chair (figure 194). The dark tropical wood is

194. WRITING CABINET AND CHAIR (1903–1904) KOLOMAN MOSER
Macassar ebony, Madagascar ebony, boxwood, mahogany, ivory, tortoiseshell; 56 × 47 × 23½ in.
Austrian Museum of Applied Arts, Vienna (H 2305); Photo: Gearld Zugmann/MAK

195. CASKET/BOX (1912) KARL ADOLF FRANZ
Pearwood, ebonized pearwood, abalone; 6½ × 12¼ × 6¾ in.
Austrian Museum of Applied Arts, Vienna (W.I. 1177); Photo: Georg Mayer/MAK

surrounded with a running border of small black and brown stripes. The doors and drawers are clearly defined by the clean lines of the marquetry borders. The contrast with the contemporary design of French Art Nouveau is pronounced.

The Weiner Werkstätte spawned a creative outpouring in Vienna. One young designer of note was Karl Adolf Franz. Like Moser, Franz enhanced his furniture with geometric pattern. One oval cabinet features fronts with a series of abalone ovals inlaid into ebony rectangles (figure 195). These rectangles are put together in a checkerboard pattern with other rectangles made up of vertical black and brown stripes. In its geometric patterning, I find the decoration to be reminiscent of the Tutankhamen coffer (figure 102). Built around 1912, this cabinet is quite characteristic of Viennese design, emphasizing clean lines and interesting materials.

‿

In 2003 a desk commission I had was driven by the client's interests, which led to a different design concept than I was pursuing. As the client and I looked at various decorative possibilities for marquetry, we recognized that her interior wasn't right for a pictographic marquetry design. She wanted something that would feature interesting materials but not call too much attention to itself. I thought of the pyramid chest of drawers with the mother-of-pearl banding based on the Wimmer-Wisgrill design that we recently completed (figure 185). I found some solid white oak with a lovely curl and matched this with a profusely patterned oak burl veneer. I wanted

something bordering the two cuts of oak, and I chose zebrawood, which has the same tones as white oak. Bordering all the zebrawood, we inlaid 3/16-inch stripes of abalone shell. The overall effect is functional and satisfying (figure 196).

The abalone shell on the writing desk and the mother-of-pearl on the pyramid chest of drawers piqued my interest in using shell in more designs. We built a sideboard with goldfish swimming across the drawer fronts: natural wood tones of yellow and red fish with fins of mother-of-pearl and abalone, all on a background of very black ebony (figure 197). Underwater plants are

196. DESK AND CHAIR (2001) SILAS KOPF
Oak, oak burl, zebrawood, and abalone shell; 30 × 64 × 26 in.
Photo: David Ryan

depicted with dyed woods. I cut the marquetry using bevel sawing. The fins include spines of natural wood that separate the segments. My intent was to use the boldness of the shell to create a rhythm across the frieze. Inlaid details are made from a polyester that simulates ivory.

ↄↄ

Pianos: I was approached by Steinway and Sons about designing an art case piano in 1989. Steinway had had Wendell Castle design a piano to commemorate the building of their 500,000th instrument. They were searching for other designers to do pianos and revive a long-dormant program in art case production. They inquired at Wendell's gallery in New York about other craftsmen who might make special pianos. The gallery director recommended they talk to me.

At the beginning of the twentieth century Steinway built many art-case pianos. In that era before radio, a piano was thought of as the home entertainment center. Many middle-class homes would have had one, and many upper class homes would have had a fancy one. Perhaps the fanciest of them all was a piano designed by the English painter, Lawrence Alma Tadema (figure 198). He designed a special Steinway in 1882 for Henry Marquand, the first president of the Board of the Metropolitan Museum. Parts of the piano were painted by Alma Tadema, and the surfaces were extensively inlayed. Making custom cases was a specialty of Steinway a hundred years ago, involving the services of many outside designers, such as the Herter Brothers and Tiffany Glass.

I made a visit to the Steinway factory in Long Island City to discuss the process. I got a basic tour and an understanding of how the pianos are built. They were interested in a Model L, which is the largest of their domestic grand pianos.

My primary design concern was to maintain the integrity of the musical instrument and not do anything that would affect its acoustics. I wanted to do a floral motif, something that could be accessible to a range of possible customers (figure 199). I decided on a series of "windows" on the vertical surface of the bent rim. They would be small enough to cut individually on my saw without difficulty, to be jointed together afterwards in the longer frieze. The flowers are oversized morning glories, the vine appearing to cross from window to window, naturally connecting the elements. I opted not to put anything on the top because of the way the lid functions. (Sometimes the lid is fully closed. Sometimes, the 18 inches or so closest to the pianist is flipped over—and it doesn't hinge exactly perpendicular to the side. And sometimes the lid is propped open either 6 inches or 2

197. GOLDFISH SIDEBOARD (2001) SILAS KOPF
Granadillo, ebony, mother-of-pearl, faux ivory, and marquetry; 35 × 73 × 18 in.
Photo: Dean Powell

198. MODEL D, STEINWAY AND SONS PIANOFORTE (1884) SIR LAURENCE ALMA-TADEMA, DESIGNER
Ebony, sandalwood, ivory, coral, mother-of-pearl, boxwood; 40¼ × 104¼ × 59¼ in.
Sterling and Francine Clark Art Institute, Williamstown, Mass.; Inv. (1997.8)

feet. With all these possibilities it is difficult to get a harmonious arrangement of marquetry on a lid.)

Steinway let me choose a very beautiful veneer for the basic wood of the piano. We acquired a highly figured flitch of walnut burl. For the background of the morning glories we used a golden-toned laurel burl. The basic wood for the flowers is holly, which contrasts nicely with the laurel. I also designed the legs and the lyre (which holds the foot pedals). It was important to me to maintain all the balance points and relationships as they exist on the standard Model L. This way we could be sure that it would be first and foremost a musical instrument. The

legs are a wishbone shape. They are built of solid wood, veneered with the walnut burl, and trimmed along the edges with a border of holly.

A few years later Steinway came back and asked me to work on a design that could be done as an edition to commemorate the fiftieth anniversary of the Aspen Music Festival. I designed legs with an aspen leaf motif that could be reproduced in limited number with a laser cutter.

Aspen Piano was seen by clients of mine and we talked about it over dinner. I told them that originally I had had the idea of doing a much more elaborate design with aspen trees running around the rim of the piano, but

199. Morning Glories (1989) Silas Kopf; Model L, Steinway and Sons piano
Walnut, walnut burl, laurel burl, holly, and marquetry; 40½ × 58 × 70½ in.
Photo: courtesy of Steinway and Sons

200. ASPEN TREES (2002) SILAS KOPF;
MODEL L, STEINWAY AND SONS PIANO
Walnut, Macassar ebony, and marquetry;
40½ × 58 × 70½ in.
Photo: courtesy of Steinway and Sons

that the concept was too involved to do as an edition. They were intrigued with my original design and asked if I would be interested in doing some drawings and approaching Steinway about the possibility of doing the more elaborate aspen piano.

Having gone through the process of working on a custom piano, I was aware of some of the design limitations. For the aspen piano I wanted the marquetry motif to be continuous down the leg (figure 200). However, the legs have to be detachable, or such a heavy object can't be moved. This meant that the marquetry had to be carefully cut so there would be natural breaks in the design. The marquetry was also being glued directly onto the solid rim. The rims are made of maple and all the grain runs horizontally. Therefore it expands and contracts in height, and the face veneers should also run horizontally. My design called for a series of aspen trees that would rise vertically and break the background into smaller parts. This allowed me to work on the individual areas on my

saw (with its throat limitations) and ultimately assemble the parts into the long frieze.

In 2005 I started the design for a very unusual piano (figure 201). It was to be made and sold as a fund-raiser for the Henry David Thoreau Institute in Concord, Massachusetts. I was asked to design and build a piece using some of the wood from the area around Walden Pond. Early on, we decided to work in as ecologically conservative a manner as possible. We were not going to use any tropical woods; whenever possible we would use wood either from Massachusetts or able to grow there. I thought of the great intarsiatori of Renaissance Italy, who made such wondrous pictures with a limited palette.

The design incorporates a series of plaques glued to the rim of the piano. Ten depict trees and shrubs that Thoreau wrote about; an eleventh plaque is a portrait of the author. Above the plaques is a long quote from *Walden.* On each leg is a pond scene: one with fish, one with a frog, and the third with a turtle.

☙

201. WALDEN WOODS (2006) SILAS KOPF; MODEL D, STEINWAY AND SONS PIANO
Walnut and marquetry; 40½ × 61¼ × 107¾ in.
Photo: courtesy of Steinway and Sons

American Marquetry

In 2003 I was asked to participate in a show at the Milwaukee Art Museum called, *Skin Deep: American Marquetry Furniture.* Three woodworkers represented three different centuries of American furniture: Nathan Lombard, Peter Glass, and myself.

I had paid only casual attention to marquetry in American furniture, regarding it as a provincial imitation of European work, as in the the bell flowers and shells that adorn Early American pieces based on Hepplewhite designs. I had assumed that many of these decorative elements were purchased from itinerant craftsmen to make undistinguished furniture a little fancier.

The show in Milwaukee made me aware of the great legacy of American marquetry. I saw something distinctive in the work of Nathan Lombard, who worked in Massachusetts at the end of the eighteenth century in what is called the Federal style. Federal pieces definitely have European roots, but in the hands of someone like Lombard they took on much more of an American look. One of Lombard's most famous pieces is a secretary/bookcase built around 1800, now on display at the Winterthur Museum in Delaware (figure 202). The upper doors of the piece are decorated with symmetrical marquetry eagles that become the focal point of the piece.

The nineteenth-century representative in the *Skin Deep* exhibition was a German immigrant named Peter Glass. He learned cabinetmaking and marquetry in Bavaria before coming to America as a 20-year-old in 1844. He settled in Boston and worked in a piano factory. Eventually he moved to Wisconsin, where he farmed and built furniture.

Glass's work was not high style; it might be thought of as folk art. He, like many immigrants in this period, made wooden objects decorated to var-

202. DESK AND BOOKCASE (1800–1805)
NATHAN LOMBARD
Cherry, mahogany, basswood, white pine;
92½ × 42½ × 21¼ in.
Winterthur Museum, Winterthur, Del.; Bequest of Henry Francis duPont; Photo: Winterthur Museum

ious degrees, often in geometric patterns. These objects can be perfectly charming and also uniquely American. This folk art has sometimes been referred to as "men's quilting." It was a way for farmers to spend the long winter months making useful and interesting objects. The pieces can appear amateurish when placed side by side with professional cabinetwork, and certainly the marquetry is not particularly skillful. Yet they have an engaging integrity (figure 204).

One of the most interesting of these folk pieces was a secretary built in the 1860s by Frederick Hazen in Spring-field, Massachusetts (figure 203). He worked on the piece for seven years. Over 18,000 pieces of veneer are used, including wood with historic links, such as timber from Independence Hall and Mount Vernon.

At about the same time as Peter Glass came to America (and interestingly my German ancestors) another young man came to New York from Württemberg. Gustave Herter was later joined by his younger brother, Christian. Together they established a powerhouse design company that manufactured furniture for the rich and famous of America.

203. SECRETARY (1862–69) FREDERICK STEDMAN HAZEN
Mahogany veneered with marquetry; 81¼ × 42¾ × 19½ in.
Collection of Robert and Marjorie Hirschhorn; Photos: David Stansbury

204. WORKSTAND (1897) PETER GLASS
Mahogany, cedar, walnut, and marquetry; 29 × 20½ × 20½ in.
Milwaukee Art Museum, Milwaukee, Wis.; Gift of Friends of Art (M1997.168); Photo: Larry Sanders

**205. AESTHETIC MOVEMENT
CENTER TABLE (1877–78)
HERTER BROTHERS**
Ebonized, inlaid, carved, and gilded
maple, gilded bronze fittings;
30¼ × 56 × 35 in.
*Virginia Museum of Fine Arts, Richmond,
Va.; The Adolphe D. and Wilkins C.
Williams Fund (90.30); Photo: Katherine
Wetzel–Virginia Museum of Fine Arts*

Herter Brothers furniture was at first indistinguishable from furniture being built on the continent. By 1870 the firm was making extraordinary objects that incorporated many influences.

In the latter half of the nineteenth century so many Germans lived on the lower east side of Manhattan around Tompkins Square that the area was known as Kleindeutschland (Little Germany). This is where Henry Steinway opened his piano factory in the 1850s. Hundreds if not thousands of skilled cabinetmakers were available in the neighborhood. The Herters also drew on these workmen to build the complicated pieces of furniture they designed.

The Herters used marquetry decoration to create elegant and opulent pieces. During the 1870s Americans were greatly interested in Japan. The insular island nation had only recently been opened to Western trade and Americans were fascinated with the culture. The company designed a series of pieces with stylized marquetry chrysanthemums on an ebonized ground. A center table now at the Virginia Museum of Fine Arts is decorated with small stylized flowers on the black ground, which was a hallmark of Herter Brothers marquetry (figure 205). The graphic effect resembles that of a textile design.

The Herter Brothers employed skilled marqueteurs who could execute more traditional and painterly designs. A pair of pedestals at the Detroit Institute of Arts have wonderful mar-

quetry pictures of plants and butterflies (figure 206). I wasn't aware of these pieces when I built my *Garden Cabinet* (figure 72) or *Roses and Butterflies* (figure 211), but the comparisons would be apt.

At the turn of the century while the Herter brothers were catering to an elite clientele, the American middle class were furnishing their homes with the simple, honest furniture of Gustav Stickley, made in the Craftsman Style.

These pieces were often made of oak, with sturdy joinery and no embellishments. They were affordable, and the Stickley factory produced thousands of pieces for the growing American population.

Among Stickley's designers was an architect named Harvey Ellis. While Ellis admired the Craftsman aesthetic, distinguished by its stark simplicity, he occasionally designed furniture for Stickley that had some inlay. At the

206. PEDESTALS (1877–78) HERTER BROTHERS
Maple, birdseye maple, mahogany, and marquetry; 53½h × 23½ × 23½ in.
Detroit Institute of Arts; Founders Society Purchase, Gibbs-Williams Fund, Beatrice Rogers Fund, Edward Rothman Fund, Lewis Acquisition Fund, and Elizabeth and Allen Shelden Fund; (inv. 1992.213.1); Photo: Detroit Institute of Arts

207. Fall Front Desk (c. 1903–04) Gustav Stickley Workshops and Harvey Ellis
Quartersawn white oak, copper, pewter, and exotic wood inlays, unfinished poplar;
46 × 42 × 11½ in.
Virginia Museum of Fine Arts, Richmond, Va.; Gift of Sydney and Francis Lewis (85.70);
Photo: Katherine Wetzel–Virginia Museum of Fine Arts

Virginia Museum of Fine Arts in Richmond an oak desk designed by Ellis has an inlaid motif made of copper and pewter (figure 207). The oak is fumed in ammonia, which darkens it, making the metal stand out in greater contrast.

Through my work and study, I have learned a great deal from how things have been done historically. At the same time I am open to new things based on older objects that I like. I am also willing to combine different elements and different approaches in trying to get a new look. Some ideas get "filed" and don't appear again for years.

I like to use chairs as objects for marquetry exploration. They have become like the jewelry boxes I was making when I first started working. The marquetry on chairs is basically limited to the backs, as it was limited to the tops on boxes. Chairs are difficult pieces to make because of all the angles involved in making them comfortable. Often the chairs we made were single pieces to go along with desks, but occasionally we would get a commission for a dining set or a game table.

In 1999 I was commissioned to make a set of dining chairs in a Modernist design (figure 208). The clients had two basic interests: They wanted the chairs to be mostly black, and they wanted bright colors in the marquetry. We ruled out solid ebony and chose to dye the wood black. The brightly colored objects could have been flowers, but we settled on animals: insects, reptiles, and amphibians, amongst flowers and other vegetation.

I had stopped using dyed veneers some years earlier. At the time I decided that I liked the challenge of working with natural wood tones, and the bright colors struck me as strident. But I found these chairs very pleasing when they were done. They are obviously wood, but a little bolder than most of the marquetry I had been doing.

208. Set of Dining Chairs (1998) Silas Kopf
Ebonized cherry and marquetry of natural and dyed woods; 41 × 18 × 19 in.
Photo: Billy Cunningham

209. Side Chairs with Animals (2000) Silas Kopf
Narra and marquetry; 41 × 18 × 19 in.
Photo: David Ryan

Not long after finishing that dining set, I was commissioned to do another set of chairs. The clients saw the black set and asked for animals on theirs as well. They too liked the black background and the dyed veneer, but they wanted the framing parts of the chairs to be in natural wood (figure 209).

Another set of chairs was part of a game table (figure 210). In this case the client was an opera lover and requested a music theme. I chose to depict hands playing a different instrument on each of the four chairs: an oboe, a violin, a trumpet, and a piano. The idea went back to the mantle clock we had made years earlier (figure 82).

The angles involved in making chair parts make them difficult to jig up, so we cut two extra sets. This was an

210. Game Table and Chairs (2001) Silas Kopf
Ash, ebony, holly, and marquetry; 29½ × 42 × 42 in.
Photo: David Ryan

211. ROSES AND BUTTERFLIES (2001) SILAS KOPF
Ash, bird's-eye maple, walnut burl, and marquetry; 41h × 26 × 24 in.
Photo: Dean Powell

opportunity to make basically the same chair, but with different marquetry. I chose a complicated floral motif similar to that of the *Garden Cabinet* that we had built years earlier (figure 72). One chair has a bird's-eye maple background, the other has a walnut burl background (figure 211). The theme is the same on each chair: roses and butterflies. The marquetry on one side is a mirror image of the marquetry on the other side, as if the marquetry extends through the whole one-inch thickness. Using a floral motif on a chair back was a way of acknowledging my early inspiration, Louis Majorelle (figure 26).

Chairs can be a sensual and tactile experience. Majorelle's chairs and *Roses and Butterflies* invite the user to explore the sculpture of the arms. Mortise-and-tenon joints for the parts need to be cut when the elements are big blocks with flat planes. Only after the joinery is complete can the curves be sawn, and unexpected things can happen in shaping wood. An exposed knot or other flaw can mean having to reject a part. In making a run of sculpted chairs it is wise to make extra parts. We built a set of twelve dining chairs, which fortuitously resulted in a complete extra set of useable parts. The marquetry for the large group of chairs depicted morning glories, but for the single chair I made a drawing of myself and cropped it to fit in the odd triangular space on the backsplat of the chair.

One thing I try to do after finishing each piece is to stand back and say, "What would I do differently next time? How can I make it better?" Sometimes you are too close to a piece to make a judgment right away and you

212. PARABOLA 2
(2006) SILAS KOPF
Thuya burl, copper, brass,
mother-of-pearl, abalone;
67 × 34 × 13 in.
Photo: David Ryan

should go back after a year or so and perhaps look at a photo and then ask the question. I hope it is obvious that I try to be open to the influence of historic objects. Sometimes I need to be open to my own work. Ideas that are dormant for years can make a worthy reappearance. For instance, I had always liked *Parabola* (figure 163). Years later we brought the form out of storage and made another piece from the old shape. This time the cabinet veneer is thuya burl, and the only marquetry is in a clock face at the top of the arch (figure 212). The face is decorated with rings of brass and copper, cut from tubing.

Among the rings are dots of mother-of-pearl and abalone shell; the voids are filled with black epoxy. With the epoxy leveled, the dots appear to be inlaid into the black ground.

We have made a series of cabinets on stands that use the same elliptical form. In the first piece, for the Milwaukee Art Museum exhibition, the decoration is of mixed flowers on a Macassar ebony ground (figure 213). These flowers are similar to many flowers that I have done over the years. I liked the rounded format of the cabinet and the way that the viewer is tempted to keep walking around the piece to see what's around the corner.

213. Elliptical Garden Cabinet (2002) Silas Kopf
Mahogany, Macassar ebony, and marquetry; 64 × 22 × 17 in.
Photo: Milwaukee Museum of Art

214. Aloha Shirt Cabinet (2003) Silas Kopf
Maple, bird's-eye maple, and marquetry; 64½ × 22 × 17 in.
Photo: David Ryan

About a year later we used the same elliptical format to make another cabinet (figure 214). For many years my wife, Linda, had jokingly suggested that I should design Hawaiian shirts because I wear them all the time. I decided that the cabinet on a stand had about the right proportions. The key in fabric design is creating a pattern that can be repeated indefinitely. In this case seahorses run in diagonal groups over the surface. In the background are wavy leaves of kelp in dyed woods. The ground is a profusely patterned bird's-eye maple. We used a banding with thin dark lines above and below the cabinet to emphasize the horizontals. It also accents the curves because as the lines go around the corners they get closer together.

The third incarnation of the elliptical cabinet on a stand uses the cracked ice pattern that we used on the tables for the *Inspired By China* exhibition (figure 96). The wrinkle here was to combine three different woods (figure 215). Running through the center in a random wave is a group of polygons in English brown oak. Bordering the center group are pieces cut in white oak.
We cut the outer set of shapes in ash. The woods all have approximately the same straight-striped grain pattern and blend together.

In 2003 we built a desk that was to have no pictographic decoration on the top (figure 216). It was a very complicated piece to build. The construction is similar to the lectern (figure 160). But this time two coopered

215. Cracked Ice Ellipse (2006) Silas Kopf
Ash, white oak, English brown oak, East Indian rosewood;
64 × 22 × 17 in.
Photo: David Ryan

216. Three Mile Island Desk and Chair (2004) Silas Kopf
Machiche, Sapele, Satinwood, and marquetry; 30 × 60 × 28 in.
Photo: David Ryan

"barrels" close up rather than open. The veneer is a beautiful quilted sapele. A parquetry border around the sapele on the top includes mother-of-pearl parts in the center of each motif. The only place we used a standard marquetry image is inside the drawer, where a fancy fountain pen appears.

Round pieces of furniture can be awkward to use in decorating a home; most cabinets have flat backs to sit against a wall. Working on pianos led me to appreciate pieces of furniture that aren't rectilinear. Marquetry decoration can create a narrative, leading the viewer to explore the entire piece. The elliptical cabinets encouraged that exploration. In 2007 we built *Bad Hare Day*, a larger oval cabinet with rabbits chasing a fox (figure 217).

In 2004 I returned to using oysters as a design element. I had a long limb of walnut and was about to get dozens of pieces cut from it. Previously I had used oysters as a parquetry element, where the edges of the pieces were

217. Bad Hare Day (2007) Silas Kopf
Walnut, Macassar ebony, and marquetry; 41 × 62 × 29 in.
Photo: David Ryan

218. Falling Oysters (2004) Silas Kopf
Ebonized ash, purpleheart, walnut; 56 × 21½ × 12 in.
Photo: Dean Powell

squared and then joined in rows (figures 164 and 166).
Falling Oysters uses the wany-edged profile of the oyster as
it was originally cut from the limb (figure 218).
I used four sets of pieces set in a line and splayed like a
deck of cards. At the top of the panels the oysters are
spaced closely together. As they descend, they separate, as
they'd do if falling. I deliberately chose groups of oysters
that have knots, so you can follow the relationship among
the pieces and mentally reconstruct the limb.

I have occasionally combined several different
marquetry elements in the same piece. *Nasturtiums*

219. Nasturtiums (2006) Silas Kopf
Granadillo, shedua, parquetry banding, and marquetry with wood, copper, brass, mother-of-pearl, and abalone; 42 × 61 × 19 in.
Photo: David Ryan

features marquetry reminiscent of stained glass with black borders surrounding all the marquetry parts (figure 219). The stylized leaves are made of wood, the flowers are brass and ebony, and the butterflies are shell. The panels are all slightly curved to soften the design. To create strong horizontal lines, we manufactured a toppo banding of cherry, maple, and bog oak (see Appendix 3: Banding). The banding borders all the veneered panels and also accentuates the legs.

❧

I am often asked if there are technologies that will make my marquetry work obsolete. I have several times explored using laser cutting, guided by computers, and found that the machines can do remarkable things.

My first experience with laser cutting involved a client who wanted a writing table with a musical theme (figure 220). I designed a border around the top consisting of a series of forty walnut trumpets in silhouette on a maple ground, each trumpet about four inches long. I discovered that trying to cut all the necessary detail around the valves was almost impossible. Someone suggested I talk

220. REMEMBERING LOUIS (1993) SILAS KOPF
Walnut, maple, ebony, and marquetry; 27 × 62½ × 24½ in.
Photo: David Behl

to a man in a neighboring town who did laser cutting, mainly scale architectural parts for three-dimensional models. I took my little sketch of the trumpet to him and he scanned it into the computer. He was able to make the lines even crisper than they had been in my sketch, and we tried a sample.

First he cut the trumpet. Then the maple. In the lighter maple I was able to detect a very slight burned edge. In the walnut this browning was virtually invisible. The cutting of even the finest detail was excellent. When we put the parts together, only a very slight line around the trumpet was visible. In fact, the fit was even better than I wanted. I was hoping for a little space, which I was

planning to fill with a black mastic. That proved to be a small hurdle, as he typed into the computer an increase of 3 percent in the size of the opening in the maple. Presto! It was exactly what I wanted. And in no time I had forty identical motifs.

I have subsequently used laser cutting for lettering, which is very easy to lay out on the computer. I also designed another desk with a repeated theme (figure 221). I didn't mind the little scorching of the marquetry parts. The thin line between the lighter woods just becomes another design element.

The value of the laser cutter lies in the machine's ability to make duplicate parts over and over. Setting up

" — Henry David Thoreau

Sugar Maple

DETAIL OF FIGURE 201. WALDEN WOODS PIANO (2006)
SILAS KOPF; MODEL D STEINWAY AND SONS

the scan is as time consuming as cutting the parts on a saw. So to make one picture using the computer doesn't offer an obvious advantage over sawing. And then there is that little bit of burning. But if you are going to be making many identical pictures, the machine is amazing. It has also been a remarkable tool for cutting parts extremely accurately, such as the trumpets on the desk or the lettering on the *Walden Woods* piano (figure 201).

ભ

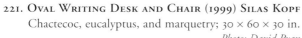

221. Oval Writing Desk and Chair (1999) Silas Kopf
Chactecoc, eucalyptus, and marquetry; 30 × 60 × 30 in.
Photo: David Ryan

I have been working for more than thirty years making furniture and marquetry. It has been an adventure in learning the craft, as well as educating myself in its history. The future is a blank slate upon which I will make some marks. I suspect that I will continue to explore the legacy of furniture decoration that spans 5,000 years. Big parts of the world have their own traditions, about which I know very little. My goal is to incorporate new ideas that test the limits of tools and materials while creating interesting and provocative furniture.

I'll continue looking into the past while keeping an eye on the future. There are museums to visit and books to read. If I can inspire people to similarly explore marquetry and inlay in both the workshop and the museum, I will have done my job.

⌀

1.2

ALL APPENDIX PHOTOS (EXCEPT PAGE 206): RICK MASTELLI

Wood is hygroscopic, absorbing and releasing moisture in response to changes in relative humidity. As a result, it expands and contracts—in width, across the grain, and also to a lesser extent in thickness—but almost not at all in length. In a temperate climate, where the air can be laden with moisture in summer and bone-dry in winter, this uneven dimensional response is a critical consideration in wood designs and constructions.

One way of making a panel stable is to glue sheets of wood veneer together, orienting the grain direction of each layer perpendicular to its neighbor, creating plywood. The thinness of the sheets minimizes the force of the movement, and the cross-grain construction locks the fibers together, providing dimensional stability. Plywood is made in a variety of qualities.

Dimensionally stable material can also be made by combining wood chips with an adhesive and pressing the mixture into sheets. This chipboard is dimensionally stable, once again, due to the minimal size and offsetting grain direction of the elements, locked by the glue. As with plywood, the quality of these sheets varies—from waferboard, where the chips are relatively huge, to fiberboard, which is essentially made from wood dust and glue.

Veneer is made in one of two basic ways: It can be sawn, or it can be sliced. Most commercially available veneers are sliced. The thickness can vary. The look of a sawn veneer is that of solid lumber. Sliced veneer can look different, depending on the orientation of the log on the slicer and the direction of the slice. Veneer can even be peeled off a log rotationally, like a roll of paper towels.

Veneers are generally glued to a dimensionally stable panel, such as plywood or fiberboard. Until the invention of modern adhesives, the only glue available was hide glue, made by boiling animal connective tissue. Hide glue is heated in a pot and then brushed onto the wood. As the glue cools, it sticks. A smooth, tight bond can be achieved by

1.1

rubbing the surface with a veneer hammer. Larger panels were traditionally glued in a press. To ensure a good bond here, the plates of the press would be warmed, to remelt the glue, and as the plates cooled, the veneer would stick.

Hide glue has many advantages. It can be loosened with heat and moisture, making repairs possible. Hide glue can be used to glue difficult shapes that would otherwise require a two-part form. Instead of metal plates, bags of sand could be heated and used to conform to compound shapes and make a veneer stick.

Various modern adhesives are now used for veneering. Aliphatic resins and urea formaldehyde resins require sustained pressure. A screw press (**1.1**) or a vacuum bag is an ideal tool for veneering with these adhesives. Curved

parts can be made out of thinner sheets of veneer or plywood, using a two-part mold in a screw press (**1.2**) or a one-part mold in a vacuum bag.

Once a marquetry picture is assembled in a sheet (see Appendix 7: Bevel Cutting), it is treated like any other veneer. Whatever method of gluing it, the panel will be the same, with one exception. The marquetry panel will have slightly different thicknesses across the picture. Not only does the thickness of the individual pieces of veneer vary, but tape, applied in several layers here and not at all there, contributes to the irregularity. Therefore, to even the pressure over the panel in the press, it is important to sandwich the panel in a flexible blanket. A thin sheet of neoprene is ideal.

☙

APPENDIX 2: PARQUETRY

Parquetry is a form of marquetry in which contrasting geometric shapes are pieced together in a repeating pattern. The key to parquetry is cutting multiple identical parts at once. Each part could be cut individually. But cutting multiple parts simultaneously is not only quicker, it produces more consistently accurate results.

Most parquetry involves polygons, such as squares or rhombuses. These straight-sided shapes can be cut using a special tool called a veneer saw, which has a curved bottom that puts only a few of the teeth in contact with the wood at a time (**2.1**). The veneer saw is flat on one side; the other side is beveled to reach the point of the teeth, which are sharpened by filing with a 60-degree file (**2.2**). The flat side of the saw rests against a fence, and the blade is drawn over the wood in a series of pull-strokes until the veneer is cut free.

CHECKERBOARD

A checkerboard is an easy parquetry project. It has 64 squares in two contrasting veneers. The first step is to place the two veneer sheets on top of one another and cut a straight edge on them (**2.3**). To guide the veneer saw, a fence is cut from a piece of solid wood thick enough to comfortably support the flat side of the veneer saw. This fence should be ripped to the width of the desired square (in our example 1¼ in.).

With straight edges established, the fence is placed on the straight edge of one of the pieces of veneer and a cut made along the parallel edge of the fence. The result is a strip with parallel edges, 1¼ in. wide (**2.4**). Repeat until there are four strips of each color (**2.5**).

Next, tape the eight strips together, alternating the colors (**2.6**).

Now a straight line is crosscut exactly perpendicular to the outer edge using a combination square and the wooden fence (**2.7**). This straight line then becomes the edge to start another series of parallel cuts, creating a series of strips made up of the two contrasting colors (**2.8**).

Alternating strips are turned end-for-end and taped together (**2.9**). The eight strips will join together to make the 64-square checkerboard (**2.10**).

2.1

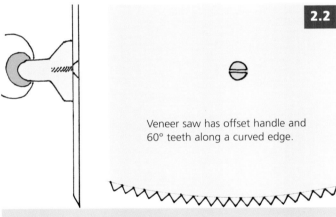
2.2

Veneer saw has offset handle and 60° teeth along a curved edge.

2.3

2.4

2.5

2.6

2.7

2.8

2.9

2.10

POWER-SAWING PARQUETRY

The power tablesaw can also be used to accurately and efficiently cut parquetry parts. The principle of gang-cutting is the same as for the veneer saw.

The tablesaw is not an obvious tool for cutting veneer because the sheet would dangerously shatter if you tried cutting it as you would thicker solid stock. The operation is made safe and accurate by making a jig to fit on the tablesaw bed. A sheet of plywood, with a pair of runners screwed to the bottom that fit snugly into the parallel tracks in the tablesaw bed and a kerf (or slit) the exact size of the sawblade, supports the veneer through the cut. The veneer is further stabilized by covering it with a piece of waste wood. The sawblade is raised just above the thickness of the veneer (**2.11**). When the jig passes over the sawblade, it will accurately cut a straight line without chipping out the veneer.

A fence is accurately screwed onto the jig parallel to the sawblade and at a distance from the blade equal to that of the desired parquetry part. The straight edge of the veneer is pushed over to the fence, and a properly sized strip is cut. One could now easily go on and make the checkerboard, as was done with the veneer saw (**2.12**).

In this example we are making a more complex pattern called the "Louis cube," a form of parquetry that was used frequently on Louis XV furniture. The pattern requires three colors and a way of making rhombuses of 60/120 degrees.

The parallel strips are taped together alternating the three colors. A fence is then screwed onto the jig at 60 degrees to the sawblade. An initial cut is made, cutting a straight edge at the angle on the striped sheet. The sheet is then slid over to the first fence, and the cutting proceeds, creating strips made up of the three colors of rhombuses (**2.13**).

These strips can then be assembled to make a number of different patterns, including herringbones. To make the Louis cube, the strips are disassembled by pulling the tape apart. This frees the individual rhombuses, which can then be re-assembled into the illusionary cubes (**2.14**). The pattern can grow as large as desired by continuing to add parts.

❧

2.11

2.12

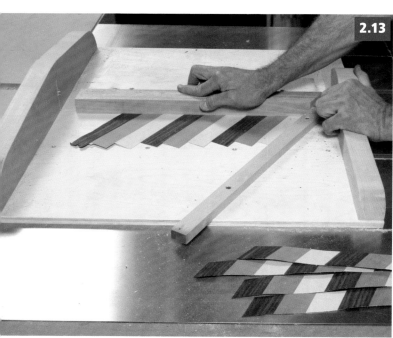

2.13

2.14

APPENDIX 3: BANDING (TARSIA A TOPPO)

Simple bandings of geometric designs (*tarsia a toppo*) can be made in a manner similar to parquetry. The key is setting up a system where multiple parts can be cut from packages. Contrasting materials are glued together, cut apart, and rearranged to create different configurations (**3.1** and **3.2**).

Banding starts with sheets of material. The sheets can be made by re-sawing boards into thinner stock (**3.3**). Fine lines can be added to a design by using commercially prepared veneers. The sheets are arranged in a pattern of alternating species, then glued back together, making a new board, striped in cross section (**3.4**).

This board can then be resawn into thin striped strips (**3.5**). In this example the strips are cut to the same thick-

3.1

3.2

3.3

3.4

3.5

ness as the original parts. The next step is to glue these strips onto a veneer that is the same thickness as the dark lines in these strips. These six individual composites are once again glued together (**3.6**). The result is a square loaf constituting a grid in cross section.

To slice this loaf, a simple jig can be made from a piece of plywood that runs in the groove on a bandsaw table. A fence is screwed to the plywood, and a stop is clamped to the fence, creating an offcut of the desired thickness (in this case approximately ¹⁄₁₆ in.). The loaf is then sliced, like bread, over and over producing a set of identical tiles that can then be used as banding (**3.7**).

The loaf can also be cut on an angle, thereby elongating the square into a rectangle (**3.8** and **3.9**).

The design possibilities for banding are unlimited. The wood can be glued together, changing the grain direction so that pieces can display end- or side-grain orientations. Pieces can be cut and stacked at an angle to create herringbone patterns. The parts can be very tiny, as in Tunbridgeware (pp. 130–131). This is also the method used to make the delicate rosettes that decorate the sound holes in fine guitars.

The method used to cut the tiles from a loaf is exactly the same as the techniques used to cut oysters (pp. 136–138), which are thin sections (round or oval, depending on the angle of the slice) of tree limbs (**3.10**).

❧

3.6

3.7

3.8

3.9

3.10

4.1

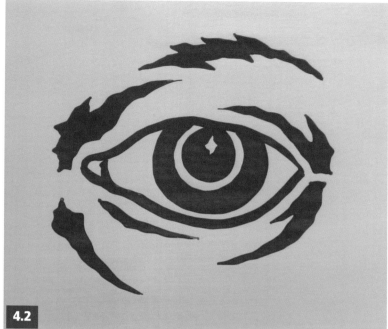

4.2

4.3

Boulle work is produced by cutting two contrasting materials in juxtaposition to one another and then interchanging the parts. The lighter parts are put into the darker background (**4.1**), and the darker parts go into the lighter ground (**4.2**). In this way the marqueteur gets two panels from one cutting.

Traditionally, the materials for Boulle work are a lighter-colored metal, such as brass or pewter, and a dark wood, such as ebony, or a darkly-mottled tortoiseshell.

Once a design is selected, sheets of the materials are cut to the same dimensions (**4.3**). In this case the panels will be made of brass and ebony. The wood should be slightly thicker than the metal. That way, in leveling the final panel the softer material is taken down to the harder material.

The materials are prepared by first roughing up one side of the metal. Brass can be easily scratched using an old hacksaw blade secured in a simple handle (**4.4**). This will become the side that gets glued to the substrate. The wood parts of the design may have short grain that might shatter or fall apart during the cutting. Hide glue is therefore brushed on one side of the wood and a piece of newsprint is stuck

4.4

4.5

4.6 **4.7**

4.8

to it (**4.5**). _The combination of the glue and the paper will help hold little pieces of wood together.

The two sheets are taped together with the "up" sides in the same orientation to one another. This means the scratched side of the metal and the side of the ebony without the glue and paper are oriented the same way. The brass should be on the bottom because it is stronger and can better support the cutting. A piece of wax paper can also be inserted between the sheets to lubricate the sawblade (**4.6**). The packet is completed by putting waste veneers on the top and bottom. An ideal choice is a softer wood like poplar (**4.7**). The motif is glued on top (**4.8**).

Wherever there is an independent part of the motif, a hole needs to be drilled to insert the sawblade through (**4.9**). The holes will be visible in the final product so they should be only slightly larger than the sawblade and placed at a point on the line where they won't be obvious. The saw kerf will be visible as well, so the blade should be as small as possible. There is a trade off between the strength of the blade and the size of the kerf. The metal being cut is hard enough to be tough on a blade, and a blade too fine can easily break. But a blade that is too stout will leave an unsightly gap in the final picture.

In the seventeenth century, when Boulle work first became popular, the panels were cut using a simple handheld fretsaw (figure 108). In the nineteenth century, a chevalet with a cantilevered arm (figure 110 and **5.7**) made cutting the parts more efficient. Today, the power scroll saw is the most common choice.

Cutting proceeds from the interior parts to the outer parts (**4.10**). In a design of concentric circles, for instance, the smallest diameter must be cut first. If you were to start from the outside, the pattern would fall apart and there would be no way to cut the smallest circle. After a part is cut free it is set aside in a tray (**4.11**).

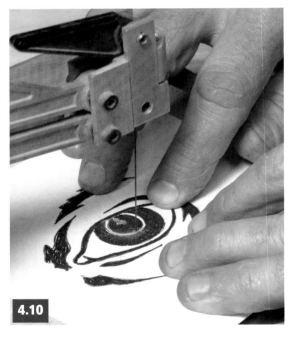

4.9 **4.10**

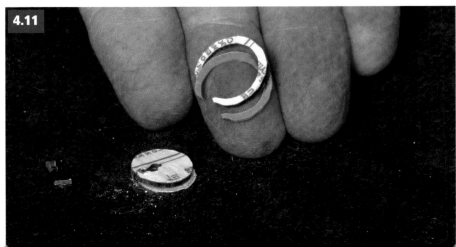

4.11

Occasionally, after a lot of the parts have been cut, the packet will become quite flimsy. It can be stabilized by gluing another waste veneer to the bottom, thereby providing a solid base again. It can also be a problem cutting very small parts. As soon as they are cut free, they can fall through the hole in the table and be lost. The problem can be avoided by slipping a waste piece of veneer or cardboard under the packet part-way through the cut, to reduce the size of the hole in the table.

When everything has been cut, the two motifs are ready to assemble. A piece of paper is glued to the up side of both background sheets (the unscratched side of the metal and the paper side of the wood). The individual parts can then be taken from the tray and glued into the proper spot (**4.12**). A dab of hide glue is all it takes, as hide glue requires no sustained pressure to adhere. The clean part of the wood and the scratched part of the brass should be visible. A gap the size of the saw kerf will surround each part, which should be centered in the space. The pictures are assembled from the outside in, so the spaces shrink until the final piece is put in place (**4.13**).

The panels are then ready to glue to the substrate. The pressing is like any other marquetry panel; however, the adhesive needs to be one that bonds with metal. Fish glue was used traditionally. In this example I use epoxy. (This is somewhat controversial, as restoration specialists don't recommend using any adhesive that can't be reversed. But epoxy appears to form a long-lasting bond, and I have decided to use it on Boulle work). A dark sawdust, such as ebony, is mixed with whatever adhesive is chosen. This fills the gap of the kerf and makes the line practically invisible.

The panels are cleaned up using scrapers, files, and sandpaper (**4.14**). It's important not to work too long in one area, or the friction can heat the metal, which can break the glue bond. Polishing proceeds to the desired level of finish.

❧

4.12

4.13

4.14

APPENDIX 5: PIECE BY PIECE

The traditional method developed in the eighteenth century for cutting multiple motifs is the technique called piece by piece—in French, *élément par élément* (**5.1**). Packets of veneers are put together and the designs are glued to the packet and then cut out. This is an evolution of the Boulle technique, where the contrasting materials are put together and cut in a packet, then assembled. Here the packets contain only one species, and the parts that border one another are not cut at the same time.

PREPARING THE PACKET

In the piece-by-piece method all the veneers are prepared as they are for the Boulle process. Small pieces of veneer can be quite fragile, particularly if the wood fibers are short grain. Sometimes short grain is preferred for effect, and sometimes it is unavoidable because of the curved shape of the piece. Either way, the veneer can be strengthened by gluing paper to the surface. Hide glue and paper will help bond the fibers together and keep small parts from chipping away.

To assemble a packet, a number of veneers are cut to the same size and stacked together. A waste veneer goes on each side of the packet, for support. Ideally, this veneer is a little thicker and should be easy to cut—1/16-in. poplar is ideal. Additionally a couple of pieces of wax paper can be added to lubricate the sawblade (**5.2**). The packet is taped together. At this point the name of the species and the grain direction should be written on the top of the packet.

The packet can be as large as the marqueteur feels comfortable cutting. A larger packet that isn't completely used on one project can be used again on another project. Additionally, the number of layers of veneer can vary. The thicker the packet, the more challenging the cutting. But more pictures can be produced. A professional might cut as many as twenty-four layers, making the packet as much as an inch thick. In this example I have chosen six layers.

A number of duplicate patterns are needed to cut apart so the individual parts can be glued on the packet.

5.1

5.2

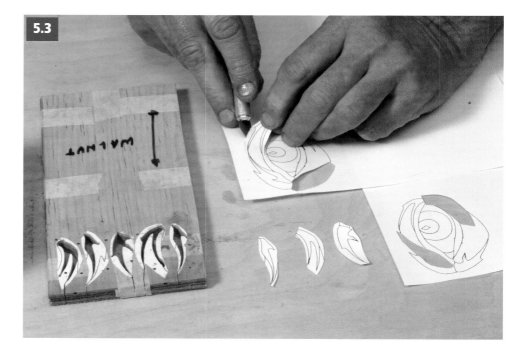

5.3

White space is left surrounding each motif, so there is no confusion about the line to be cut. Hide glue is then used to adhere the pattern to the packet in the desired orientation (**5.3**). (Note that a previously prepared packet can be used again and again until it is finally too small to hold. In this example a set of parts has already been cut from the walnut packet).

The tape holding the packet together does not squeeze the veneers together tightly enough by itself. Thin brads secure the packet. Pilot holes are drilled in the waste areas close to the patterns. The brads are driven through and then clipped off and peened over, thus stapling the packet tight (**5.4** and **5.5**). The packet that will serve as the background veneer is similarly prepared, this time with the brads on the inside of the motif (**5.6**).

The Chevalet

Piece-by-piece marquetry requires very accurate sawing. The sawblade is much larger than that used for Boulle work because the the material is much thicker. The bigger blade means a bigger kerf. The size of the kerf is not critical, however, as each individual shape is cut with the kerf on the waste side. What is paramount is that the saw cut accurately and perpendicularly. If the blade is not running square, the shape of the motif will not be the same from the top to the bottom of the stack; instead, the size will get incrementally larger or smaller through the stack.

The tool that was developed in the nineteenth century to address this concern is the chevalet (**5.7**). It has a number of adjustments that allow the marqueteur to easily cut packets with the precision necessary to get perfect results.

The sawblade is held in tension in a wooden frame mounted horizontally. Attached to the back of the frame is a steel rod that fits in bushings on the chevalet superstructure, allowing the saw to slide back and forth. The metal rod hangs from a cradle that allows some side-to-side movement, which helps in following the line of cut. The arms of the cradle have two adjustments. On the sawyer's side the arm can

5.4

5.5

5.6

5.7

5.8

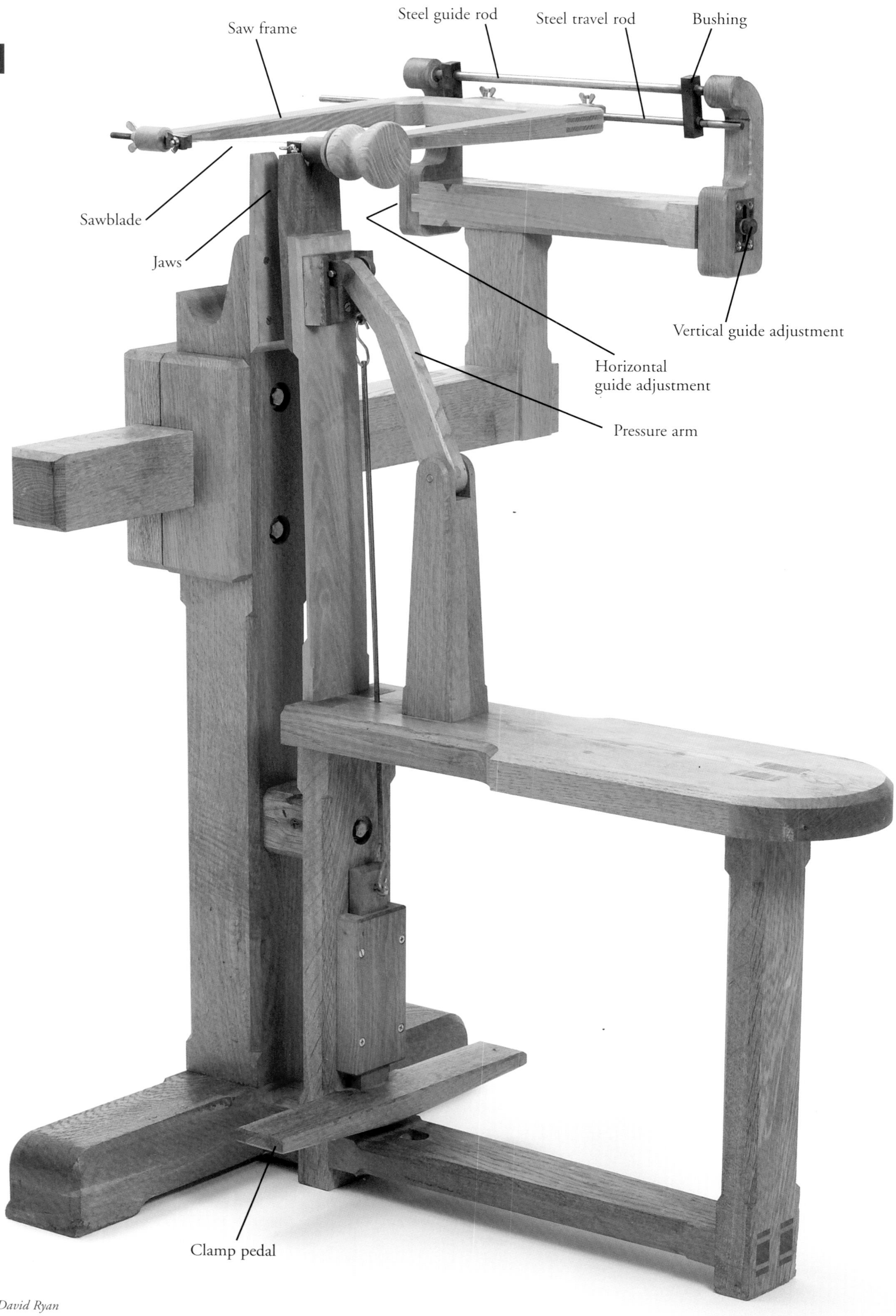

Saw frame

Steel guide rod

Steel travel rod

Bushing

Sawblade

Jaws

Vertical guide adjustment

Horizontal
guide adjustment

Pressure arm

Clamp pedal

Photo: David Ryan

be raised or lowered. On the far end the arm can be adjusted to the left or right. Between these two adjustments the saw-blade can be made to run exactly per-pendicular to the work (**5.8**).

The chevalet developed from an earlier tool for securing veneer during fretsawing (figure 108). Clamping is controlled by the sawyer's feet. Pushing down with the heels pulls an arm mounted on a pivot forward, pressing a movable jaw against a fixed jaw. One hand can then reposition the work between clampings (the jaws relax open upon raising the heels), while the other hand moves the saw back and forth when the work is secure.

SAWING THE PACKET

Sawing begins once all the design's pat-terns are glued onto the packets. The saw needs to just take the line, with the rest of the kerf on the waste side. If some of the line is left, the piece will not fit properly. If the kerf goes over the line, a gap will be evident in the final picture. Precise and accurate sawing will result in a picture whose joints are the size of the fine line of the drawing.

Sawing commences on the right side of the packet and proceeds in a clock-wise direction (**5.9**). This way, the wood is supported by the rest of the packet until the very end of the cut. At that point it is necessary to reach around the packet and stabilize the wood with your fingers until it is cut free.

The background is cut similarly, except that a starter hole must be drilled for the blade to be inserted through, and the kerf will now be on the inside (**5.10**). When cutting is complete, the parts are set aside in a tray. In this example there are six iden-tical parts (**5.11**). All of the individual components that go into the picture are treated the same.

ASSEMBLING THE PICTURE

A piece of paper is glued to the front face of one of the background pieces using hide glue. This will create a recess, open from the backside, that is ready to receive the individual pieces of the marquetry picture. One of the pieces on the perimeter is selected and

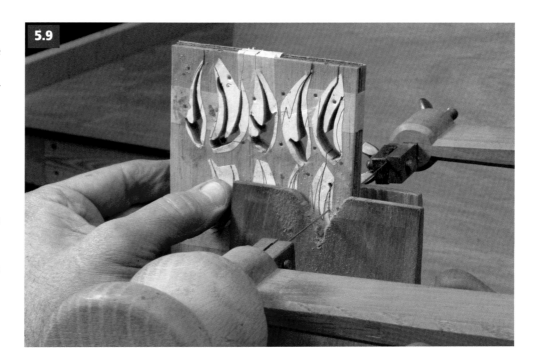

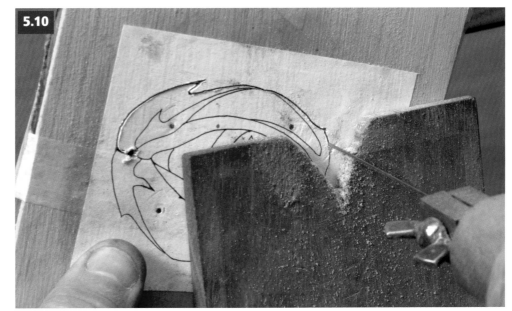

APPENDIX 6: SAND SHADING

glued into the recess. The process continues from the outside in, adding one piece at a time (**5.12**). Finally the very center of the picture (the tiny highlight in the pupil) is glued in place (**5.13**). The other five pictures are assembled in exactly the same way.

The final step is to clean the back of the picture with a little sanding. The marquetry is now ready to glue into a panel. Once the picture and panel are secure, the paper on the front of the picture can be scraped off.

Marquetry parts can be shaded as they have been traditionally, by dipping them into a pan of sand heated on a hot plate. The sand is hottest at the bottom, and therefore the deeper the piece is thrust into the pan, the darker it will become. The edges of the wood, having more surface area, also get a little darker. The beauty of the technique is that the shading is gradual, and therefore very effective in producing a three-dimensional illusion.

The finer the sand, the more evenly it will shade the wood. The wood can be dipped into the sand using tweezers (**6.1**). Or the sand can be scooped out of the pan and the veneer passed through it for more control (**6.2**).

Care must be taken not to scorch the wood too much, or, like charcoal, it will lose its structural integrity. Some surface charring of the wood will disappear after the panel is glued up and the top surface is scraped away. It is best to monitor the shading by dipping the veneer in and out of the sand until the desired shade is reached.

5.12

5.13

6.1

6.2

APPENDIX 7: BEVEL CUTTING

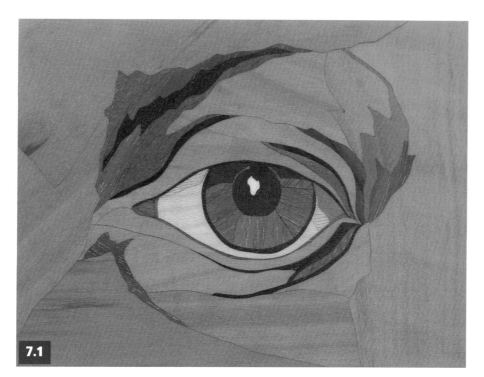

7.1

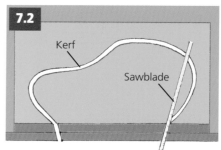

7.2

Cutting at an angle through two veneers at once creates matching beveled edges on both object ▢ and background ▢ layers.

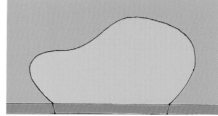

The beveled object fits into the beveled background with no gap; the saw kerf disappears.

Bevel cutting (also called double-bevel cutting) is a method of sawing marquetry that can easily produce an intricate picture with no gaps between the pieces (**7.1**). The process is similar to Boulle work, where the saw line becomes the border between the parts. But instead of the kerf being perpendicular to the surface, in bevel cutting the kerf is angled so that when the two parts are pieced together, the gap is eliminated.

Bevel cutting has several advantages. Unlike cutting a packet, as is done with the piece-by-piece method, the marqueteur can see (and orient to best effect) the grain and figure in the wood as he works. Extremely fine details can be added easily. And because the bevel results in the two pieces overlapping, flawless joints can be produced even by a relatively inexperienced sawyer. The disadvantage of the method is that only one picture can be made at a time.

Bevel cutting is an additive process. The marqueteur starts with two pieces of veneer, one of which will fit into or be joined to the other. The veneer being added is set on top of the receiving veneer, and the saw cuts through both at once. The gap created by the sawblade collapses when the top piece

7.3

falls into the lower one (**7.2**). The waste parts are set aside and the two pieces secured with veneer tape (a thin paper tape made sticky by moistening with water). Now the two pieces act like a single piece of veneer, and the next piece can be added to the picture. The picture is built part by part, taping each piece to a growing assembly, until the picture is complete.

The angle of the bevel is a function of the thickness of the sawblade and

the thickness of the veneer. A finer sawblade requires a more vertical cut. Conversely, a thinner veneer requires a more angled cut. The blade chosen needs to be fine enough to make tight turns, in order to cut fine details, but not too fine, or it will easily break. Similarly the veneer needs to be thick enough to allow the cut to be close to vertical. With a veneer thickness of $\frac{1}{32}$ inch and a blade size of 2/0, the angle will be 13 degrees.

The example pictured starts with a drawing of a human eye (**7.3**). A group of veneers is selected to represent the flesh tones, as well as the pupil, iris, and white of the eye. The woods range from holly for the highlight in the center of the pupil, to ebony for the pupil itself. The other woods include maple, cherry, walnut, and imbuya. I also need tracing paper, black carbon paper, and "white carbon" transfer paper. The carbons will be used to transfer the drawing from a tracing to the wood itself.

A marquetry picture requires a line drawing as a key for the different

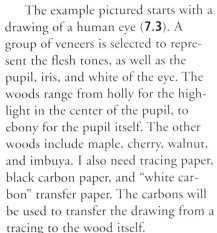

and allow the picture to grow outward. This way the marquetry parts are always added to the perimeter. The first two parts of the eye are the pupil (ebony) and the small highlight (holly). Using the tracing-paper line drawing and the carbon paper, I draw those two parts on the piece of holly.

The ebony is placed under the holly and the beveled cut made on the line (**7.5**). The holly piece is laid into the ebony background (**7.6**) and secured with veneer tape underneath.

Working my way outward, the iris is next. The tracing-paper drawing is lined up with the ebony/holly assembly, a piece of walnut is laid under it, and the border of the pupil and iris is transferred to the wood using the white "carbon" paper. Note that the tracing-paper drawing is flipped over to get the mirror image of the original drawing. It is preferable to work from the backside, because all the parts will be held together with tape on the "front" of the assembly. The clean backside (up for sawing) is eventually glued to the panel, and the taped face is scraped clean and finished.

In my line drawing, I segmented the iris so that the grain of several pieces of the walnut veneer will radiate from the pupil, like the structure of an actual iris (**7.7**). The saw cut is then made, which establishes that part of the circle of the pupil where the iris touches it (**7.8**). The bevel cut ensures that the parts will fit perfectly (**7.9**). I tape them together and proceed around the iris, adding a total of five pieces of walnut (**7.10**).

Bevel cutting can be done using a handheld fretsaw, but it is most easily accomplished with a power scroll saw. The table is tilted to the correct angle, and both hands are free to maneuver the veneer through the sawblade (**7.11**). The picture proceeds, adding oversize pieces that are then cut back in subsequent additions. The lower edge of the white of the eye is defined, for instance, with the addition of a piece of walnut. Then, a piece of Brazilian imbuya is laid under the assembly, and the upper eyeline is cut (**7.12**). The

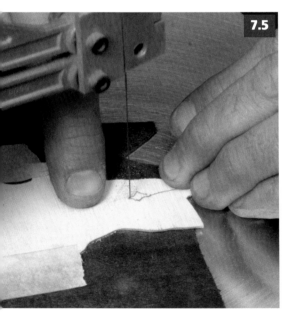

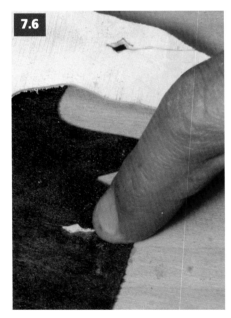

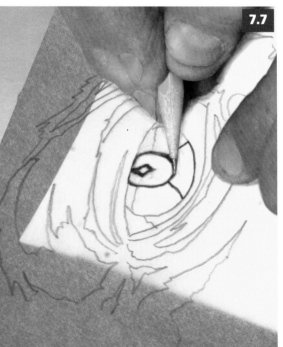

woods selected. Using tracing paper, the original shaded drawing is broken down into lines designating different color and tonal areas. The drawing will be more or less complicated depending on how many veneers comprise the palette being used. Here I have five different tones for the flesh, and I am drawing lines to create the borders between the tones (**7.4**). Sometimes subtly different tones meld together to create a gradual transition, and other times woods of high contrast are juxtaposed for dramatic effect.

Technically, bevel cutting can begin with any piece of the picture, but practically it is easiest to start in the middle

7.8

7.9

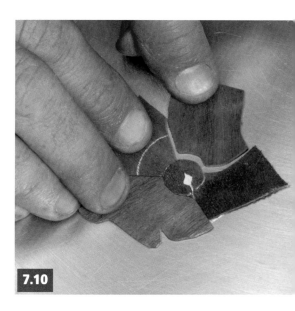

7.10

7.11

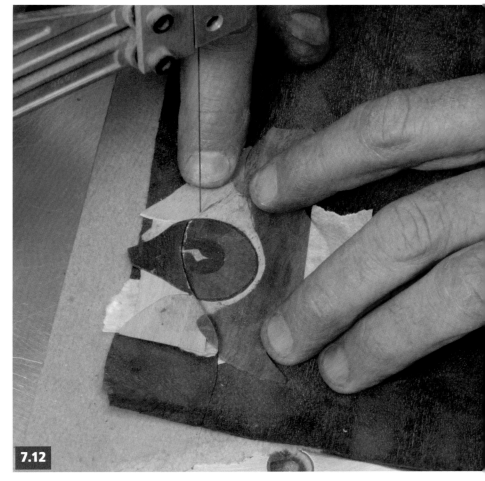

7.12

7.13

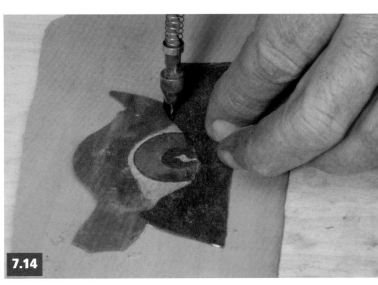

7.14

7.15

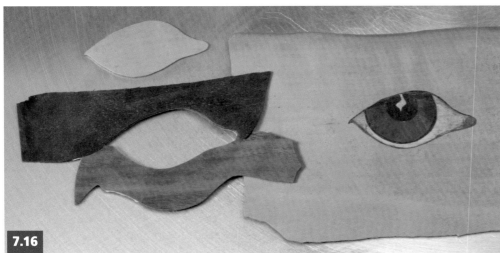

7.16

7.17

imbuya piece is taped (on the front) in position (**7.13**).

To surround this assembly, a piece of cherry veneer, which will be the first flesh tone of the eye, is placed under it. A hole is drilled through both layers in order to insert the sawblade (**7.14**). By cutting around the perimeter and leaving a little of the darker walnut and imbuya (**7.15**), a very fine line, only about $\frac{1}{32}$ in. wide, defines the top and bottom of the eye.

Here is an obvious advantage of bevel cutting. I am able to add this fine detail without having to handle tiny pieces of veneer. The detail is created by cutting back close to an established line where the veneer is already joined to the assembly. The cut goes completely around the perimeter, creating a space in the background veneer that is exactly the same shape is the eye. By cutting in the correct direction in relation to the table tilt, the eye and the cherry surround fit together with no gap (**7.16**). (The cherry waste piece in the shape of the eye will fit in the space between the imbuya and walnut waste, but the gap will be twice the thickness of the saw kerf.)

One piece at a time, the process continues until all the details have been added. If a significant build-up of tape on the front side compromises sawing or risks achieving even pressure in the press, you can temporarily add masking tape to the clean backside of the assembly, peel off the veneer tape from the front, and retape it more sparingly. The marquetry picture is ready for pressing into a panel (**7.17**).

❧

CHRONOLOGY

SILAS KOPF

Born: 1949, Warren, Pennsylvania

Education:

A.B. Princeton University (architecture), 1972
Apprentice to Wendell Castle, 1974–1976
Studied at the École Boulle, Paris, 1988

Awards:

1988   National Endowment for the Arts–Craftsman's Fellowship
1996   New England Craft Foundation Fellowship
1997   Boston Society of Arts and Crafts Fellowship

Selected Exhibitions:

1980   Don Muller Gallery, Northampton, Mass.
1982   Pritam and Eames Gallery, East Hampton, N.Y.
1983   Snyderman Gallery, Philadelphia, Pa.
Pritam and Eames Gallery, East Hampton, N.Y.
Gallery Henoch, New York
1986   Workbench Gallery, New York
Wisteriahurst Museum, Holyoke, Mass.
1987   Gallery Henoch, New York
1988   Gallery Henoch (solo exhibition), New York
1989   *Artful Objects*, Ft. Wayne Museum, Ft. Wayne, Ind.
1990   *Contemporary Still Life*, Gallery Henoch, New York
Gallery Henoch (solo exhibition), New York
1991   *Art That Works*, national touring exhibition
1992   Gallery Henoch (solo exhibition), New York
1993   *The Forest Refined*, Trenton City Museum, Trenton, N.J.
1994   *Conservation By Design*, national touring exhibition
1995   Art Miami, Miami Beach, Fla.
Gallery Henoch (solo exhibition), New York
1996   International Exposition of Sculptural Objects &
Functional Art (SOFA), Chicago, Ill.
1998   Gallery Henoch (solo exhibition), New York
1999   Gallery Henoch, New York
2001   Gallery Henoch (solo exhibition), New York
2002   *Skin Deep*, Milwaukee Art Museum, Milwaukee, Wis.
2003   Gallery Henoch (solo exhibition), New York,
2006   *Inspired By China*, Peabody Essex Museum, Salem, Mass.
2007   Gallery Henoch (solo exhibition), New York

DETAIL OF FIGURE 73: COLLECTOR'S CABINET
(1999) SILAS KOPF
Photo: David Ryan

Featured Works by the Author

1977   *Bamboo Cabinet* (figure 24)
1979   *Dogwood Coffee Table* (figure 22)
1980   Marquetry Jewelry Boxes (figure 19)
       Blanket Chest (figure 23)
1984   *Hands on Plane* (figure 60)
       1498–1984 (figure 61)
1985   *Enthralled* (figure 83)
       Primal Woodworking (figure 4; detail on p. 66)
       Tea Cabinet (figure 63)
       Linda (figure 79)
1986   Fall Front Desk (figure 6)
       Wine Cabinet (figure 62)
       Fall Front Desk with Cat (figure 65)
       Lego Cabinet (figure 81)
1987   *Azalea Cabinet* (figure 70)
       Typewriter Desk (figure 76)
       Sasha (figure 78)
       Mantle Clock (figure 82)
       Parquetry Bookstand One (figure 94)
1988   *Hadley Chest with Tulips* (figure 5)
       Trompe l'Oeil Desk with Violin (figure 66)
       Baseball Cabinet (figure 90)
       Parquetry Bookstand Two (figure 95)
       Student exercise: Piece by piece (figure 109)
       Student exercise: Boulle work (figure 111)
       Half Round Cabinet (figure 168)
       Floral Sideboard (figure 170)
1989   *Aquarium Fall Front Cabinet* (figure 67)
       Phone Cabinet One (figure 84)
       Bricolage (figure 86; detail on p. 66)
       School Desk (figure 156)
       Morning Glories; Model L, Steinway and Sons piano
         (figure 199; detail on p. xv)
1990   *Music Cabinet* (figure 1)
       Iris Coffee Table (figure 68)
       Dad (figure 80)
       Magazine Coffee Table (figure 92)
       Coffee Table for Ann and Joel (figure 93)
       Grape Vine Commodes (figure 180)
1991   *Formication* (figure 153)
       Faces Fall Front Desk (figure 157)
       Fishscale Chest of Drawers (figure 159)
       Lectern with Faces (figure 160)
       Cardinal Cabinet (figure 71)
       Argus (figure 154)
       Parabola (figure 163)
       Oyster Desk (figure 164)
       Game Table for Chess and Go (figure 167)
       Boulle Cabinets with Daffodils (figure 181)

1993   *Phone Cabinet Two* (figure 85)
       Cuckoo Clock (figure 87)
       Remembering Louis (figure 220)
1994   *Cracked* (figure 162)
       Fall Front Desk with Sasha (figure 166)
1995   *Urban Theme (Life Is A Rat Race) Corner Cabinet*
         (figure 161)
       Nest of Birds Chest of Drawers (figure 169)
1996   Traditional Boulle Cabinets (figure 183)
1997   *Dog Sideboard* (figure 182)
1998   *Garden Cabinet* (figure 72)
       Trompe L'Oeil Collector's Cabinet (figure 91)
       Set of Dining Chairs (figure 208)
1999   *What a Knucklehead* (figure 9; detail on p. 69)
       Collector's Cabinet (figure 73; detail on p. 213)
       Oval Writing Desk and Chair (figure 221)
2000   *Hadley Chest with Apples* (figure 69)
       Side Chairs with Animals (figure 209)
2001   Desk and Chair (figure 196)
       Goldfish Sideboard (figure 197)
       Game Table and Chairs (figure 210)
       Roses and Butterflies (figure 211)
2002   *Pondering Floyd Collins Blanket Chest* (figure 88)
       Pyramid Chest (figure 185; detail on p. 144)
       Elliptical Garden Cabinet (figure 213)
2003   *Sloppy Paint Job* (figure 8)
       Four Arts (figure 89; detail on p. 5)
       Aloha Shirt Cabinet (figure 214; detail on p. xiv)
2004   *Panthers* (figure 97)
       Antelope Cabinet (figure 179)
       Three Mile Island Desk and Chair (figure 216; detail
         on p. x)
       Falling Oysters (figure 218)
2005   *Bees and Tulips* (figure 155)
2006   *Cracked Ice Tables* (figure 96)
       Walden Woods; Model D, Steinway and Sons piano
         (figure 201; detail on p. 191)
       Parabola 2 (figure 212)
       Cracked Ice Ellipse (figure 215)
       Nasturtiums (figure 219)
2007   *Bad Hare Day* (figure 217)

REFERENCES

TECHNICAL REFERENCES

Joyce, Ernest. *The Encyclopedia of Furnituremaking.* New York: Drake Publishing, 1970.

Hawkins, David. *Techniques of Wood Surface Decoration.* New York: Sterling Publishing, 1987.

Hoadley, R. Bruce. *Understanding Wood.* Newtown, CT: Taunton Press, 2000.

Lincoln, W. A. *The Complete Manual of Wood Veneering.* New York: Charles Scribner, 1984.

Patterson, James E. *Pearl Inlay.* Athens, OH: Stewart MacDonald, 1991.

Robinson, Larry. *The Art of Inlay.* San Francisco: Miller Freeman, 1999.

Square, David Shath. The Veneering Book. Newtown, CT: Taunton Press, 1995.

MARQUETRY – TECHNICAL

Bruggermann, Erich. *Kunst und Technik der Intarsien.* Munich: Calwey GmbH and Co., 1988.

Lincoln, W. A. *The Art and Practice of Marquetry.* New York: Charles Scribner's Sons, 1971.

———. *The Marquetry Manual.* London: Stobart and Sons, 1989.

Massie, Frédéric and René Maubert. *Reconnaître la Marqueterie Boulle.* Paris: Adam Brio, 1990.

Ramond, Pierre. *La Marqueterie.* Dourdan: *Edition H.* Vial, 1981.

———. *Marquetry (English Translation).* Newtown, CT: Taunton Press, 1989.

FURNITURE HISTORY

Borger, Louise Ada. *Complete Guide to Furniture Styles.* New York: Chas. Scribner's Sons, 1969.

Morley, John. *History of Furniture.* Boston: Little Brown and Co., 1999.

Riccardi-Cubitt, Monique. *The Art of the Cabinet.* London: Thames and Hudson, 1992.

Smith, Edward Lucie. *Furniture: A Concise History.* New York: Oxford University Press, 1979.

Watson, Francis, introduction. *The History of Furniture.* New York: Crescent Books, 1976.

EGYPT, GREECE, and ROME

Baker, Hollis. *Furniture in the Ancient World.* New York: MacMillan Co., 1966.

Carter, Howard. *The Tomb of Tutankhamun.* New York: Excalibur Books, 1972.

Killen, Geoffrey. *Egyptian Woodworking and Furniture.* Princes Risborough: Shire Publications, 1994.

Lucas, A. and J.R. Harris, *Egyptian Materials and Industries.* Mineola, NY: Dover Books, 1999.

Petrie, W. M. F. *Arts and Crafts of Ancient Egypt.* London: Foulis Co., 1910.

ITALIAN RENAISSANCE INTARSIA

Brizzi, Giovanni. *Il Coro Intarsiato dell'Abbazia di Monte Oliveto Maggiore.* Rome: Silvani, 1989.

Haines, Margaret. *The Sacretia Delle Messe.* Florence: Cassa di Risparanio, 1983.

Raggio, Olga. *The Gubbio Studiolo and Its Conservation, vol. 1.* New York: Metropolitan Museum of Art, 1999.

Wilmering, Antoine. *The Gubbio Studiolo and Its Conservation, vol. 2.* New York: Metropolitan Museum of Art, 1999.

CLASSIC FRENCH FURNITURE

Chastang, Yannick. *Paintings in Wood– French Marquetry Furniture.* London: The Wallace Collection, 2001.

Huth, Hans. *Roentgen Furniture.* London: Sotheby Parke Bernet, 1974.

Pradère, Alexandre. *French Furniture Makers.* Malibu, CA: Getty Publishing, 1989.

Ramond, Pierre. *Chefs d'Œuvres des Marqueteurs (vols. I, II, III).* Dourdan: Edition H. Vial, 1996.

———. *Masterpieces of Marquetry (English translation).* Malibu, CA: Getty Publications, 2000.

Roubo, J. A. *Le Menuisier en Meubles 1772.* Paris: Inter-Livres (reprint).

Scheurleer, Theodoor. *Pierre Gole: Ébéniste de Louis XIV.* Paris: Faton, 2005.

Stortmann-Dohler, Rosemarie. *Jean-François Oeben 1721–1763.* Paris: Perrin et fils, 2002.

ART NOUVEAU

Bouvier, Roselyne. *Majorelle.* Paris: La Bibliotheque des Arts, 1991.

Duncan, Alastair. *Art Nouveau Furniture.* New York: Clarkson Potter, 1982.

Garner, Philippe. *Émile Gallé.* New York: Rizzoli, 1972.

Schmutzler, Robert. *Art Nouveau.* New York: Abrams, 1962.

ART DECO FURNITURE

Bréon, Emmanuel and Rosalind Pepall, ed. *Ruhlmann-Genius of Art Deco.* Somogy Éditions d'Art, 2004.

———. *Ruhlmann: Master of Art Deco.* New York: Abrams, 1983.

Camard, Florence. *Süe et Mare et la Compagnie des Arts Français.* Paris: Éditions de l'Amateur, 1993.

ARTS AND CRAFTS FURNITURE

Lambourne, Lionel. *Utopian Craftsmen.* Peregrine Smith, Salt Lake City, UT: 1980.

Naylor, Gillian. *The Arts and Crafts Movement.* M.I.T. Press, Cambridge, MA: 1971.

OTHER FURNITURE

Baroni, Daniele and Antonio d'Auria. *Kolo Moser: Graphic Artist and Designer.* New York: Rizzoli, 1984.

Muhlberger, Richard. *American Folk Marquetry.* New York: Museum of American Folk Art, 1998.

WHERE TO FIND MARQUETRY

The figure captions in this book tell where each piece illustrated can be found. Here are the places where outstanding collections of furniture or marquetry are worth a special visit.

UNITED STATES
Metropolitan Museum of Art, New York.
The museum has an outstanding collection of furniture from around the world, including many fine examples of classic French and English furniture. And don't miss the Gubbio Studiolo.

Frick Collection, New York.
This gem of a museum has several masterpieces by Boulle and Riesener.

J. Paul Getty Museum, Los Angeles.
The museum has some of the finest examples of classic French furniture anywhere (and that includes France).

Virginia Museum of Fine Arts, Richmond, Va.
An excellent collection of Art Deco and Art Nouveau furniture.

Detroit Institute of Arts, Detroit, Mich.

National Gallery of Art, Washington, D.C.

Winterthur Museum, Wilmington, Del.
Fine examples of early American furniture, showing the way marquetry was used as decoration.

FRANCE
The Louvre, Paris
One of the great museums in the world and home of some of the great pieces of French furniture.

Musée des Arts Decoratifs, Paris
The museum is the repository of French design history with excellent examples from all periods.

Musée d'Orsay, Paris
The collection focuses on late nineteenth- and early twentieth-century painting and decorative objects.

Musée Nissim de Camondo, Paris
The collection displays classic French furniture in a domestic setting.

Musée Jacquemart-André, Paris

Musée Cognac-Jay, Paris

Musée de l'École de Nancy, Nancy
Worth the pilgrimage to see the work of Gallé and Majorelle.

Château de Versailles, Versailles
Royal furniture set in original interiors.

GREAT BRITAIN
Victoria and Albert Museum, London
The V&A is one of the great collections of decorative objects in the world. Furniture abounds from all periods, with delights around every corner.

Windsor Castle, Windsor
The royal family has been collecting decorative art for centuries and has some wonderful example of European furniture.

Leicester City Museums, Leicester
The work of Ernest Gimson is preserved in the city's collection.

ITALY
Duomo of Siena
This cathedral has a choir decorated with intarsia panels by Fra Giovanni.

Monte Oliveto Maggiore, outside of Siena
The choir has the finest work of Fra Giovanni.

La Collegiata, San Quirico d'Orcia
This little church houses the intarsia of Antonio Barili.

Duomo of Florence
Florence is one of the great art centers of the world and the cathedral is a treasure. Both the choir and sacristy feature stunning examples of intarsia.

Ducal Palace, Urbino
The studiolo is one of the great masterpieces of intarsia art.

S. Maria in Organo, Verona
Verona is the home of Fra Giovanni, and he decorated the choir in the church.

THE NETHERLANDS
Rijksmuseum, Amsterdam
The museum has outstanding examples of Dutch and other European decorative art.

AUSTRIA
Oesterreiches Museum, Vienna

Museum für Angewandte Kunst, Vienna

RUSSIA
The Hermitage, St. Petersburg
Russia's finest museum has great decorative objects from throughout Europe.

PORTUGAL
Museu Calouste Gulbenkian, Lisbon

SPAIN
Museo Nacional de Artes Decoratives, Madrid

DENMARK
Danish Museum of Decorative Art, Copenhagen

SWEDEN
National Museum, Stockholm

EGYPT
National Museum, Cairo
If you want to see the furniture of Tutankhamen then you must make the pilgrimage to Cairo.

And of course... Stunning pieces of marquetry can be found in museums and collections throughout the world. This list represents only a glimpse of where some great decorative art can be found. Go out and explore!

Page references in **bold** represent illustrations.